Other Books by Frank McKinney

The Tap

Dead Fred, Flying Lunchboxes, and the Good Luck Circle

*Frank McKinney's Maverick Approach to Real Estate Success:
How You Can Go From a $50,000 Fixer-Upper
to a $100 Million Mansion*

Make It BIG! 49 Secrets for Building a Life of Extreme Success

BURST THIS!

Frank McKinney's Bubble-Proof Real Estate Strategies

FRANK McKINNEY

Health Communications, Inc.
Deerfield Beach, Florida

www.hcibooks.com

This book is designed to provide accurate and authoritative information on the subject of real estate investment strategies. While the author and publisher have used best efforts in preparing this book, they make no representations or warranties with respect to the accuracy or completeness of its contents, and they specifically disclaim any implied warranties of merchantability or fitness for a particular purpose. No warranty may be created or extended by sales representatives or written sales materials. As each individual is unique, questions relevant to specific situations should be addressed to an appropriate professional to ensure that it has been evaluated carefully and appropriately. The author and publisher specifically disclaim any liability, loss, or risk that is incurred as a consequence, directly or indirectly, of the use and application of any of the contents of this work.

To contact the author, please visit Frank-McKinney.com.

Library of Congress Cataloging-in-Publication Data

McKinney, Frank.
   Burst this! : Frank McKinney's bubble-proof real estate strategies / Frank McKinney.
       p.   cm.
   Includes bibliographical references and index.
   ISBN-13: 978-0-7573-1383-7 (hard cover)
   ISBN-10: 0-7573-1383-3 (hard cover)
1. Real estate investment—United States. I. Title.
   HD255.M3728 2009
   332.63'240973—dc22

                                                                           2008049568

HCI, its logos and marks are trademarks of Health Communications, Inc.

Publisher: Health Communications, Inc.
        3201 S.W. 15th Street
        Deerfield Beach, FL 33442–8190

This book was printed on recycled paper.

The Leadership in Energy and Environmental Design (LEED) Green Building Rating System™ of the U.S. Green Building Council encourages and accelerates global adoption of sustainable green building and development practices through the creation and implementation of universally understood and accepted tools and performance criteria. This book is part of Frank McKinney's efforts to educate the public about these practices and standards.

Cover design by Robert Mott, Robert Mott Designs.com
Interior design and formatting by Lawna Patterson Oldfield

To all the naysayers, pundits,
and bubble-heads:
Go ahead. Try and burst this!

To all you bubble-proofers:
May you continue to exercise
your risk threshold like a muscle.
Eventually it will become stronger
and able to withstand
greater pressure.

We feel most alive when experiencing extremes for the first time,

in our pursuit to live the dichotomies found in life,

not by merely existing in the "comfort corridor."

CONTENTS

ACKNOWLEDGMENTS

Considering this is book number five for me, and I've created a set of acknowledgments for each one I've written, you'd think that I would have covered everyone who is anyone in the prior four. Not so fast, my friend.

I released two other books on the same day as *Burst This!* Their titles are *The Tap* and *Dead Fred, Flying Lunchboxes, and the Good Luck Circle*. The first is a spiritually based book that expands on the biblical wisdom from the Gospel of Luke: *To whom much has been entrusted, much shall be expected*, teaching you how to succeed in the business we are all in, the business of life. Therefore, in *The Tap*, I acknowledged those who had helped me form the principles found in it, those who'd shown me how to experience "Tap Moments." *Dead Fred* is my first young-reader fantasy novel. In this deeply imaginative book, I recognized those who had helped me never lose the little boy inside, which is a key element to fostering creativity.

In my 2006 bestseller, *Frank McKinney's Maverick Approach to Real Estate Success*, I saluted those who'd contributed to my twenty-year journey of becoming known as a real estate "artist" who creates the most beautiful oceanfront estate homes in the world and who makes markets where they hadn't existed before. And finally, the acknowledgments in my first bestseller, *Make It BIG! 49 Secrets for Building a Life of Extreme Success*, thanked those who'd helped shape the way I look at life in general: people from my grade-school teachers to my mentors.

So, in adding up how many names I'd mentioned in the first four books, it became clear to me that I would have accomplished very little in my life without the help of every one of those 247 "angels." That's twenty-five pages in total attributed to people who made my life what it is! Staggering numbers, but true.

While I am fiercely independent (I write all my books and design our homes from a tree-house office—alone), and am not a partner guy, it dawned on me when compiling these acknowledgments that I am fairly needy. I recall my Badwater Ultramarathon race experiences where I ran 135 miles through the Death Valley desert, nonstop in the middle of July—three times. If it hadn't been for my crew, I never would have finished—and maybe not even survived—what's been called the most difficult footrace in the world by *National Geographic* and the Discovery Channel. My crew helped me do it three years in a row. They said I was high-maintenance, and I guess it was true.

When I say I'm needy, I mean I need to surround myself with a great team. Those 247 people were significant contributing factors to my success. Please read the other four books—heck, there's a good chance you'll find the name of someone you know in there.

So who is left to thank, and why acknowledge them here?

Let's begin with my simple criteria. If someone contributed to my belief that real estate bubbles are most often self-created and assisted me in devising strategies to bubble-proof my own real estate investments, then they are here. If they helped me through tough times in my real estate career, you will find them. If they helped with any aspect concerning the compilation of this book, they are here. That's it.

Who bubble-proofed Frank?

I want to save most of the exciting and meaty content for the "most obscene four-letter word" chapter, yet I must acknowledge my late father Frank McKinney for instilling in me a very conservative core. I'm not talking political leanings; I'm referring to fiscal conservatism, not living beyond my means, taking that "lunch pail" approach, and not allowing my perceived ability to get ahead of my actual competency.

You can't bubble-proof without adequate financing. I want to thank my bankers at Bank of America for growing with me over the last twenty-five years. Joe Silk, Maxie Washington, Mark Maller, Doug Bose, Dan Langelier, Chris Willis, Brian Joyner, Bill Kennedy, Lauren Chaney, Lynn Parker, and many others had the "interpreneurial" vision that saw us making markets, and backed us up with responsible lending practices. No wonder Bank of America is one of the few remaining strongholds in the financial arena. I suggest you contact them with your real estate lending needs, as they "get it" and have the money to lend.

I want to acknowledge my brother, Bob, who is a very accomplished real estate investor and owner of the largest Weichert Realtors franchise in the Midwest. Although he is ten years younger than I am, we've grown up in this business together. On many occasions I've tried to encourage him to move from Indiana and join me in Florida to work with me. He is far too successful to ever accept that offer. Bob helped me fight when I felt I had no more in me. As recently as the end of 2008, when even my world began to look vulnerable, Bob brought back the survivalist instinct in me—a trait that is critical to any bubble-proofing mindset. While times remain uncertain, and we are experiencing markets that have no historical reference point, Bob has helped me navigate through storms in the past, and he will be there for this and any future seismic shifts in our shared field.

I want to thank my mom, Katherine McKinney, for never suppressing the risk taker in me. While she certainly turned gray far too early (because of the daredevil days of my youth), she allowed me to pursue a career that brought me closer to my family and closer to God, which sustained me as a good little altar boy in her eyes.

When contemplating bubble-proof strategies, and sharing them for the first time, your family is unbeatable. In addition to my brother, I want to thank my four sisters, Martie, Marlen, Madeleine, and Heather. It is nice to see that their real estate purchases have been immune from significant degradation in value, and even flourished, because of our talks.

I want to thank all those people who showed me what *not* to do by overextending, overleveraging, and underimproving their properties. I learn a lot by observing success, but witnessing failure and storing away the reasons why is also invaluable. I will not name names, but, rest assured, you do not want to be on this list.

In the same breath, I want to thank those select few who have bought our oceanfront homes since we began creating our artistry in 1991. You provided guidance and even mentorship long after the sale. All of you have provided invaluable input that is now reflected in every Frank McKinney home.

Who believed *Burst This!* was more than just another real estate book?

I want to thank all of the hardworking people at HCI Books, my publisher. Their belief that the concepts found in *Burst This!* were distinctly different from anything else that had been published—and their willingness to publish not only this book, but the other two I wrote and released simultaneously—speaks volumes. I specifically want to thank Peter Vegso, Thomas Sand, Pat Holdsworth, Paola Fernandez, Kim Weiss, Carol Rosenberg, Michele Matrisciani, Andrea Gold, Kelly Maragni, Lori Golden, Sean Geary, Mike Briggs, Craig Jarvie, Christine Zambrano, Gina Johnson, Sydney Stevens, and Manuel Saez.

Books don't sell themselves. Circulating the message of *Burst This!* around the globe is a large undertaking. I want to thank my publicists, Jane Grant and her team of Daniel Grant, Adam Singer, and Savannah Whaley of Pierson Grant Public Relations, for their tireless efforts and enthusiasm for this work.

I want to sincerely thank Karen Risch for her invaluable input in this book. She more than helped me with *Burst This!* and *The Tap*. Sure, she is supposed to be a "ghost" and remain anonymous per our contract, but there is no way I could have captured all this content without her expertise. She must be acknowledged, along with her colleagues at Just Write: Victoria St. George and Nancy Brand Patel. Karen and I sure had fun working on these books; she even helped a bit with *Dead Fred*. I also want to thank Robert Mott for his imaginative work on the book cover. Take a look; it's simply amazing!

We need to bubble-proof for more than just ourselves. If you have a child, or will in the future, simply being a parent is reason enough to read and apply the strategies that follow. My daughter,

Laura (a.k.a. Ppeekk, pronounced "Peekie"), is turning into quite the up-and-coming real estate investor. Without her careful attention to the fish in our giant aquariums, energy monitoring, and interior-design help, our margins wouldn't be what they are. Ppeekk is the love of my life, and I sure hope you pick up a copy of *Dead Fred, Flying Lunchboxes, and the Good Luck Circle* to see what the power of spending imaginative time with your kids can do.

There is no one who has seen me fly so close to the sun, so near that the skin on my face was ready to peel off, as my beautiful wife, Nilsa. From that first fixer-upper to our multimillion-dollar mansions, Nilsa has been the stabilizing force in my life. As I risked more, she stood tall above any challenge, oftentimes with a rosary grasped between her fingers. Few know she is the interior designer for our artistry. Always a force behind the scenes, Nilsa makes our homes magnificent. She also understands that in order to bubble-proof, you must sacrifice today for a better tomorrow. My wife has done just that, including living with me in a one-room studio that was so small you could flip your pancakes from the shower. She never once complained or asked for more. Nilsa, I love you very much and look forward to continuing to make markets and make ———————— with you.

INTRODUCTION
A Beacon of Realistic Optimism and Opportunism

In an old folk tale, an unsuspecting chicken freaks after an acorn drops on her head. "The sky is falling!" Henny Penny, a.k.a. Chicken Little, screeches to anyone who will listen. Evidently, chickens are considered experts on the sky (they must *watch* and *talk about* it a lot), because Chicken Little gathers a crowd, all nervously awaiting the big crash.

How does the story end? A fox comes along, lures the gaggling group under his roof as "protection," and then proceeds to eat all of Chicken Little's followers for dinner. She escapes in that version, but in another one, the fox gobbles up everyone, including the hysterical little hen. The moral of the story, depending on which ending you like:

> Don't believe everything you hear, or
> Have some courage and don't be such a chicken.

* * *

When I decided to write this book, it was when real estate values in the United States, and even around the world, continued declining at an alarming rate. As I looked to the different U.S. markets, people who previously had been swept up in the excitement of escalating property values were now depressed, panicked, or both. On every one of the dozens of news channels, it was easy to find some talking head insisting that the bubble had finally burst, the mortgage meltdown was in full swing, banks were failing, the credit crunch was here to stay, the government was going to throw in over a trillion dollars to stem the problem, and real estate prices would never recover.

The sky was falling, or so they said.

The chicken littles were running around everywhere, squawking. If you've ever watched chickens in a flap, you know they kick up a lot of dust and poop all over everything. It's a pretty good metaphor for what was happening among these so-called expert analysts. They threw around statistics and projections and complex studies like so much chicken manure, and they obscured the true trends by continually pecking at only certain parts of the country or scratching only short periods of time. The outlook for real estate was starting to stink, and it was largely due to the load of crap they were dumping onto it.

What really ticked me off was that the experts constantly neglected to mention one very important fact: **real estate is a commodity with recurring cycles**. Let me say that another way: Real estate markets will always have cycles of up and down, both regionally and nationally. At any time in history, those who get caught up in the greed associated with boom times or the fear associated with bust times are the ones who ride the roller coaster, experiencing flash-in-the-pan success or losing their shirts. But those who take a contrarian approach are the ones who steadily build the legacy kind of net worth that can sustain generations. They are the Trumps, the Zells, the Buffetts—the moguls and mavericks—and, yes, the

McKinneys you read about. It will be you, too, when you put what you learn in this book to work.

For nearly twenty-five years, I've been taking the contrarian approach, making new markets in real estate and creating opportunities where no one else recognizes them. Today, I'm known as the "real estate rock czar," "the king of ready-made dream homes," and the world's first real estate "artist," delivering magnificent oceanfront properties to the world's wealthiest, who clamor for the opportunity to own them. My business has not only survived four of the most recent down cycles (which we'll examine in great detail later in this book, along with the two downturns that came before that), but my company has also profited and thrived during *all* cycles of the market. So, as the country became gripped with fear during the most recent real estate and capital-markets implosion, many reporters, real estate investment clubs, and market mavens sought me out as a beacon of realistic optimism and opportunism. I offered a resounding counteropinion to the prevailing point of view, and I backed up my position with my own results and even with my current actions in the face of fear. I could say unequivocally that I always put my money where my mouth is, something few "experts" can claim.

Right at the depths of the cycle, I was fully invested in creating two multimillion-dollar oceanfront estates, Acqua Liana ($29 million) and Crystalina ($30 million), both designed to set new standards of environmentally responsible building practices for ultraluxury homes. During what some considered the most uncertain of times, I was shouldering huge amounts of risk. Nearing completion as this book went to press, Acqua Liana was conceived, constructed, and finished down to the gold-plated toothbrushes in the master bathroom, fine linens on the beds, and soft Egyptian-cotton towels in the closet—all without a buyer in mind. Similarly, Crystalina would be undertaken, as all my projects are, as a *speculative* investment.

Even before Acqua Liana and Crystalina were in the works, I'd spent over two years designing and permitting the world's most expensive oceanfront spec home, to be priced at $135 million. The Manalapan Residence sprawls over nearly 70,000 square feet, with fourteen bedrooms, twenty-two bathrooms, and a sixteen-car garage. I was slated to break ground only when a prudent amount of debt had been retired.

With three oceanfront properties in various stages of development during the bust cycle, my own money, reputation, and company were on the line throughout the whole turmoil—just as they were in the previous three downturns, just as they have been for the past quarter-century. I was (and still am) repeatedly asked, "How are you able to get eight hours' sleep every night?" or "How do you keep a full head of hair?"

More than once, when I've stepped up to a public urinal, someone has taken his place right next to me and said, "I just wanted to see if those things were really made out of brass."

Most often, people ask me, "How is it that you continue to pursue such big, new projects at a time like this?"

Whenever this comes up, I have to smile. It's always "a time like this." Welcome to the world of high-stakes real estate, where risk walks arm-in-arm with opportunity.

So I regularly respond, "I create my own reality and markets to go along with it. I recognize what's going on 'out there,' but I don't want to be associated with that reality. I'm more concerned with what's going on 'in here,' so I'm going to make my own reality and a fortune at the same time."

Acqua Liana ("Water Flower"), $29 Million

Our oceanfront artistry: the largest and most opulent, certified-green home ever constructed.
(http://www.Frank-McKinney.com/acqua_liana.aspx)

I've never denied the inherent challenges—figures don't lie—but I do argue with pervasive negativity, the presumption that when numbers are down, they'll stay down. We aren't that little old lady in the Life Alert commercial. We may fall, but we can get up. Nor are we what I swear is the same old lady in the Clapper commercial. We can't "clap on" or "clap off" our sentiment when it comes to our opportunist's approach to the market. If you're an opportunist—and I argue in this book that this is the strongest position you can take in real estate—then you approach every new market scenario with the question of how you can best profit or protect your wealth, not how to run for the exits any time someone yells, "Fire!"

Besides, while things may sometimes look grim from the bird's-eye view (and we know what happens to those who listen to squawking birds), for the individual investor, the down times have always held tremendous opportunity. Lots of people prosper in boom times, of course, but many set themselves up to make even bigger money during a crisis/correction.

Why not do both now?

In my frustration with the dire predictions, I've confronted the naysayers. Have you noticed how nearly all the "expert" studies rise to consciousness only when the pundits are portraying a fiery doom? How they conveniently appear during a downward cycle that they are unable to recognize is inherent to real estate? Why is it that their crystal balls get so swollen and hazy when values are set to elevate?

It's typical of overeducated, pompous, self-consumed academics with too much time on their hands, far too many cups of latte in their systems, and too many capital letters before or after their names: Ph.D., Dr., D.S., D.A, and so on. (Ask me sometime what D.S. or D.A. stands for.)

These authorities put food on the table based on their ability to formulate intimidating, Ivy League–sounding, and completely biased studies. How dare we doubt them! Yet these experts have yet to earn a single dime through full-time investing in the commodity they profess to be so astute about: real estate. Aren't I more of an authority on real estate than the pundits? Who has the most on-the-ground experience?

I hereby propose that from now on we let those people succeed in *watching* and *talking about* the market while we succeed in seizing the opportunities such markets present.

Yes, we should read their gospel (certainly, learn all you can—I do), but I also have to ask one question: **if you were going to invest your life savings in real estate, who would you choose to advise you, these supposed experts or me?**

Although my disagreement and irritation with the academic analysts led me to start writing *Burst This!* during what I've called "the Great Real Estate Depression of '08 and '09," it isn't a book only for the tough times, nor only for the good times, nor only for any other specific time. It's a book about how to profit in real estate *any time.* I know that sounds like a tired statement, but I can back it up with nearly twenty-five years of stellar results.

Keep *Burst This!* at the front of your bookshelf, and plan to come back to it ten minutes, ten days, or ten years from now, whenever you need a dose of realistic optimism and practical wisdom. It's about enduring principles and practices that I've used to increase my personal wealth, year over year, ever since I got started in this business by buying foreclosures and rehabbing crack houses so many years ago. From the beginning, I've worked consistently to get where I am now, and the lessons I learned from that first deal, and every deal I've done since, still have bearing on what I do today. And let me be clear: real estate is what I do every day, day in and day out. There are plenty of books in circulation by real estate *theorists* (notice how close that word is to *terrorists*—they both love inspiring fear), who are no better than snake oil salesmen. Most of these "experts" haven't actually been on either side of a real estate transaction since my hairstyle was popular.

I wrote about my first twenty years in the real estate business in my second bestseller, *Frank McKinney's Maverick Approach to Real Estate Success.* Since its publication, I've received thousands of wonderful letters from readers telling me how they've used the book as a guide and done extremely well by following it during all kinds of regional market fluctuations, including the most severe one that happened recently. How will *Burst This!* be different? Here, I promise to go toe-to-toe with the experts, dismantle their theories, and offer you the best of what I have in concrete, actionable advice for how to make it big in real estate, in all economic conditions—even in the middle of the "biggest financial crisis since the Great Depression of 1929," maybe ever—whether you're a first-time home buyer or a seasoned deal-maker.

Do I have a crystal ball to foretell the future? Many say I do, especially my bankers. Truth be told, I really don't. But do I have the experience and the foresight to guide you through any kind of real estate cycle? You bet. If you're still sitting on the sidelines and wondering when the right time will be for you to get into the market, get back into the market, or make a new market . . . if you want to capitalize on the predictable upswing that always comes after a downturn . . . if you know the smartest move you can make is following strategies that weather anything the market throws your way . . . then you're in exactly the right place at the right time.

In Part One, "The Confident Contrarian," *Burst This!* will

- reveal the **mindset and psychology** you need to take smart risks in any kind of market;
- show you exactly what to look for so you can **anticipate and make market trends;**
- set the record straight on **what's really happened with real estate** investments, both for the short and long term.

I take you on a factual real estate retrospective, a postmortem of the housing markets, from the midseventies to today. Together, we'll look at **six distinct real estate cycles** over the last thirty-six years, sifting out critical, recurring trends that highlight significant opportunities while signaling where history might repeat itself. You'll get the **evidentiary truth**, not the fear-mongering or sugar-coating, on real estate's ups and downs. You'll see exactly how I've successfully handled these predictable cycles with **timeless financial and investment strategies**. I'll also pinpoint the types of real-estate investments that have consistently shown **immunity to the market's volatility**.

In Part Two, "The Market Maker," you'll get the lowdown on how to find, fund, and finish a great property.

- These chapters walk you through the real estate fundamentals of **locating, negotiating, buying, and improving**—plus how you can create opportunities and completely avoid bursting your own bubble.
- I'll tell you about the one kind of real estate deal I would return to if I lost everything tomorrow—and why you or I could stick with this and **make good money at that level forever**.
- And I'll caution you about **the real estate weapon** that, if used sensibly, can help you rise above the competition, but if used irresponsibly, could cause you to self-destruct. Hint: it's the very same thing that took down some of the big national banks recently.

In Part Three, "The Artist and The Closer," it's all about **closing the loop and closing your buyer**. It's about who you are in the real estate world, what you stand for, and the brand that is you. This part of the book offers you a complete system for selling any property, which I call the **"Grade School Compass Approach to Marketing, Promotion, and Sales."** Yes, it's as simple as it sounds. Implementing its 165 distinct elements requires diligence, attention to detail, and a bit of creativity, but it's entirely adaptable to your situation, whether you're ready to move up from your first starter home or working to close the deal on your fiftieth multimillion-dollar property.

Part Four, "The Enlightened Absolutist," reveals the single most important spiritual principle of my astronomical success. I share with you how compassionate capitalism and responsible stewardship have led to the greatest rewards I've given and received. I also provide you with a set of simple actions you can take today that will accelerate your ascent both personally and professionally.

I guarantee that when you have turned the last page in *Burst This!* and you promise to diligently apply what you've learned, you'll be able to dominate your chosen real estate market and do so with far greater confidence, backed up by a proven plan for making it big. By the time you've returned this book to your bookshelf (no sharing—your friends and associates must buy their own),

- you'll fully recognize that **you can create opportunities** as easily as you might create your own bubble;
- you'll be ready to **do your next deal (and every one thereafter) safely and with complete confidence** that you can not only buy right, but you can sell like no other, too; and
- you'll **turn that bubble mentality inside out**, transforming it into a force field that protects and bubble-proofs your real estate investments forever.

Go on, you can say to the markets and the pundits and anyone else who challenges your ability to succeed with real estate: *Just try and burst this!*

I promise you, they won't stand a chance.

PART ONE

THE CONFIDENT CONTRARIAN

When everyone else is racing for the exits,
that's when you should be calmly
walking through the entrance.

Although I'm most often referred to as the world's first real estate "artist," I'm also considered a realist and an optimist, yet always an opportunist. (That's quite a few "ists.")

To succeed in real estate, it's unwise to approach your craft as only a flipper, wholesaler, retailer, builder, renovator, contractor, short seller, or any of the other labels you might stick on yourself. You must consider yourself a real estate *opportunist* who is educated and ready to profit in any market, using many applications, under any condition.

Burst This! is designed to help you understand all the roles you must play as an opportunist.

As I write this from my tree-house office, I'm carving out a new niche as the "green giant," the guy who creates oceanfront masterpieces that combine opulent luxury and environmental responsibility, and in Chapter 1, you'll see how this is just as much a part of the American Dream as the charming three-bedroom, two-bath with the nice lawn and picket fence. More important, you'll see how the American Dream safeguards two crucial market segments and how you can profit from them.

In Chapter 2, I share with you how you can boost your own risk tolerance—how you can gain the confidence you'll need to take prudent risks in any kind of market. This is the realist talking. Yet to do what I do, I have to live in my *own* reality, not the media's or anyone else's. That's the optimistic and opportunistic side—something you'll read more about in Chapter 3—which will keep you ahead of the curve, not looking at its backside.

In Chapter 4, we examine six historical cycles of the real estate market in detail. Don't worry: I won't bury you in charts and graphs and numbers, but I will give you the unvarnished truth about recurring ups and downs. I will use real estate's past to help you predict your real estate future.

Let's start with a simple analogy, which you should keep in mind as you read the next few chapters: Think of certain segments of the real estate market as blue-chip investments. "Blue chip" stocks are those offered by companies that are considered safe places to put your money—leaders in their class that are in healthy financial shape. Much real estate is a Pfizer, a Coca-Cola, a Cisco. It's a Dow Chemical, Apple, Microsoft, General Electric, Bank of America, or Google.

What defines a blue chip is that it makes steady money for investors over time. In a single month, or even a single year, prices may dip and investors may sustain short-term losses, but if that happens, it reflects *undervaluation*, not depreciation. There's a big difference in the definition here. In other words, for a period of time, a blue chip can be sold for less than it's been worth historically: it's a bargain because the investment is backed by a still-strong entity that remains profitable and the best of breed in its class.

For the confident contrarian, recognizing the aberration represents a significant opportunity.

As one example, consider Microsoft's antitrust issues of 2000–2001. Imagine that someone you knew well, someone with a sharp financial mind and your best interests at heart, had come to you in December of 2000 and told you Microsoft had dropped to twenty dollars a share, and that it historically had been more than double that. This person said that although it might not get up to fifty dollars again, it surely was undervalued now. This low price was counter to its historical performance. Wouldn't you have wanted to buy some shares? Maybe a lot of them? Using your backward-looking crystal ball, I bet you would.

You could have bought that stock, closed your eyes and gone Rip Van Winkle, then woken up a little less than *three years later* (not even the twenty years old Rip spent snoozing under his tree), and your stock would have been worth more than thirty dollars a share.

A more recent example would be Warren Buffett, the richest man in the world at this writing, taking a large stake in General Electric and Goldman Sachs—once again taking a contrarian's approach, investing in best of breed while they were suffering from declining share price in the face of much fear. Buffett follows and profits from a simple rule of buying: "Be fearful when others are greedy, and be greedy when others are fearful."

"Be fearful when others are greedy" refers to occasions of *overvaluation*, which occur even among the blue chips. Who can forget the dot-com bubble, when many investors' excitement got them so jacked up that they were willing to pay obscene prices for anything even remotely related to the Internet? The blue chips that were developing products and services for the World Wide Web got a price bump from that run-up, too. And when the correction occurred, when investors realized the emperor wasn't wearing any clothes and started unloading the stocks that were *overvalued*, the blue chips' prices normalized, too. However, those prices didn't bottom out and go to zero like so many of the dot-com stocks (the ones that had no earnings but once boasted a high-share price just because of the ".com" in the company name). Those investors who got out before the bubble burst—who sold before the market could no longer sustain inflated prices and share prices dropped like a stone—made out like bandits. The same held true during the recent market correction. So many quality companies were devalued just as a matter of course, not based on any real depreciation. Contrarians like Buffett stepped in to feast.

Throughout this book, when I talk about a "bubble," I'm referring to any market condition where people are excited about a commodity and therefore paying more for it than what it's worth. Of course, that "worth" can be hard to figure. In a bull market, demand (and greed) keeps driving prices up, up, up. In a bear market, flagging demand (and mostly fear) drives prices down. It takes a cool head, a commitment to making your own markets, a realistic review of historical values, and an ability to shut out the noisemakers (the pundits and panderers) to avoid getting caught in the greed and fear cycles of the masses.

Yes, you need to protect yourself against market bubbles, and I'll be helping you do that in this first part of the book. Yet there's something incredibly important you need to realize right now: **The bubble you most need to protect against is *the one you might create on your own* by overpaying, overextending, overleveraging, overimproving, underimproving, getting overexcited, or not marketing properly. *Burst This!* will definitely help you pay the right price for the appropriate number of properties, using responsible debt without introducing damaging emotion, while insuring you improve for maximum appeal. Most important, it will help you market like nobody else.** Although there's plenty to be learned by studying the trends generated by the emotional reactions of the majority of investors (in general, what *not* to do), the most important trend for you to follow is your ability to make markets while making the most of any situation.

1

THE AMERICAN DREAM
WILL NEVER DIE

When TV shows and entire channels made it big by showing viewers how to flip, sell, move up, fix up, stage, and landscape your house for greatest curb appeal and highest profit, they were riding the wave of the new decade, all the way up to late 2006. At the turn of the twenty-first century, home loans were cheap, people began using their own houses like personal ATMs, and getting into the real estate business had become as easy as picking up that free lollipop on your way out of your local bank. People who wanted a new place for themselves and people who wanted to invest in real estate were in full-on Mardi Gras mode. Times were pretty darn good, prices were rising steadily, and it looked to most as if the party would go on forever.

Then the mortgage and credit crisis hit, and home values began to drop precipitously after 2006, an inevitable swing of the pendulum. I was intrigued when these TV programs didn't shut down along with many of the subprime lenders. The shows' producers and their audiences' appetite for more seemed unfazed by what was happening in housing markets across the United States. At the same time, I noticed that attendance continued to rise at the many real estate investment seminars and club meetings I was keynoting across the country.

Interesting, I thought at the time. *These television folks and many real estate investors seem to understand what's happening better than the financial analysts, who sound like they get their forecasts from a Magic 8-Ball: "Outlook not so good."*

Unlike the perky carpenters and interior decorators on TV, the so-called experts were talking as if no one would ever buy a house again. Irritated by what I considered a lot of self-serving noise from the pessimistic pundits, I often wondered, *Don't those guys learn from the past?*

As the ol' 8-Ball would say, "Don't count on it."

In fact, interest in real estate doesn't disappear when times get tough, which is something savvy real estate investors understand. Demand doesn't die; it just starts to run scared, like the rest of us. Once it's safe to come out again, that pent-up demand always explodes, and the market cycles back into rebound and growth mode . . . at which point the analysts and theorists clam up and go back to their ivory towers, and the talking heads switch gears from preying on people's fears to running up their greed, and the cycle starts all over again.

What will never disappear, nor will it ever burst, is people's innate desire to own a part of the American Dream. We could get into a lengthy psychological/sociological dissertation on what that means, exactly, but it's unnecessary. All you have to do is close your eyes, and the symbol of all that is good about the American Dream will pop right into your head. It's a single-family home: a three-bedroom, two-bathroom, single-story, nicely renovated place with a freshly mown lawn behind a crisp, white picket fence. It's the prototypical entry-level home, the kind gainfully employed people usually buy in their late twenties to midthirties when they're thinking of starting a family and getting a dog.

This segment of the real estate marketplace is recession-, bubble-, and almost-anything-else-you-could-possibly-imagine-proof. The American Dream will never die, because owning a piece of it is one of the most compelling ideals we have. It's been with us since the country was founded, and it helped drive exploration and expansion. The right to own property is even protected by our Constitution under the Fifth Amendment. ("No person shall . . . be deprived of life, liberty, or property, without due process of law; nor shall private property be taken for public use, without just compensation." But make no mistake: That right *must* be earned responsibly; it's not an entitlement. You have every right to pursue the American Dream, but no inherent right to achieve it. More on this later in the book, where I go more deeply into the subject of debt.) The American Dream resurged and solidified at the end of World War II, when the veterans came home with the hope of restoring normalcy, stability, and even legacy to their families. The emblem of that hope was and still is home ownership, especially first-home ownership.

Whether you're a beginning investor, seasoned pro, or first-time home buyer yourself, take some comfort in knowing that this kind of house—the starter home—presents a market opportunity you can take to the bank over and over again. In fact, if the bottom were to fall out of the ultra-high-end market I make today, if my critics were to be proven right and I found myself dumpster diving (yes, someone actually predicted that), then you can bet that I would return to the starter-home market segment, where I made excellent money for the first six years of my nearly twenty-five-year real estate career.

The same principles that were at work back then still apply now:

- **Real estate is all about the local market.** Some regions experience price spikes and drops based on the local economy, but there's no such thing as a national real estate market. You don't have to study national statistics or economic indicators to make good buying and selling decisions in your local market. You don't need to travel the country looking for great opportunities; you can be an expert on the five- to twenty-mile radius around your own home and do very well in real estate. (What is the entry-level home in your area? It probably costs less than $300,000, and it may cost *a lot* less than $300,000, especially if you're in the Midwest or Great Plains states, or some places in the South. A great way to find out is to meet with a realtor or visit a real estate investment club in your town, something I'll address more in Chapter 2.)

- **You make your money the day you buy, not the day you sell.** Regardless of your market, your improvements, and your ability to sell, the price you negotiate for the property determines your potential profit margin from the outset. *Overpay and suffer the consequences.* A well-bought property is like an annuity that pays off handsomely. I actually celebrate our "buy" days more than the "sell" days because I know I have created a tremendous opportunity. (You'll learn the exact, simple formula for computing and securing your profit margin in Part Two of this book.)

- **If you market like nobody else, you can make up for earlier mistakes.** You might not have secured the absolute best location, you might have paid a little more than is optimal, or you might have overlooked a couple of improvements that would perfect the house, or even overimproved where you shouldn't have—this can happen because of inexperience, budget limitations, budget overruns, or any number of other reasons. But if you become the master marketer I know you can be, you'll still turn a very respectable profit. (Part Three's "Grade School Compass Approach" shows you how in great detail.)

These three precepts have carried me through since my first investment property purchase in 1986, when I bought a fixer-upper for $36,000 in Palm Beach County, Florida, within ten miles of where I was living at the time. It was a crack house, a dilapidated two-bedroom, one-bath, 620-square-foot junker in a neighborhood overrun by drug dealers, prostitutes, and their customers, but when I saw it, I saw opportunity, not blight. I knew I could not only make that house the nicest little crack house on the block, but I could also improve the neighborhood. I could make a new market, set a trend, and do some good for the people who lived nearby. So I used the $30,000 I'd saved while working as a tennis pro, together with $6,000 I borrowed from family and some of my tennis students, to take on the house and its renovation. I sold it six months later for $63,500, netting a $7,000 profit.

That was my first big real estate deal, and I don't say that with tongue in cheek. In all my years in real estate, I don't think I've ever felt better or more proud than I did on that closing day at 10:30 AM on the fifth day of December in 1986. What I gained from the process of locating, negotiating, buying, improving, marketing, and selling this first house remains invaluable to me, and *Burst This!* gives you everything I've learned since that stellar day, and then some.

By the way, the last time I checked, my buyer from that first deal still lives there, and the neighborhood has come up considerably. Not long ago, comparable houses on the same block were selling for $200,000.

Over the next few years, I did more deals and learned more about what worked and what didn't. I bought and renovated several nearby houses along Bankers Row in Delray Beach, Florida, which is where my wife, Nilsa, and I were married in 1990. In fact, we both believed so wholeheartedly in what we were doing to revive that area, and had fallen so in love with one of our properties there (a 1920s Italianate home we'd bought in 1989 for $75,000, with an original fountain in the front and cozy guesthouse out back), that we decided to make it our first home together as husband and wife. We held our wedding reception in the romantic courtyard, I carried her over the threshold at the end of the evening, and our wedding night was the first night we spent there. We were delighted to put down roots in such a beautiful place, and I'm not at all embarrassed to admit that we'd completely bought into our own hype about what an up-and-coming neighborhood it was. We'd found our dream home, for sure.

A few years into our wedded bliss, I went to Nilsa and said, "Honey, I'm tired of working on so many houses every year, having twenty electric bills, twenty water bills, and managing so many different work crews and hiring so many different plumbers with their pants falling down, and I just can't do it anymore. Let's do just one. I know this business, so let's take a chance and buy this falling-down oceanfront house I've found on the beach. So it's $750,000 instead of $75,000. It looks so much like what we've been doing, with its two weeks' worth of uncollected newspapers strewn across a front lawn that hasn't been cut in months, its broken windows, and toppled mailbox. When we're done with this one, we can retire, and not put ourselves out ever again. I promise. Besides, it's just one more zero added to the acquisition."

No doubt Nilsa raised an eyebrow at me for the "never again," "we can retire," and "just one more zero" comments, but to her credit, she said yes. She knew that I wasn't a fly-by-night character with no plan, I wasn't a dreamer, and I wasn't about to make a stupid choice. A calculated risk, yes. A confident, contrary investment, yes. She believed in me, she believed in us, and she believed we could do it together. Yes, yes, yes.

She agreed even though it would mean selling our lovely home, the car, and some of our clothes—and still having to borrow a considerable sum—to close the deal. In order to "sacrifice today for a better tomorrow," we sold our place on Bankers Row in 1991 for $250,000.

Turns out we were right about the neighborhood again. The woman who bought our house resold it for $540,000 a few years later, and I recently saw it on the market again for $1.5 million.

We bought our oceanfront fixer-upper, Driftwood Dunes, for $775,000 and began work right away, cleaning up the yard, getting the exterior in shape, and putting up signs so that when a potential buyer came by, at any time, the place would be in its best possible condition. Meanwhile, we moved ourselves into a studio apartment that was so small you could flip your pancakes cooking on the kitchen stove while you were standing in the shower. But when we realized we could save money on rent by living in the small guest quarters above the garage of Driftwood Dunes, we quietly moved in. Because we didn't want our presence to prejudice a potential buyer, we lived there under the radar, keeping our clothes in the trunk of our car or in a locked shed, showering outside, and using only a microwave—again outside, to keep any food smells from the house. The house was always kept in immaculate condition, but whenever there was an unscheduled showing, it was like a fire drill. I would shove my half-eaten bowl of Fruity Pebbles under the bed while Nilsa ran to slam the trunk of the car shut. We lived like gypsies for quite a while as we sunk all our available capital into the real estate business. All told, seven years of a transient existence passed from the time we moved out of Bankers Row until we decided to buy our own home again, the 1930s beach house on 2.35 oceanfront acres where we still live today.

It was a huge leap from investing in properties in downtown Delray Beach to putting all our money on the oceanfront with Driftwood Dunes but, as it turns out, it was also exactly the right thing to do. We skipped over the volatile midrange market—the McMansions and other four-bedroom-plus houses may seem like the logical next step, but, while there are certainly exceptions to every rule, that's one real estate segment that rarely qualifies for blue-chip status. The starter homes and the high-end homes do qualify, as the real estate market is something like a herd of horses, where the top horse and the bottom horse have established positions. They graze peacefully while those in the middle of the herd get beat up, biting and kicking one another just to get a decent patch of grass.

In the midrange of real estate, the law of supply and demand can work against you. The homes remain out of reach for first-time buyers, and buyers in this market often rely on an unrealistic and irresponsible amount of debt to fund their lifestyles. They also count on an irrational rate of annual appreciation while they're convinced their job status will always be safe. When combined, these factors can cause uncomfortable fluctuations in price and ability to repay debt should even a small shift take place—in the market or in their lives. As recent history has shown us, this is often a volatile cocktail.

So we went straight from solid entry-level to high-end homes, and after eighteen excruciating months on the market, Driftwood Dunes sold for $1.8 million in 1994. Since I hadn't sold a property for more than $250,000 in the six years prior, it certainly was considered the stratosphere for me, as it was the most expensive deal I could have done at the time. This gave us a glimpse into the other bubble-proof segment of the market, at the opposite end of the spectrum from the entry-level home: the ultra-high end. While $1.8 million may not quite have qualified for that bracket (nowadays, I define the *ultra*-high-end segment as properties valued at $15 million and above for most areas), it was close enough for me to see exactly where I wanted to go.

What makes the ultra-high-end market segment so stable? Since the Roman Era, there has always been a class of people with vast amounts of wealth, who can afford to live like royalty—and pay cash for it. Those are my buyers now, the $50-million-and-up-in-net-worth club, an admittedly small group, totaling only about 50,000 in the world, or about .0000007 percent of the earth's population. Sometimes bankers and other doubters like to remind me of that tiny number, and that my chances of success are equally as small, but then I remind them that there are only a few estate homes magnificent enough to compete for these people's attention and desire, and I like my odds even better when we start narrowing it down into upscale, temperate locales. Only Beverly Hills, Bel Air, Malibu, parts of Hawaii, Southern France, the Italian Riviera, and a few others can compete with Palm Beach County, where my artistry is showcased. And if the buyer is specifically looking for something in Florida? Forget about it. Now we've narrowed the field to those five to ten other properties in the same league as my masterpieces. Doing the math, I like my chances.

So I'm competing among a handful of people who do what I do: designing, building, and selling the most opulent mansions around. I'm considered one of the best in the world at this, mostly because it allows the real estate artist in me to express my gifts in a way few investors can. I absolutely love real estate, and the ultra-high end affords me the opportunity to create spectacular oceanfront homes while making markets that haven't existed before. I enjoy the suspense of knowing *today could be the day* . . . for the big sale, for a groundbreaking purchase, for the grand new idea, for a unique opportunity. I assure you, I know I am alive *every day!*

Since Driftwood Dunes in 1991, we've stayed on the oceanfront, creating art in the form of the world's most magnificent multimillion-dollar estate homes, each set on the sun-drenched canvas of Palm Beach, on Florida's Gold Coast. Every new project is inspired by exotic locales and infused with vivid imagination. The sales prices have occasionally set records, and we've steadily increased them. After that first oceanfront sale, we went from $1.9 million to $6 million to $12 million, and then to $30 million and $50 million, with thirty-four multimillion-dollar sales on the way. Over the last ten years, the average selling price for our artistry has been $15.3 million, and the average time on market for these masterpieces has been an astonishingly low 54.5 days, compared to the high-end industry average of $5 million and fifteen months respectively.

As this book is released, I am just completing and nearing the sale of our $29 million Acqua Liana estate (http://www.frank-mckinney.com/acqua_liana.aspx), a direct ocean-to-Intracoastal masterpiece hailed as the world's largest and most expensive silver-certified "green" home. I'm also working toward completion on another large ocean-to-Intracoastal home where we hope to break our own $29 million green price record with the $30 million Crystalina estate (http://www.frank-mckinney.com/crystalina.aspx), where I'm building the first gold-certified, multimillion-dollar spec home

Crystalina ("Crystal Clear Views"), $30 Million

Crystalina entices ever-changing waterscapes and luxuriant landscapes into every room of this artistic triumph. It has been designed as the first-ever home of its size and price to be gold certified by the USGBC. (http://www/Frank-McKinney.com/crystalina.aspx)

in the world.

Am I ahead of my time by introducing green building at the highest end of the market? Am I attempting to set a trend before my buyers are fully ready for it? Maybe. But all I need is one buyer for each property, someone who loves a direct ocean location with a turnkey masterpiece that reflects the architectural influences of the South Pacific: the thatched roofs and innovative incorporation of water and glass throughout the homes, both for stunning beauty and to highlight the estates' connection with the ocean and its surrounding environment. (*Acqua Liana* means "water flower," and *Crystalina* loosely translates as "crystal clear views.")

Acqua Liana, for example, features the first-ever glass water floor with hand-painted lotus flower motif on the glass tiles below. You peer through eighteen inches of crystal clear water, where artistry is appreciated "under foot and under water," and the scene is accentuated with trailing bubbles. The water floor gives way to an open reflecting pond with nine-foot, hand-blown glass chandelier suspended above, all set before a soaring twenty-four-foot, floor-to-ceiling water wall affording ample views of the Atlantic. You walk under an arched aquarium wet bar—walk below with exotic fish above!—to explore the rest of the 15,071 total square feet of the home, including the 2,180-square-foot oceanfront master bedroom and dual kitchens (one for caterers and one for the owners' family). Out back, there's also a two-bedroom two-bath guesthouse adorned in bamboo and partially submerged in a lagoon.

For the fortunate few, that's the American Dream, just as much as the cute ranch house on a tree-lined street is for someone else. As someone who invests in real estate, you're delivering the American Dream to those who desire to own it just as much as I am.

You're playing an important part in ensuring its vitality, and making plenty of money in the process. At the same time, you're living your own version of the American Dream, the one that affords those who will work hard the opportunity to build whatever life they choose for themselves through free enterprise and capitalism. Long live the dream!

Your Chapter 1
BURST OF INSPIRATION

• Take a moment to consider why you're interested in real estate and what *Burst This!* has to offer. Is it your career, and you're working to improve your performance and results? Are you just getting started and looking to seal your first deal? Are you buying a place for yourself? What is your version and vision of the American Dream, and how will you deliver it?

2

TAKE OFF THE ROSE-COLORED GLASSES AND PLANT A ROSE GARDEN

The first time I agreed to enter a demolition derby, I didn't know any better. Sure, I knew it was about slamming the pedal to the floor, driving with all the testosterone one could muster, and smashing cars, but my prior experience with the sport was nonexistent.

For the ten months leading up to the Durango Demolition Derby in Colorado, one of the largest and most well known in the country, my friend Eddie Cairo, his pals, and their wives built the car. That's right: it took almost a year of weekend wrench slinging and blowtorching to give the ride its best chance to survive dozens of bone-crushing hits that would normally land the occupant in the emergency room, or worse.

With all that they'd invested, I had to ask, "Hey, guys, why isn't one of you doing this? I haven't lifted a wrench to help you—not that I'd know what to do if I did—but why me?"

Eddie shrugged. "Oh, well, we figured you'd be the one with the guts to drive it, plus half of our wives won't allow it, and the rest of us are either too big or too scared to do it." He laughed. "So why not put the crash test dummy—er, you, Frank—in the driver's seat?"

I didn't know if his vote of confidence was a compliment or an insult, but I was psyched to be driving in this crazy competition, and I was honored that they'd let me behind the wheel to drive for them.

"Well, that sounds like a challenge I could handle. Let me do a little research."

Eddie shook his head and laughed at me again. "Yeah, it's 'a challenge,' all right."

Six months later, as I watched the first round from the stands with Nilsa and our daughter, Laura, I started to sweat. Oh, the carnage! When we saw one car attempt to slam backward into another, but then somehow ride right up onto the hood and crash through where the windshield would normally be, we couldn't take our eyes off the driver who had a spinning tire inches away from his face—and we all realized just how dangerous this could be. After all, the objective is to disable, demolish, and otherwise destroy your competitors so you are the last one moving—and you do it with five-thousand pounds of steel and wheels. Laura started crying and Nilsa turned sheet white.

It scared me, too, but I was getting pumped. I couldn't wait to get inside the car, where Eddie and company had stripped out anything unnecessary, including the glove box, the upholstery, the radio, even the rearview mirror. (Though I jury-rigged a makeshift rearview mirror because I couldn't back up otherwise, as I couldn't turn my head in the stiff neck brace I'd wear.) When I finally strapped into the stripped yet rigid car, sporting fire-retardant suit and gloves, said neck brace, kneepads, mouth guard, and helmet, I thought my heart was going to burst an artery. I only wished my race suit came with a diaper.

What am I doing out here? The thought crossed my mind more than once as I sat in that 1991 Caprice Classic cop car, appropriately (prophetically?) painted with the number eighty-six. But who would be eighty-sixed: them or me?

When the green flag dropped and my heat began, I was determined not to embarrass myself or my crew, who had worked so hard, or my friends and family, who were all watching. I slammed the pedal to the floor, driving most of the time in reverse to protect the radiator, engine, and front wheel axle. The first hit slammed my head into the neck rest so hard that it bent (the neck rest, not my head).

The all-out smashup seemed to last for an hour, but it was actually fourteen minutes that concluded with one testosterone-fueled, full-length-of-the-corral, head-on collision with another car. The impact caused me to see black for a short time, but when I came to, I was ready to go again.

However, the car wasn't. Mangled and undriveable, it had to be towed back to the pits with three flat tires, the frame compressed into the wheel wells, the cooling fan dislodged and thrown into the car with me, all cooling fluid lost, and a dead alternator and battery. The crew would have forty-five minutes to repair the car if we were going to make it into the "last chance" heat, where all those who hadn't qualified for the finals could take one last run and try to move on to the final round. While the crew banged away with sledge-hammers, used a backhoe to pull out the frame, changed the tires, battery, and alternator, then replaced fluids and started applying duct tape everywhere, I sat down, feeling bummed and thinking the fun was over. That car did not look like it could be revived.

Two minutes before the heat was supposed to start, the car fired, and I raced out to take her into the corral. We were the last to speed onto the dirt, and as I sat there revving the engine, I couldn't comprehend how the crew had done it. Not only had they repaired the car, but it was running better than it had in the first heat!

We put out competitor after competitor. By the end, I was driving on two flat tires, and my radiator hose let go, spraying me with scalding water. But the car kept on going. It came down to just two of us, me and one other car that stalled in the corral. The other car was declared the winner, even though ours was the only one to drive out, albeit in reverse, as the transmission had lost all forward gears and I couldn't see out the front due to the hood being smashed up higher than the roof of the car. We appealed to no avail and were ranked number eleven out of forty for the entire derby. The top ten went to the finals, but my crew held their heads up. It was a fine effort for the day: we'd gone out there guns ablazing and come back with a complete heap of metal. That's what the derby's all about. And there is always next year. . . .

Why should you care about my foray into this crazy crash-and-burn sport? Like most high-risk endeavors, it has several parallels to real estate. **First, your team—not you alone—determines your success from the start.** Their trust in you puts you behind the wheel, their expertise can compensate for any lack of experience you may have, and their skill and understanding carry you through whenever there's a setback. A crash, even a big one, doesn't have to put you out of the running if you have a great crew in the pit.

You can easily see how analogous this is to the people who work with you, whether we're talking about office help, project managers, contractors, consultants, engineers, construction workers, or any of the other people who help make your success possible. The sheer number of details to be overseen and nailed down require you to be

Demolition Man

A sedan turned compact car: Is this the front or the back?

surrounded by people you trust and who will do an excellent job for you, for your potential buyer, and for their own personal and professional satisfaction.

You can also draw a comparison between the pit crew and your family. I can't possibly overstate how especially important the support and encouragement of your significant other is to your self-confidence and, therefore, the success of your real estate ventures. Whether your partner in life is also a partner in your profession or not, he or she is like the crew chief, in that this person deeply affects your ability to bring your best to each contest. I've watched some mediocre players rise to the height of their abilities because they had someone in their corner who always wanted the best for and from them, but I've also watched many people's promising careers tank in the wake of an unsupportive spouse.

Quite frequently, when I'm keynoting a real estate investment event, I'll notice a few people who look like they'd rather be anywhere else, and I'll know immediately that they're married to someone who dragged them there under loud protest. I'm no Dr. Phil, but this kind of relationship dynamic has to be addressed, so I give these couples the same advice I would give you if you found yourself in the same situation: I'd never tell you which to choose, the real estate business or the marriage, but you've got some thinking to do. Maybe some marriage counseling to attend. Maybe some career counseling. Maybe both. A great marriage and a great real estate career can each be so rewarding, and there is no need to sacrifice one for the other.

You can't go at this alone. You must do this together.

I've always said Nilsa isn't the woman behind my success, but instead the woman who stands beside me in success. In addition to being our talented interior designer for all of our estate homes, and a far better personnel manager than I ever will be, Nilsa is the one person I can always count on to believe in me. In the first chapter, I told you how she was willing to put it all on the line, how she said yes when I asked her to put her faith in me and put our lifestyle on hold so that we could sacrifice then for a better future. That certainly wasn't the only time she took big risks with me, for me, or on me.

While self-confidence begins with you, it's definitely carried through by surrounding yourself with people who believe in you. You need their support as you pursue the other important factor to success in demolition derbies, real estate, or life in general: **Gently yet often exercise your risk threshold like a muscle so that it becomes stronger and better able to withstand greater and greater**

pressure. If you have read any of my prior books, that theme may sound familiar, but I want you to focus on that statement for a moment. Repeat it to yourself, and then write it down.

The primary difference between me and others who'd like to do what I do, but don't (or don't do it successfully), boils down to my appetite for and willingness to take bigger and bigger risks. Speculation—the process of conceiving, creating, and completing these estate homes without a buyer in mind—is nothing *but* risk. From the time I acquire the opportunity to the time I sell a finished masterpiece to a buyer, I assume all acquisition costs; pay all the contractors, subcontractors, and consultants; cover all utilities and insurances; buy all the premier materials; and fully furnish the home. My thumbprint is on every inch of a 15,000-square-foot home, as I supervise every last detail down to the artistically folded edges of the toilet paper in every bathroom. With only 50,000 people in the world who are qualified and *might consider* purchasing from me, supposedly my odds of succeeding are incredibly small. Yet I've never lost money on a for-profit real estate deal.

Am I scared of something going wrong? You bet. Every day. I worry. I doubt. I second-guess my decisions. But to me, that's just a sign that I'm pursuing an opportunity worthy of my attention. If I were coasting along, I'd start thinking something wasn't right, that I wasn't pushing myself, that I was taking the easy way out and cheating myself in the process. The truth is that I live with fear nearly all the time, especially in these most challenging times, but I've gotten used to it. My risk tolerance is as fortified as the roll cage in my demolition-derby car.

Years ago, during those eighteen months when we had Driftwood Dunes on the market, almost all my capital was still tied up in that house. You might think that the logical thing would have been for me to return to renovating foreclosures because it was something I knew I could do to bring in some cash. But it was clearly time to take another calculated risk. We wanted to push into the ultra-high-end market, not keep doing what we'd always done, so I used the equity from the Dunes property to buy another lot on the oceanfront and immediately got to work with planning, designing, and permitting a 12,000-square-foot mansion. The risk paid off: Chateau D'Amoureaux sold for $5.9 million less than a year after we sold Driftwood Dunes.

Other than the amount of money on the line, things haven't changed for me since that old Caprice Classic was nearly new. As we were nearing completion on our $29 million ocean-to-Intracoastal estate, Acqua Liana, the safest bet was to wait for it to sell before devoting any resources to its sister project, the $30 million Crystalina. Why? Because I'm not absolutely certain the market is ready for either property: Will potential buyers think they might be sacrificing something with a "green" mansion? Do they (mistakenly) believe that you can't have the ultimate in luxury and the ultimate in environmental responsibility under the same roof? I'm banking on the absolute "wow" factor of what we've created at Acqua Liana to show them the truth, but are my buyers ready to believe it? I have to believe they are; the last time I checked, those were leaves growing on the trees outside my window, not $100 bills.

Even though I'm acutely aware of this uncertainty every night before I lay my head on the pillow with thoughts of "what if?" dancing in my head, by the next morning, a whole new set of "what if?" questions come to mind. What if today is the day Acqua Liana sells? What if today is the day some of our available land sells? What if today the economy shows signs of improving? Always the opportunist, I wake up every day knowing that there is no such thing as a home that stays on the market forever, and today I am one day closer to an eventual sale. And sure enough, many days turn out to include one of those "extraordinarily golden moments" that keeps me moving ahead with the one thing I have become pretty good at: taking risks that few understand.

So even though I currently don't have the funding to complete Crystalina if Acqua Liana doesn't sell in a timely manner, we are ready to continue what we've already started there when Acqua Liana sells because of my strong conviction based upon nearly a quarter-century of crystal-ball predictions that have come true. Notice I wrote *ready to . . . when. . . .* There are many factors at work that go into such a risky decision, and right now as I sit here in my tree house, many are undetermined. There is the cash-availability issue with the degradation of the credit markets, the psyche of the high-end buyer, the shift in consciousness toward that buyer, the pummeling our South Florida market is taking, and more. It's a risk definitely worth taking, as Crystalina has been fully designed and permitted, but it is not prudent for me to actually break ground until I have responsibly created enough cushion. That's where I implement my "three Rs": Responsible Risk=Rewards.

Yes, I've always had an appetite for risk. I used to emulate Evel Knievel in my backyard as a kid, setting higher and higher jumps and somehow surviving plenty of dangerous stunts. I spent my teen years breaking the speed limit and doing other things that turned my mother's beautiful head of black hair to white, and paid the price for it with more than a few nights in juvenile hall. In my adult life, I've found legal—yet no less daring—ways to feed my need for speed. Not that long ago, I jumped my motorcycle over a replica of the first house I sold, evidence that I never outgrew my admiration for Evel Knievel.

Launch[3]

To celebrate my second book release and my twentieth anniversary of making markets in the real estate business, we threw a blowout party where I launched myself and my bike over a replica of the first house I bought and sold, landed on the spot where we were launching our next multimillion-dollar spec home, and also launched what would become my second bestseller, **Frank McKinney's Maverick Approach to Real Estate Success.**

Plus there's the demolition derby . . . and racing my dirt bike around the path in my backyard . . . and driving a golf cart with a flaming Christmas tree tied to the back . . . and doing extreme sports like the Badwater Ultramarathon, a 135-mile nonstop footrace through Death Valley in blazing-hot summer.

One of the most popular chapters from my first bestseller, *Make It BIG! 49 Secrets for Building a Life of Extreme Success*, was the one that asked readers to assess where they were on a "risk continuum." At one end is the phobic who's frightened by the prospect of getting out of bed in the morning for fear that the floor will be cold, and at the other is the daredevil who seeks out every opportunity for risk and reward, often with no regard for their personal well-being.

Risk Continuum

phobic  *daredevil*

Everyone falls somewhere between these two extremes. Where are you now?

Those who skew toward the phobic end of the spectrum are those who allow the fear that always accompanies an opportunity to stop them from moving forward. Those who tend toward the other end feel the fear and still feel *compelled* to move toward the opportunity. So an important question to consider is who you think has the fuller life: the phobic or the daredevil?

Since the answer to that question is probably glaringly obvious to you, perhaps this is an even more important question: **how can you build enough confidence to consistently move forward in the face of fear?**

Which brings us back, again, to the demolition derby. You know, after that first year of nearly making it into the finals, I knew I had to return. Yet it had left me feeling pretty banged up, fairly cloudy-headed, and numb down my entire right side. At the time, no one but

Nilsa knew how badly injured I was. While I was still headachy and my face was experiencing something like a Novocaine hangover on one side, Nilsa and I were concerned about what I might have done to myself. As it turned out, the paralysis was temporary, probably from a concussion.

When I had lunch with a friend just before my most recent Durango Demolition Derby, I told her about the injuries I'd sustained in the last one. She's a physical therapist, and she looked at me like I was nuts.

"Why, exactly, are you driving in the derby again this year?"

"Because I remember how great it was last year, and I've learned from what I did wrong. I'll be easier on the machinery and not go after anyone head-on."

As in real estate, I chose not to let the risks keep me from doing what I love to do, but I'm always learning from my mistakes. If my margins got burned on some piece of property, would I never go back in the game, or would I simply learn from what took place and do a better job with the next acquisition?

I believe in preparation and the value of research, but only in the service of action. In the weeks before participating in one of these derbies, I look at tapes of previous years' competitions. I watch every heat. I watch the winners and the losers. I study like there is such a thing as a Ph.D. in "derbology." I scrutinize the weld lines. I watch the tires being affixed. I learn what to hit where and with what part of the car. I can't lift a welding torch or use a torque wrench, and I'm a laughingstock when it comes to working on my own car, but my role is to learn as much as I can—and then *get behind the wheel*. I do my homework, but I don't overthink it to the point of inaction. Otherwise, I'd be stuck in the mud, sitting on the sidelines, or getting slammed on all sides.

This year my goal was to make the finals, which we did, ending up in sixth place out of forty cars—not bad for a guy who didn't know squat a little over a year ago. I have set my mind to making the top three at next year's race (which would actually deliver prize money and trophies), with an overall win the following year. This will occur only when the power of team combines with the power of the mind, and with a willingness to take risks in the face of known and unknown danger.

BUILD CONFIDENCE, AND THEN GET BEHIND THE WHEEL

So I'm a daredevil—maybe that's true. But I'm no fool. I believe in taking risks, but I also believe in study, practice, and gradual progress. I studied six months for the first demolition derby, and my plan is to gradually do better each year, over four tries. I'm not so foolish as to say, "Next year I'm going to win the whole thing!" I know every time I compete I'll be learning something that will give me greater success the next time. It's the same with the Badwater race in Death Valley. Every time I've competed, I've looked to better my time and my experience. But the only way I can even step onto the Badwater course is after six months of intense physical and mental preparation, and with a team that supports me every step of the way.

The same holds true in real estate. My very first deal made me a grand profit of $7,000 on an investment of around $50,000 and six months of backbreaking work. But it was some of the most important money I've ever earned because it validated that *what I was doing worked*. It taught me the basics that I use today in my multimillion-dollar properties. I was perfectly happy to keep doing the same kinds of deals for the first six years of my career, and then I applied those exact, timeless principles to the oceanfront real estate market.

You, too, should be willing to start slow, start small, and build your confidence over time and over several deals. Real estate investing isn't the lottery; you're rarely going to have the "big win" that sets you up for life. Instead, it's a process of finding the right properties at the right prices and then selling them at a profit and, most important, building your confidence and knowledge with each deal. You're aiming for an upward spiral of progress that takes you from win to win. It's a far better way to go than jumping in with no preparation other than an idea and a lot of hope. If I had done that with the demolition derby, I'd have been a pancake after the first round. If I'd done that with Badwater, I would have been toast—almost literally—within a mile or two. And if I had done that with real estate, I might still be making tiny profits on lousy deals and hoping that the next one would be my big score. Or I'd be out of the business altogether.

My latest property, Acqua Liana, follows the principles of buying right, selling right, building confidence, and learning. This is the first time I have built a completely green property, and I had to learn a lot about construction materials, costs, and issues that I'd never dealt with before. However, what I learned on Acqua Liana will cut down my construction time by 12 to 15 percent on its sister property, Crystalina. And I'm certain that I will learn a great deal from marketing Acqua Liana that I can apply when it comes to selling Crystalina, as well.

When you invest in real estate, I don't advocate jumping into your first (or fiftieth) deal without doing some research first. You need that research to ensure you're taking a smart risk (not creating your own bubble by overpaying, overextending, overleveraging, or getting overly excited) and also to build your confidence. At the same time, you need to realize that there's a time for research and there's a time to act. When I did my first deal, I probably over-analyzed. It was six months before I put any money into a property. I'd go to the courthouse steps, where foreclosures were auctioned in Palm Beach County, and just watch the bidders. I had to work up the courage to put my own hard-earned money on the line, and I figured the best way to learn was to see what other people were doing and then do it better. Looking back, it was a great education, although it taught me more about what not to do than what to do. When I finally developed enough confidence from watching the auctions, I went out and made dozens of offers on places that met my criteria for a good purchase, and eventually one of those offers was accepted.

You don't need to spend as much time as I did watching and waiting. **My advice to you is to take three months, but not longer than six months, for your research** to give you the assurance that you know enough to move forward. Do *not* fall prey to taking what I call the "spreadsheet approach" to life, a.k.a. "paralysis by analysis." This is the common practice of overanalyzing every possible variable and forecasting every permutation and scenario. While I love the fact that we have so much information at our fingertips on the Internet, if you let yourself get overwhelmed with data, you'll start seeing all the reasons not to invest and never get in the market. You have to step out of what I call "cubicle mentality," looking only to make your life certain and safe. When I bought my first crack house, the only certainty I had lay in my own ability to do whatever it took to renovate and sell the house at a profit. Whenever I put my money into a multimillion-dollar spec home project—with up to two years to create the masterpiece in a difficult market that some say has "burst," and naysayers telling me I'm bound to go broke this time—the only certainty I have lies in my ability to tolerate risk, combined with my consistent experiences of coming out on top. I don't know what the economy will be doing when my property is completed and is ready for the fortunate few, but I do know that I can make a market even in the toughest conditions. It's never with a guarantee, but I have faith and believe.

Spending too much time and doing too much research won't help you make a better decision; it'll just give you more reasons not to take the risk. Overthinking is often just a prolonged excuse to allow fear to run the show. Without being consciously aware of it, you are actually looking for a reason to say no. And if you look long enough, believe me, in today's information society, you will find it!

Don't let the need to know turn into the need to "no." Realize that complete certainty isn't a realistic objective, nor is it even healthy. Instead, strive for *clarity* on the three criteria that are most important: 1) Is this an opportunity you believe in with all your mind and heart? 2) Do you see this as that annuity that will pay off handsomely for you and your family? 3) Does it make financial sense according to the formula provided and detailed in Part Two of this book?

I don't believe in the "ready, fire, aim" approach to life. I do believe in good preparation, appropriate analysis, detailed planning, and bold execution. I believe in doing my homework, relying on my intuition, saying, "I want to make a go of this," and then making the leap.

Here's how to avoid overanalyzing, overthinking, and thereby overlooking a great opportunity during that three- to six-month learning phase.

• **Get your head—and your assets—in order.** Make sure you're ready to dedicate the time and effort it will take to do the deal. If you're just starting out, you'll need to be willing to put a good amount of money into something that may take months to produce a profit. Can you deal with that timeline? Do you have access to the money you'll need for carrying costs until you sell the property? Do you have a contingency fund? It used to be that potential investors could just pull equity out of their homes or other properties and use them as down payments on their investment real estate, but in today's financial market, you'd better be sure your financing and funding is firmly in place before you put in a bid. You must be very conservative when it comes to your ability to carry your property.

More important, you must assess your risk tolerance. If you've invested in real estate before, how have your previous deals affected your psychology? If you made a killing in the bubble market of 2006, you'd better not assume it will be as easy in today's market and jump in without adequate preparation and analysis. On the other hand, if you invested in 2007 and had to sell at a loss, you may be overly cautious about getting back in until the market "comes back." But there are good deals to be found in every market cycle, and you need to be prepared to look for them and seize them when they appear. Make sure your risk tolerance is high enough to get you into, or back into, the game.

Finally, choose one investment system or strategy. Clear your bookshelf of all the wonderful books and tapes you may have accumulated and focus on one method. I see so many people who get excited about a particular kind of real estate, whether it's short sales, foreclosures, rehabbing, wholesaling, retail, apartment conversions, etc., only to jump ship to another method or sales category before they've really done anything or learned enough. Pick a method and plan to stick with it for at least six months of active investing. Don't let yourself be distracted by the great deal your friend just did or the latest speaker, seminar, or book—including mine—that promises you faster and better returns. To do well in anything in life, you have to be willing to put in sufficient time and effort to get good at it.

- **Begin to attend local real estate investment club meetings.** Real estate investment clubs didn't exist (or I didn't know about them) when I got started, so I had to learn about investing the hard way, through months of study on the courthouse steps and a lot of mistakes. You can shorten your learning curve considerably by attending a good local real estate investment club. First of all, the people in the club should know a great deal about your local community, which is the most important research you can do. (As we'll discuss in Part Three, all real estate markets are local, and your best deals will be found within a five- to twenty-five-mile radius of your home.) Second, real estate investment clubs offer informative guest speakers who are experts on many strategies and topics. The clubs often do bus tours to see potential properties and neighborhoods; they conduct visits to local home improvement stores to help you learn about budgets; they'll turn you on to foreclosure lists and introduce you to financing sources; you'll get tax advice about how to structure your corporate entity, and more. You also could have the chance to partner with other investors who have had some success in your market. Of course, at every club you need to be smart about whom you choose to associate with, and beware of the product promotion, but most good clubs offer a great fast track to real estate education. The easiest way to find one in your area is to do an Internet search on "Real estate investment club in [your community]."

• **Do the right kind of research.** You must become an expert in your local marketplace, not in national housing trends or how much home values have fallen in the state next door. It's awfully easy in our 24/7 news cycle/Internet world to get distracted by this housing report and that projection, and forget that all you're looking for is the right property in the right neighborhood that you can buy at the right price. Choose the neighborhoods where you want to invest and become an expert in the real estate there. Know what properties are going for, which banks are financing the deals, which realtors handle the kind of properties you are focusing on, and so on. Spend your three to six months becoming *not* a real estate expert, but an expert on your local marketplace.

• **Create your investment plan.** Lay out clearly and exactly how much you have to invest, what kind of property you're looking for and where, how much you're budgeting for improvements/renovations, marketing costs, closing costs, and so on. Make sure to include contingency funds in your budget. Create a timeline for acquiring, renovating, and selling the property, and then add at least two to three months. Even if you've invested in real estate before, your plan must reflect both current and anticipated market conditions for when you sell the property. Creating a good, solid, smart plan is as important as knowing your market, and you'll be getting important help on all of this in Part Two.

- **Start by back-testing a single purchase.** Talk to a local realtor and real estate investment club members who might assist you by locating a few great buys that you could have made (you'll get criteria for this in Chapter 6), but don't purchase anything yet. Then narrow your list down to one property. You want to see, if you had purchased a particular property and improved it according to your prescribed budget, could you have sold it for a reasonable profit? Then do it all over again with another mock purchase. Do not exceed more than five tests. If you feel you would have profited in three of the five, you are ready. "But Frank, I still have a 40 percent chance of losing money, so I'm not ready." Oh yes you are, believe me. When it's for real—with real money, not monopoly money—you'll be right.

Remember, you need to do this for only three to six months. **When you're ready to enter the market, make lots of offers, but start with one deal.** Don't overextend yourself by snapping up multiple properties. If you are just starting, I want you to see one deal through to completion before you move on. Look for The One. Complete it, and then look for The Next One. As you gain confidence, you'll be tempted to take on additional properties even at this early stage. *Resist it.* Even if you've been doing this for a while, you're far better served by focusing on only the number of properties that you can reasonably manage, both financially and logistically. Always know that you are in the business of risk, and the smart money never puts it all out there without a reserve to hedge against the worst-case scenario. Chapter 8 will give you even more details on safeguarding against the irresponsible overuse of debt.

Not long ago a friend of mine, David Dweck, said, "Frank, you must see everything with rose-colored glasses, given the amount of risk you're willing to take." He was surprised at my response: "That's ridiculous. I've never worn rose-colored glasses in my life. I pride myself in seeing reality as it is. I know exactly what I'm getting into with every deal and with everything I take on. I'm a realistic optimist. I make my own market. I take a patch of barren ground and plant a lush garden with the properties we create. I don't need rose-colored glasses; I turn reality into a rose garden of my own creation."

You, too, must combine realism, optimism, and risk tolerance to turn your real estate investing from a patch of dirt into a beautiful rose garden of profitable properties. You need to get your head and assets in order, do locally based research, learn what you can from other people, and then practice by doing a simulated transaction on a property or two. Consider all of that to be tilling the soil before you plant anything—that is, before you put your money on the line. But you can't wait forever before you plant and expect the garden to grow on its own. If you do, all you'll get is a patch of weeds. Put on the glasses of the realistic optimist and start planting. You'll be surprised at how quickly your garden will grow.

Your Chapter 2
BURST OF INSPIRATION

• Where are you on the risk continuum, closer to phobic or daredevil? What can you do this week to exercise your risk muscle so that it can be strengthened to withstand greater and greater pressure?

3

WHY A PH.D.
IN PARADOXICOLOGY
IS REQUIRED

My formal education stopped after a less-than-stellar sojourn through four high schools in four years (I was asked to leave the first three), but after twenty-plus years in real estate, I believe I have earned a Ph.D. in what I call "paradoxicology": the ability not just to deal with the extreme paradoxes of life but to celebrate and profit from them. You can see a clear example of this in the invitation I sent to a select group not too long ago . . .

How would you like to be one of the fortunate few at the premier grand unveiling of Acqua Liana, the world's largest and most expensive certified "green" home, priced at $29 million? Considered the hottest ticket in Palm Beach, the event is invitation-only and will be attended by more than 500 VIPs, media people, politicians, million-dollar real estate brokers, and book industry executives. The evening's festivities include a theatrical and illusionary unveiling, live entertainment, gourmet cuisine, and the "Friday the 13th Manalapan mojito."

43

This was the introduction to our latest big event, which included not only the grand unveiling of Acqua Liana, but also a launch party for *Burst This!* plus two other books, *The Tap* and *Dead Fred, Flying Lunchboxes, and the Good Luck Circle*, which I was releasing at the same time. The next morning, special guests rose with the sun and enjoyed a business breakfast like no other—meeting businessman and billionaire Rich DeVos, and later a business seminar featuring my "Leave-Your-Fears-Behind Coffin Exercise." (It's best I don't divulge too much about that part here. The surprise is half the impact, and if you're ever inclined to do it with me, I'd hate to spoil it for you. Suffice it to say that it involves a coffin, a eulogy, a promise that has yet to fail, and a chance to lay your fears to eternal rest.)

Some of the people attending our events are donors who support the Caring House Project Foundation. From time to time, they also accompany us to Haiti, the poorest country in the western hemisphere. Together, we've toured Cité Soleil, the poorest suburb in the city of Port-au-Prince, which is an unforgettable sensory experience. We've worked at a feeding center, visited an orphanage and a home for the elderly, and toured the villages that the Caring House Project Foundation has erected there. We've had communal meals with the people who live there, and sat down in front of a warm fire to share stories and conversation with these people whose lives appear to be so different from our own.

The contrast of the ultraluxury accommodations of our multi-million-dollar mansions to the bare essentials of the $5,000 concrete homes we build in Haiti (along with the sights, sounds, and smells that come with immersing yourself in the poorest city in the Western hemisphere) reminds me of the wild swings of the pendulum we can experience in real estate markets. These tours are

Stability and Self-Sufficiency Begin at Home

Just a two-hour flight away from our Florida oceanfront masterpieces, we build entire self-sufficient villages in the least developed country in the Americas, Haiti, with the generous support of donors to the Caring House Project Foundation (http://www.frank-mckinney.com/caring_project.aspx).

designed to illustrate that there's never just one side, whether we're talking about the price of housing or quality of life or, for that matter, economic theory.

Possessing an unshakable understanding that seeking out the dichotomies found in life *tends to reward the brave* is what I call having a Ph.D. in paradoxicology. Let's repeat that, as it is a very important element of this book, and even more important for your life: **those who develop a deep understanding that we should live with and embrace the dichotomies presented by life are rewarded beyond common measure.** Realize that whenever things look one-sided and everyone else is focusing solely on that side, it's time to look for the other. You'll always find the opposite somewhere, and sometimes not so very far away. The self-sustaining villages we build in Haiti for the world's most desperately poor are only a two-hour flight from the opulent mansions we create for the world's most extravagantly wealthy.

Sir John Templeton, regarded by many as one of the greatest investors of all time, was known for advising people to buy at the point of maximum pessimism, also called the point of *capitulation*, when everyone else is throwing in the white towel stained red with their own blood, and to sell at the point of maximum optimism, which has been called *irrational exuberance*. This is more than just a fancy way of telling you to buy low and sell high. It's a way of looking at the marketplace as driven by mass psychology and collective emotion, where you see the lament of extreme pessimism ("we are in a real estate depression," "the real estate market is in an acute crash," "it will never recover," "it may be worse than 1929") as a green light, and the jubilation of extreme optimism ("real estate is a no-lose investment," "the market always goes up and will be up another 20 percent next year," "everyone is making money hand over fist!" "my aunt's second cousin's friend just flipped a condo and made $50,000 on her first try") as a red light. Remember Warren Buffett's counsel: When everyone else is greedy, it's time to be afraid, and when everyone is afraid, it's time to get greedy. All other conditions dictate that you proceed with reasonable caution, neither racing in nor putting on the brakes. Notice the phrase is *reasonable caution*, not *extreme caution*. Reasonable caution is a matter of doing the three to six months of research I recommended in the previous chapter.

In the early part of my real estate career, I was clearly focused on the areas of maximum pessimism, the houses nobody wanted, the seedy neighborhoods. No investor was brave enough to enter, or they were too lazy to consider a $10,000 profit worth their time. So I know exactly what Sir John was talking about. These are the areas where you can not only find severely undervalued properties, improve them, and then sell them at or above market value for significant profit, but where you can also do a lot of good. (Whether doing good is already on your agenda or not, let me encourage you to embrace this idea for the simple reason that improving not just a house but a whole neighborhood is crucial to making a market.) You could say that I'm still focusing on the areas of maximum pessimism, trying to make markets where they are thought unattainable or unworthy, building enormous homes on spec with a minuscule number of potential buyers. Or compounding the risk by choosing to make oceanfront markets in towns that aren't as well known as, for instance, Palm Beach, Boca Raton, or Malibu.

Still, the maxim holds: As long as you buy right—and I'll give you the formula for this in Chapter 6—real estate can be as certain as an annuity or a blue-chip investment. Just as the title of that chapter says, "Once You've Bubble-Proofed, You'll Celebrate Your 'Buy' Day More than Your 'Sell' Day." That's what Sir John meant when he advised that you buy at the point of maximum pessimism: **you capitalize on the fact that other people don't yet see the value concealed by overreaction, by blinding emotion.**

Remember the devastation of Hurricane Katrina in 2005? (Who could forget?) As the floods came and the water washed away people's homes and businesses, the natural response was to flee. People were dying, the city they loved was crushed, and the sheer force of this disaster was terrifying. Could we call this a point of maximum pessimism? Of course. Were people right to be pessimistic? Of course. Did that create an incredible opportunity for investors to purchase undervalued property in New Orleans and along the Gulf Coast of Mississippi? Of course.

We don't know yet exactly how long it will take to rebuild the entire city, so someone investing in New Orleans would be wise to view it as a buy-and-hold deal. Yet certain parts and parishes of New Orleans were among the few places in the country that showed significant appreciation twelve months after that fateful day in 2005. Remember that you're not going to tie yourself down to one kind of real estate label. If you were an investor living in Louisiana, and you were already familiar with the market in New Orleans, the time to buy was most certainly while things looked bleakest and the city was most desperately in need of people to come in with both a vision for the future and the cash to make it happen. In 2009, four years after Katrina leveled huge swaths of the casinos and hotels on Mississippi's coast, the casinos are operating once more and four cities in the area—Biloxi, Pascagoula, Hattiesburg, and Mobile, Alabama— produced some of the strongest appreciation in housing in the United States. Paradoxical? Yes. But the places you make the most money are often where others fail to see opportunity.

This ability to find value in undervalued real estate was one of the keys to Donald Trump's great success in the 1980s and 1990s, and well into the early part of this century. In January 1985 Trump bought one of the last undeveloped pieces of property in Manhattan, 77 acres of the Penn Central train yards on the West Side. It was considered a wasteland, a toxic dump. He paid $100 million for the land. Over the next ten years he wanted to erect Trump City, three buildings encompassing 5 million square feet of development that also included a 21-acre public park. In 1991 Trump brought in investors from Hong Kong, while he retained a stake in the project. Construction began in 1997. In 2005 the entire property was sold to the Carlyle Group for *$1.76 billion*—the largest residential real estate sale in the history of New York City. Paradoxical? Again, yes.

Nowadays many real estate investors are looking outside the United States to our neighbors in Central America for opportunities. While I spend a lot of time in Haiti and our housing projects there, just across the border in the Dominican Republic you can see developments going up right and left. The same is true in Costa Rica, Belize, the coasts of Mexico, and Panama. Housing costs are low, the climates are tropical, and many people from the United States and Canada are either moving or retiring to Central America to take advantage of the lower cost of living. These are areas many investors would never have considered when looking for great deals, but they demonstrate clearly that, with a little research and a willingness to go to locations others are just beginning to discover—to see value where most people do not—the confident contrarian can make money in every market. Paradoxical? . . . I think you get the point.

ARE THEY JUST TALKING, OR ARE THEY MAKING SENSE?

Let me ask you this: do you think that the academic analysts would be as enthusiastic as I am, or as Sir John was, about jumping into a depressed market? You know they wouldn't be, based on what they had to say during recent economic downturns. Both the media and the analysts tend to portray things as either boom ("Hurray!

Let's watch the race: everyone's making money!") or more often, bust (with even more enthusiasm, "Hurray! I mean, boo! Let's all enjoy, I mean feel bad, when the cars crash: nobody's making money!"). The truth is never so black and white. Here are the important truths every Doctor of Paradoxicology knows:

- **During the so-called bust times, buying opportunities abound.** This is when you can easily snap up valuable properties for far less than they're worth and in relatively short order sell them at a price more in line with their value, making a decent profit. (This assumes that you have some "dry powder," as in good credit and ready money to make purchases, and that you haven't overextended yourself going into the bust.) So it's a great time for some, and a lousy time for others.

- **During the so-called boom times, it's more difficult to locate a good opportunity.** You may be able to get in and out of the market and make a quick buck (or $60,000, as my sister Martie did during the run-up in San Diego real estate in the early 2000s), but the odds of getting overexcited and overpaying, then not recouping your investment, are higher. So it's a great time for some, and a lousy time for others.

What makes it a great time or a lousy time for *you* is how well you apply the confident-contrarian approach—whether you're able to keep your head on straight and make strategic purchases or sales while everyone else around you is out there just banging and crashing in the real-estate version of the demolition derby.

It's interesting: even during the so-called boom times, the media tend to put a negative spin on things, encouraging fear instead of a healthy respect for the cycles of a commodity. I remember reading the headlines for years that announced how much money people were making as real-estate prices soared in certain regions, coupled with a line just underneath that would always caution: "But When Will the Bubble Burst?" This subtext continued for nearly five years, so it was only a matter of time before they'd be proven "right," as an upward trend won't last forever. No self-fulfilling prophesy here, only time catching up to a certainty. Eventually they had a point, I guess, but how does that really help someone who invests in real estate? It doesn't. It just creates fear, confusion, uncertainty, endless second-opinion-seeking, and a false sense of, "Gee, what do they know that I don't?" Believe me, they don't know that much at all.

Even when they do know quite a lot, as with the analysts who have made their academic careers by studying market statistics, you should question both their motives and their methods.

It's now an established fact that home-price data, for example, is skewed. In particular, the often-cited S&P/Case-Shiller Index is handicapped for two reasons:

1. It examines only twenty metro markets, many of which are the most highly volatile in the country, from which it extrapolates nationwide trends. Finally, in April of 2008, S&P Index chairman David Blitzer "acknowledged his organization's overall and metro-market readings paint an incomplete picture." He must be the turnip truck driver, swerving as the rest of us fall off!

2. One of the index's authors, Robert Shiller, gets paid to be negative. He's an admitted bear whose company, Macromarkets LLC, provides data to the housing hedge funds, which make their money when people have low confidence in real estate

investments. These hedge funds lose a tremendous amount of money and business when prospects look good for real estate; Shiller's job is to cherry-pick the data so that it doesn't.

That's just one particularly annoying example. Add in the fact that analysts are, by definition, always looking at what happened some time ago—the data isn't available in real time, plus if they're studying it, they have some pondering to do—so you can severely discount the value of this stuff as instructive or constructive. While I do rely on history to indicate where a trend may begin or deviate, most of the data is strictly *informational*. If you realize that it is often also manipulated (meaning slanted to suit a particular person's hypothesis, which is just a swanky way of saying *opinion*), you really have to take it all with a grain of salt. Heck, in recent times, you needed a salt mine. You can make statistics say about anything you want if you plug in enough (or not enough) variables.

At one point, I was seriously considering putting myself on the cover of this book flipping the bird, fuzzing out my middle finger, and basically saying that *Burst This!* is about telling everyone else to stick it. *Go on, try and burst the proven track record behind everything you'll read here.* It was meant to be a challenge and an indictment of those doomsdayers that I became so fed up with. Bubble-proofing is, in large part, separating yourself from the pack, turning off the noise of the financial press, and learning to think and act for yourself. Experts and analysts, *Burst This!* Airheaded talking heads, *Burst This!* Detractors, naysayers, gloom-and-doomers, *Burst This!* Get-rich-quick schemers, *Burst This!* Certain bank executives, *Burst This!*

My friend, you say it with me: *Burst This!* (And go ahead: let that finger fly.)

Start to consider the financial analysts as sportscasters: announcers who watch the game, comment on it, even develop some pretty well-thought-out analyses of the players and what they do on the field—reflecting the approach of Don Meredith rather than Howard Cosell. Where we get into trouble as investors is when we start to confuse the analysts with the actual game we're playing. Remember, the sportscaster may predict a winner, but in no way does that glorified observer actually determine the outcome of the game.

Although I have many points of disagreement with the academic analysts, I don't think they're completely full of baloney. Even Shiller, whose pessimism during the recent downturn was particularly grating, has some insightful things to say. He took former Federal Reserve Board chairman Alan Greenspan's phrase *irrational exuberance*, which described the unfounded excitement people feel during a bubble-boom, and made it even more meaningful in an article he titled "Infectious Exuberance," where he compared investor mania with the spread of a contagious disease. He wrote,

> Bubbles are a lot like epidemics. Every disease has a transmission rate (the rate at which it spreads from person to person) and a removal rate (the rate at which those individuals recover from or succumb to the illness and so are no longer contagious). If the transmission rate exceeds the removal rate by a certain amount, an epidemic begins.
>
> Speculative bubbles are fueled by the contagion of boom thinking, encouraged by rising prices. Sooner or later, some factor boosts the transmission rate high enough above the removal rate for an optimistic view of the market to become widespread. Arguments that this boom is unlike past bubbles—I call them "new era" stories—become more prominent and seemingly credible.

Agreed. People's tendency to get excited about making money is well established. (That's called *greed*.) And notice that the context of the above is that of a follower, rather than of a market maker. The first "transmitter" (the market leader) is long gone, lounging away on a Caribbean island counting his or her profits while the last of the wannabes are jettisoned off like waste in a toilet. Where Shiller and I part ways is in how we view that proverbial "half-full, half-empty" glass of water. I say it might be approaching half-full, and he says the well is poisoned. But the truly pertinent question is this: What are you going to do about the downside of irrational exuberance? How can you profit from it, or at the very least, protect yourself from it?

Before we get to that, let me point out that there is an upside, since this chapter is about becoming more aware of life's paradoxes. Greenspan's *irrational exuberance* is a phrase describing the excitement people feel when other people are making money, and they want to get in on it, too. That alone isn't inherently a problem, though, is it? Remember the gold rush? People who raced to the California coast were probably irrationally exuberant—they didn't understand all the risks and acted quickly, throwing on a backpack and getting on a horse, galloping to find their fortunes. They were following their gut and gold fever more than anything else, but it also made them rich. There were plenty of people who went broke near the end of the gold rush, but their excitement wasn't to blame as much as it was their being late to the party. We could just as easily make this argument about every historical bubble there has ever been, as far back as the 1600s' famous "tulipmania," where people were going crazy to own Dutch tulip bulbs as investments, on up to the most recent boom cycle in real estate.

That said, how are you going to avoid creating your own bubble, much less participating in one that the masses create? Due diligence. A little number crunching. Removing emotion. Discarding deals that don't fit the formula I share with you in Chapter 6. (Realize that before I did my first deal, I tossed forty promising properties that just didn't pencil out. That's forty opportunities researched to find The One that I was sure to profit from. I want you to remember that ratio.) You're going to become a confident contrarian, turn that bubble mentality inside out, and create a virtual force field that's impenetrable by anyone else.

Specifically, as a confident contrarian, you commit to the following:

- **Look for the moment of capitulation to make a buy.** Watch for signs of surrender: the market demonstrating an uncharacteristically prolonged downturn, where you are able to buy at 25 to 50 percent or more below the peak in property values with optimism becoming scarce in your market. Closer to home, look for the unmowed lawn, the newspapers piling up on the porch, the broken windows, the flaking paint, the tilting mailbox overflowing with bills, power cut to the property, and other clear signals that a property has been sorely neglected and the owner—or bank—might be looking to unload it.
- **Be a smart bomb, not a cluster bomb.** Don't go off in every direction haphazardly. Clearly define your targets and plan in military-like detail, then act with such precision that you can't miss.
- **No greed: Be happy hitting a single.** You don't need to swing for the fences to make excellent profits in the real estate game. If you know something about how to buy right and how to market, you can average an attractive return. It's foolish to

dismiss respectable earnings simply because your nephew Petey made a killing just a few years ago. Get over it. The real estate market did.

- **Think fast and act faster.** Build confidence, and raise your risk tolerance. Believe in yourself, and do your research as outlined in Chapter 2.
- **Focus on what you can control.** You have no sway over the markets or over other people's excitement or depression. What you can control is your response to the pessimism and optimism, and also how you locate, negotiate, market, and sell your property. *Burst This!* will help you hone these skills so that you can perform them better than anyone else in your market.

In the end, what you're doing is creating your own reality rather than buying into someone else's version. If you're interested in profiting from real estate, then you'd better be the originator and guardian of what's real for you. Buck the minion mentality, the impulse to follow along like a lemming and toss all your profits into the sea. Resist the pull of the mass psychology: If the tide is coming in (a buyer's market), it's probably time to swim out. And if the tide is rolling out (a seller's market), you can still go in the water—just don't get caught in the riptide. In either case, don't put your head in the sand or lie around sunbathing. Understand the trends, even read what the analysts/sportscasters have to say, know your local market, and then go out and make *your own* market.

That's exactly what confident contrarians do to bubble-proof their real estate.

Your Chapter 3
BURST OF INSPIRATION

- Undiscovered locations are areas where you can find severely undervalued properties. Have you ever seen a place and wondered, "Why isn't this part of town more popular? This area is great!" Is there an area within a ten-mile radius of where you live that has great potential?

4

A REAL ESTATE
POSTMORTEM

As I finished reviewing the volumes of research I'd gathered for this chapter, I was alone in one of our on-site sales offices. My staff was out for the day preparing for Tropical Storm/Hurricane Fay, and since her school had been closed, my daughter, Laura, was at home with Nilsa. Whenever I looked out the window, I could see the wind bending the palm trees, the rain squalls, and ominous gray sky, but I had a tough time believing it was really necessary to shut everything down.

I spent the afternoon poring over a bunch of numbers while our neighbors were in line buying staples like bread, milk, and gas, just in case. During one phone call that day, I found myself saying that it seemed as if "better safe than sorry" was being taken way too far. Sure, I wasn't going to stand out in the rain if I didn't have to, but neither would my whole life be rearranged because of it. I'd been through serious storms before, even violated an evacuation mandate on three occasions to stay on-site overnight and secure different properties in the middle of hurricanes, and this was nothing like that. I'd pay attention to the periodic updates about what was happening, but I wasn't going to spend all day glued to The Weather Channel. I didn't have to; all I needed to do was glance out the window. The herd mentality and overreaction surrounding the non-event was disheartening.

This turned out to be an appropriate frame of mind for me as I looked at six distinct periods when investors had to weather significant economic storms: 1) the 1973 oil crisis, 2) the height of the interest rate and inflation spike that began in the late 1970s and continued through the early 1980s, 3) the credit crunch associated with the S&L crisis that began in the late 1980s, 4) the Asian market meltdown of the late 1990s, 5) the Internet bubble that burst in the early 2000s, and 6) the most recent market correction that began in the latter part of 2006.

Although I've cautioned you against overthinking, and I don't make a habit of it myself, gathering this data turned into an occasion when I was going to exercise my Ph.D. in paradoxicology and allow myself to get engrossed in the statistics. I would indulge my analytical side because I had a theory—namely, that real estate had been demonstrating predictable, recurring cycles of up and down—but I was curious to see if the numbers really supported my thesis.

I'll relieve you of the suspense right now: They did.

Real estate downturns come around about every six years, and they tend to last at most two years. I discovered that, during the last eight recessions experienced in the United States, dating back to 1948, by the time the government takes action and passes legislation to counteract the problem via some form of stimulus package, it's a good sign that the bottom of the business cycle has already occurred.

(Peering into my crystal ball, I could see the same thing happening for the recession that started in the fourth quarter of 2008 and is expected to run for at least the first two quarters of 2009.) Whether the legislation causes us to bounce back or it just coincides with the natural rebound is unclear, but I tend to believe the economic relief plays a major role.

Most important, it's *perfectly clear* that we've been through the same economic stresses many times, in varying degrees. In fact, the patterns were established many years before that first period I studied. The "tulipmania" of 1637, for example, when people borrowed huge sums to buy Dutch flower bulbs, produced what was probably our very first credit crunch associated with a bubble. Mania, panics, bubbles, you name it: they all have a fascinating history. Yet I decided to focus on events from the last half-century because most people who are reading this book will be able to relate best to more recent events, even if it's through a dim childhood memory. It's harder to identify with something that happened hundreds of years ago and sounds archaic and improbable, like people getting financially torpedoed by a flower bulb.

What did I learn from my close study of the circumstances and statistics of six recent real estate cycles? Despite the recurring problems we've had with oil, credit, and banks, as well as the consistent theme of buyers and lenders getting themselves in trouble by overdoing credit, one of the most important things I learned from recent history is that even in the worst of circumstances, you could *still* have made money in real estate! Even if you were just an average investor, even if you hadn't followed the formula I give you in this book. And if you *had* applied my bubble-proof strategy? You could have cleared a profit nearly double the average.

Just so you know, for each of the six periods, I reviewed statistics on real estate . . .

- *Median and average sale prices of houses sold*, according to the U.S. Census Bureau
- *Interest rates*, specifically contract rates on typical mortgage commitments, according to the Federal Reserve Board
- *Inventory*, also known as "units for sale," as well as the *number of units actually sold*, according to the U.S. Census Bureau
- *Months on market*, which tells you how long it was taking for houses to sell, according to the U.S. Census Bureau
- *An affordability index*, which represents ability of a typical family to buy a house, according to the National Association of Realtors

Statistics on national economic health . . .

- *Gross Domestic Product (GDP)*, according to the U.S. Department of Commerce: Bureau of Economic Analysis
- *Inflation rates*, according to InflationData.com
- *Unemployment rates*, according to the U.S. Department of Labor: Bureau of Labor Statistics
- *Per-capita personal income*, according to the U.S. Department of Commerce: Bureau of Economic Analysis

And just for good measure . . .

- *Gas prices*, according to the U.S. Energy Information Administration

I went deeper into these numbers than I ever had reason to before, studying the indicators that are commonly thought to reflect and correlate with fluctuating values in the real estate market. **The first takeaway for you is that I could make those figures say anything I want.** It's true. I could show you only the numbers that prove my point and omit anything that doesn't make perfect pictures of regularly rising values. I could throw out the one cycle I studied that didn't look anything like the other ones. (Turns out the Asian market crisis in the late 1990s had no significant impact on real estate in the United States.)

Likewise, if I wanted to, I could show you only the numbers that would make you believe, for sure, that the sky had fallen and real estate returns had been enveloped in a giant black hole, never to see positive territory again. Sound familiar? If I, the one with the stellar high school grade point average of 1.8, could have manipulated the data this way, imagine how well experts with Ph.D.s from Ivy League schools can do it!

I've chosen not to try to make my case in that way. I'm not going to confuse or dazzle you with charts and graphs or crush you with all the numbers, trying to convince you with too many equations or computations. If you're so inclined, though, you can easily study the data yourself and verify my position. All my sources are listed above, and the information is readily available online. But my advice is that unless you are having difficulty sleeping, or Letterman has an unimpressive guest list and you're just incredibly eager to do the math yourself, you can take me at my word. Unlike other analysts, I don't get paid for presenting a particular picture of the real estate market. I get paid when I create value by making my own markets and capitalizing on whatever circumstances may prevail in the present. I get paid when I'm right. I get paid when I sell. And I get paid very well, I assure you.

So, instead, I'm going to focus on the big picture, share my conclusions with you, and be as direct as possible in telling you what numbers *are* useful for you as an investor to know, and which ones aren't.

Incidentally, the effects of Tropical Storm Fay in my hometown of Delray Beach were minimal. A local church's cupola was bent out of shape, but engineers said it was primarily due to rotten wood. After tornado warnings and hurricane warnings and President Bush declaring Florida a disaster area, pretty much all that happened here locally was that it got very wet—and considering we were in a drought, that was a good thing. Granted, in other parts of the state, it was much worse. This tropical storm did what no other has ever done here, making a record four landfalls before it finally started to wane. Personal tragedies weren't absent: twelve people died, there was severe flooding, power lines were down, and the damage to property was in the tens of millions.

Still, this provides an interesting parallel to the crises I was studying. In each of the periods I reviewed, there were people who were hit hard. Some were devastated. Yet the fact remains: most of the smart money was left unscathed, and, indeed, many of the savviest investors came out better than they were at the start of a downward trend. The disasters that plagued one area left others completely alone. Real estate, like terrible weather, proves to be a local issue.

The big lesson? Start using the problems of other regions to fuel your fear about what will happen in your own area, and you'll never profit again. Be careful what you allow to influence your thinking. Beware the mind-numbing buzz, the pessimistic perspectives that prevail in media reports, the cynicism and negative sentiment. Sometimes I wonder what people will think when they look back on this time in another fifty years. I suspect they'll be asking when, exactly, we started believing that every cloud contained asbestos instead of a silver lining. "No wonder the therapists and rehab centers were doing such a booming business," future sociologists might say. "If you bought into the media's gloomy outlook, what would make life worth living?"

More to the point of this book, why would you ever put money into real estate?

According to the pessimistic pundits whenever there's a downward trend, the supply of real estate will flood the market, submerging demand, and those who've invested will be washed out to sea . . . But you know already that the American Dream will never die. Pent-up demand always resurfaces when the time is right.

My review of the six cycles centering on market correction shows that's true.

A Quick History Lesson

Of the six cycles I studied, I actively participated in real estate investing during the most recent four of them. The first two—1972 to 1975 and 1979 to 1981—occurred when I was still fairly young, but I do remember them. My father was a banker, and he talked with me about the oil embargo, inflation, elevated interest rates, high unemployment numbers, and the impact of the rising prices at the pump on the prices we paid in the grocery store. That early 1970s economic crisis was the first time I recall seeing fear in the marketplace, specifically on my parents' faces and on TV, with people at gas stations, leaning on their open car doors, parked in the long lines snaking around the corner.

Not too long ago, I saw footage from back then on the news again, when oil prices and gas shortages reemerged as a hot topic.

When I think of that time in the seventies, I specifically picture an old Chrysler New Yorker (a great demolition derby car, by the way), with its ten miles per gallon, hooked up at the pump to receive its rationed gas, with a mile-long string of gas guzzlers winding around the block behind it. During that time, unemployment was up, interest rates were up, and gas prices were up. Some consolation: housing values continued to go up, too. Yet as I looked at all the economic factors and the other five cycles, it became obvious to me that by far the worst crisis actually occurred a few years after that, from 1979 to 1981, just as disco's mirror ball stopped spinning and I started to tease up my hair and keep it there with my mom's Aqua Net.

- **Interest rates escalated** from around 10 percent to 14 percent in just a little over a year (from January 1979 to April 1980) and then kept on climbing, eventually averaging 17.73 percent just six months later (October of 1981). Think about that: many were paying in excess of 18 percent interest!
- **The number of housing units sold fell** 42 percent, from nearly 709,000 in early 1979 to just 412,000 in late 1981.
- **Gas prices went up** from $0.90 a gallon in 1979 to $1.38 in 1981—a 53 percent leap. If you adjust those values to today's dollar, the numbers start to look eerily familiar: that's a price jump from $2.57 to $3.15 per gallon in just one year.
- **The affordability index dropped** dramatically, from a rating of 97.2 in 1979 to 68.9 in 1981. (Scores of 100 or above mean that a typical, meaning median-income, family can afford a median-priced house.)

- **The unemployment rate rose** 39 percent, from 5.9 in early 1979 to 8.2 by the fall of 1981.
- **Inflation peaked** in March 1980 at 14.76 and stayed high, although it began to drop and got down to 8.91 by the end of 1981. By today's standards, that's still almost six points higher than the target rate.

It was the perfect storm: all factors combined to make a terrific mess of the economy in general and real estate markets in particular. I know people today who are still scarred from that time in our nation's history. *Everything* was expensive, from gas to food to mortgages. Who would buy a house with interest rates so high? I'll tell you who: Those desiring to own a piece of the American Dream. Those with that proverbial "dry powder," people who took care of their credit and didn't max out a dozen credit cards and could walk into a bank and obtain favorable loan terms. Those who held a steady job and had some savings. Those who didn't have to rely on pawn shops, loan sharks, or hard money lenders to come up with the down payment to make a purchase.

For everyone else, that was a bleak period, for sure. *Yet real estate values continued to rise.* As I looked at the numbers, I thought to myself that those interest rates would have made me pretty nervous, but I would love to have had the chance to profit during what most perceived as an extremely difficult period.

That's because, as I said, even the average transaction contained valuable opportunities. Let's look at a worst-typical-case scenario (in other words, buying at a "bad" time, but doing a typical deal). The average cost of a house in 1979 was $68,300. By mid-1981, the same house was worth $83,800. If you'd bought that house in '79 then chosen to sell it in '81, after only two-and-a-half years in the worst market we'd seen since the Great Depression of 1929, you still would have made $15,500 on your investment.

If you want to break all the numbers down, here's a likely scenario: On the original purchase, you would have put down $6,830 on the house—a typical down payment in those days was 10 percent. You might have financed the remaining $61,470. With a fixed-rate, 30-year mortgage, you would have been paying 10.41 percent, or if you'd gone the variable-rate route, you'd have paid an average of about 14 percent during those high-interest years.

That raises a question, doesn't it? Wouldn't the interest payments have completely eroded your profit?

Again, let's take a worst-typical-case scenario. At an average of 14 percent, the total interest you would have paid by mid-1981 would have been about $21,500. So you might think you'd have lost some money:

> $83,800 avg. price of a home on 7-1-1981
> 68,300 avg. price of a home on 1-1-1979
> _____
> = $15,500 gain in value over 2.5 years (closing costs excluded)
> − 21,500 interest paid over 2.5 years (assuming adjustable rate)
> _____
> = $ 6,000 total "loss" on the property

(Remember that at closing, the investor would have a payoff to the bank of around $61,840, less his or her 10 percent down payment of $6,830, so you could actually walk out of closing with more than the $15,500 referenced above.)

But there's more to it than that. Remember income tax? Mortgage interest is a tax-deductible expense, so the total you'd paid would have been exempt from that. This is the *cost of doing business*, which you would have more than recouped if you were in real estate for the long term, beyond that brief difficult period. In the meantime, as a homeowner or investor, you would have done all right. Not spectacularly well, but all right. You would have either made a small profit or put a roof over your head for two-and-a-half years for less than $100 a month.

Now let's say you're not average. Let's say you could get in a time machine and travel back to the dark days of 1979 to 1981 with *Burst This!* to guide your decision making. (Don't worry; you wouldn't have to copy my early-eighties hairstyle.) Here's how the whole thing would have happened differently and with a much more appealing outcome:

- **You wouldn't have paid the average price for a house.** You would have located and negotiated a lower price and bought the opportunity for no more than $45,000, essentially putting $23,300 in your pocket right then and there.
- **You wouldn't have financed so much of the investment and would have secured the lowest interest rate.** Let's say you made a still-modest down payment of 20 percent, or $9,000. The balance to finance would have been $36,000. Surely you would have secured a fixed-rate mortgage and paid no more than 10.41 percent for the duration of the loan. (I can't believe I just wrote the words *no more than 10.41 percent.* That just gives you a sense of how difficult it was back then.) Your total interest expense for the 2.5 years would then be reduced to about $9,370, cutting the previous example's cost by 56 percent.
- **You would have improved the property so it could be sold at a higher-than-average price.** At that time, you might have sunk

an additional $6,000 into the house and increased its value by $8,000 or more.

- **You would have marketed the home like no one else using the Grade School Compass Approach.** This would further boost perceived value and increase the number of potential buyers.
- **You would have sold the home at a premium.** By combining your quality improvements with your ability to market, it would have sold for at least 10 percent above comparables, or for not less than $92,000.

After paying a realtor and other closing costs of about $5,600, you would have walked out of closing with a check for $35,000. Subtract your down payment and you would have made a profit of $26,000! This sum would be ready to invest as a down payment on your next property or two. Who knows, you might even have been able to buy a home free and clear with the $26,000. I bought plenty of properties in the late 1980s for less than $10,000.

Whether you lived in that house or held it as an investment, those figures are nothing to sneeze at. What's even more interesting, if you adjust for inflation, the numbers would look like this today: you would have paid $200,000, sold for $340,000, and profited $80,000! In *this* '79-to-'81 scenario, it turns out that statistical numbers like interest rates, unemployment rates, gas prices, number of units sold, and so on, have little bearing on whether you're able to turn a profit, even in a troubled market. In reality, they may even have helped you if you'd applied the *Burst This!* approach. **The numbers that mean the most are what you pay for the opportunity (the acquisition price), the cost of improving the opportunity, and the market you're able to create with your eventual retail selling price.**

Fast Forward to Today and "The Great Real Estate Depression"

Of all six cycles, that period from 1979 to 1981 was far and away the most troubled for real estate investors, unless you want to count what's happening just as I'm writing this chapter. And I don't say that because I believe the economic factors are so much more dire now—they're not, not yet. It's just that investor confidence has been shaken hard. Not only have conditions worsened, but (yet again) media portrayals and the pundits' predictions paint the gloomiest possible picture. *Bravo!* The combination of circumstance and media circus has broken the American investor's back. Good thing this country has a strong spine. We'll see how quickly it heals.

Today, we have an average thirty-year-fixed rate hovering just above 6 percent. Gas prices are through the roof, but when adjusted for inflation, they are actually just below what we had in 1980. The good news is that unemployment, although rising, remains quite low at just above 6 percent, the affordability index is well over 100, and although home values have been down, then flat, the number of sales is beginning to rise again in many areas across the country. We've been through much worse in times past. Yet investors have indeed been rattled by the break in a seventy-seven-year run in real estate. That's right. Until 2008, **real estate values had been appreciating, year over year, for the last seventy-seven years.** The fact that prices fell hard—and then flatlined for a time—definitely left plenty of people feeling as if they'd just been tasered: "What, I'm not going to see a 30 percent return on my house this year?" "Will it ever come back?"

I really don't think those record-breaking returns will reappear, but I do think it's only a matter of time before history repeats its patterns, people get excited about real estate because prices look attractive again, and then you're off to a slow and steady climb once more. Whenever numbers are at the bottom of the cycle, though, your job is to grab the low-hanging fruit. These are the millionaire-maker days.

As I write this, I have no doubt that in a short time, we can all say to our kids and grandkids that we lived through the Great Real Estate Depression of '08 and '09, just as your grandparents might have said they made it through the Great Depression of 1929. We'll look back on this time with relief that it's over, yet for those who couldn't see what opportunity it held, they'll also feel regret.

It's better to regret what you do rather than what you don't. Still, people can be hesitant to put a toe back in the water. The view of real estate markets as "a bubble that burst" could factor into when any particular investor might be willing to believe in the value of real estate again. In most people's minds (and I'm basing this on most of the people I've met across the country in the last few years at real estate and business events), a "bubble" is what happened to Internet stocks before they burst in 2001. And we've touched on this before: What caused the overvalued dot-com stock to rise from next to nothing all the way to $300 a share was . . . drumroll, please . . . that's right, *excitement*. Our twenty-first-century version of gold fever. Hype. Irrational exuberance. *Gotta have it. My neighbor's doing it, so I'm gonna get in.*

"Easy money."

And what caused the unsustainable run of property value appreciation in many parts of the United States? The very same factors.

So a bubble's a bubble, right? Kind of. Although the same mass psychology definitely enlarged the bubble in both cases, there's a huge difference between the Internet bubble and the real estate bubble in what happened next. Similarities between the two stop here.

For most Internet stocks, the bubble burst, no question. That $300 price per share popped, and then CompanyX.com and CompanyY.com couldn't give their stocks away. Why? Because there were no *historical earnings* to support valuation. In other words, these companies were worth only the excitement they could generate around owning a piece—not for any real value they provided in the marketplace. Once people's excitement waned, these companies went bust. (If you're thinking to yourself, *But Google's or Apple's stock is still worth $400 and $100 per share respectively*, remember those companies have significant earnings to support their valuation.)

For real estate, though, *the bubble didn't burst*. It rightfully deflated some. Prices had definitely stretched the limit, but when the correction came, housing prices didn't drop back to zero. They dipped below where they had been two years before, but they didn't crash. An average home in April of 2008 was priced at $304,700, below the average in 2006 but higher than the average in 2005. Some regions have fared much better (parts of Colorado, the Carolinas, the Midwest, etc.), while others like Florida, Las Vegas, Arizona, parts of California, etc., have fared worse.

A bubble happens when people "invest for short-term capital gains rather than for the returns associated with the productivity of the assets they were acquiring," according to Charles P. Kindleberger, a financial historian and former professor of economics at MIT. His definition is a mouthful, isn't it? What he's saying is essentially what I've been telling you: a true bubble is the result of people getting excited about how much money they can make in the short term and not considering whether or not the thing they're buying has any past, current, or future real value. To prevent ourselves from being affected by this kind of excitement, we must *remove emotion* from the acquisition side of the equation, and as you will learn, this is one of the two most important elements of succeeding in real estate.

Real estate has substantial historical earnings to support valuation. Property values have averaged annual appreciation at a rate of about 6.5 percent year over year for the last thirty years, until the streak was recently broken. That year-over-year reference represents the historical earnings to support valuation—the building blocks for the foundation. This recent dip in return is a total aberration, and we will return to that normal rate before you know it. Local markets may experience declines occasionally, usually due to an oversupply of homes for sale coupled with reduced demand (most often because of job losses or tightening credit). Just as easily, they might experience an unusually high rate of appreciation (think Las Vegas, Arizona, Florida, and parts of California in 2006). Yet a national decline had been unheard of. The end to our seventy-seven-year run-up in real estate values marks a unique point in time, that point of capitulation where the contrarian in you must emerge and see the opportunities inherent in such an unusual event.

That's what happened in the early 1930s when John J. Raskob financed the Empire State Building, an amazing art deco skyscraper that was completed in a remarkably short period, just a little more than a year, at a time when the country was still reeling from the world's largest and most important depression in history. Because of laborers' desperate need for work, he was able to hire quickly and inexpensively and keep people on the job. Because he had the dry powder to capitalize on the circumstances, he profited greatly and benefited New York in incalculable ways by taking action in a time when most others were cowering in a corner somewhere. Again, it's that flash point Sir John Templeton identified as "maximum pessimism," the time when confident contrarians make their move and make it big.

The economic conditions for these kinds of moves are evident again as I write this book. Real estate investor confidence has been shaken to its core. The media promotes fear and worry at every turn. The analysts paint a bleak picture, showing you only the data that supports a negative outlook. In a word, things look *really bad*.

There's a reason the run lasted seventy-seven years. Don't expect this type of correction to happen again anytime soon.

While some may breathe a sigh of relief at that statement, I hope you're also feeling the tug of opportunity. Price declines aren't likely to make homes so affordable again in the foreseeable future. When you're able to recognize this, it means that you're starting to earn that realist/optimist/opportunist badge for yourself.

If you're reading this book during a "bust" time, I hope you can see the hidden opportunities around you, have some dry powder, and can summon the confidence to make markets when everyone else is listening to the noise of the financial analysts.

If you're reading this book during a "normal," slow-and-steady-increase-in-values time, I hope you'll stay the course and be ever vigilant, watching for a swing in trend while keeping your focus on opportunities that abound in any market. Be content with hitting a single.

And if you're reading this book during a "boom" time, I hope you're able to capitalize on the obvious opportunities without letting the prevailing excitement ruin your judgment. Remind yourself that there's a reason the average rate of return on real estate has been 6.5

percent. The pendulum always swings too far in one direction and may swing and deliver 15 percent one year, but that means you can expect it to correct and overcompensate by swinging far in the other direction, and even depreciate your property at the same rate.

At any time, **remember that the most important numbers remain acquisition costs, improvement costs, and your retail value/selling price.** This is what determines your return, not the economic indicators, nor the analysts' predictions, nor any other fact or figure you might run across. In the next part of this book, I'll be sharing with you the precise steps for securing an opportunity at the best price, calculating your improvement costs accurately (and making improvements that contribute to the value of the home), and marketing like no one else can.

THE POSTMORTEM I PROMISED

Although I'm not going to reprint all my spreadsheets here, I do want to take the time to give you a point-by-point factual real estate retrospective, an overview of the six most recent macroeconomic cycles. I'll tell you up front: some affected real estate dramatically, while others barely registered. Here's a closer look.

The 1973 Oil Crisis

The problems we were having with oil back in the early seventies weren't all that different from what we were experiencing as I began writing this book. In both cases, we were overly dependent on foreign oil, which was controlled primarily by Arab countries hostile to the United States. In both cases, prices at the pump were escalating (adjusting for inflation, the price hikes are about even today, although in July 2008 we set a new record for gasoline cost per gallon and oil cost per barrel—which still isn't that far off from where we were in the seventies). In both cases, there was the threat of production being curtailed by those in control of the oil supply.

Our first oil crisis began Otober 17, 1973, when the Organization of the Petroleum Exporting Countries (OPEC) stopped shipping oil to any nation that had supported Israel. The United States and the Netherlands were specifically targeted. The U.S. government began rationing gas and pursuing greater independence on crude oil. Prices peaked in 1980, then dropped off slowly until 1986 when things started to stabilize for a while.

In studying the economic factors of this period, I focused primarily on 1972 to 1975 and was repeatedly struck by the similarities with the situation we face today. The other striking thing about this time is that it has become an emblem of economic crisis by providing us with images that won't fade from consciousness until this generation is long gone. The gas lines. The unemployment lines. But it wasn't nearly as bad as . . .

The Perfect Storm: 1979–1981

I've already dissected this above in detail, but let me say again that multiple factors combined to make this the worst of conditions, far worse than anything we've experienced since then. I suspect that if we had anything like this happen again, it would cause a national uprising and civil revolt that would make the Boston Tea Party or even the Los Angeles riots of 1992 look like a pillow fight between middle-school girls. Inflation was high, mortgage rates were high, food prices were high, unemployment was high, time on market was high. (Most of my high school class was high back then, too, but that's another story.) Income was at its slowest rate of appreciation, and the number of houses available to buy was down—people were definitely moving into a bunker mentality. Yet the truth is you still could have done okay in real estate markets across the country. **You could have weathered the storm.**

The next time you hear someone say, "This is the worst it can get," or "We've never seen anything like this before," I suggest you pick up this book and remind yourself of all the factors that went into creating the perfect storm of economic crisis through the late seventies and into the early eighties. And then you need to ask yourself: *are today's economic troubles really as bad as all that?*

- If they are, shouldn't you be thinking about the green light of maximum pessimism, dry powder, and capitalizing on unusual opportunities instead of getting sucked into the negativity?
- And if they're not, shouldn't you be tuning out the gloom and doom and instead creating your own reality, not treating the financial media like prophets or their analyses like gospel?

The Savings & Loan Crisis

You think subprime mortgage lenders and their customers invented the credit crunch? Think again.

The worst banking collapse since the Great Depression of 1929 stretched from 1986 to 1991; in reviewing it, I focused primarily on the latter part of the cycle, from 1989 to 1991. A huge number of homes across the country, especially in the South and Texas in particular, were funded—I should say "overfunded"—through savings and loan institutions, or thrifts. Values were propped up by speculation and aggressive appraisers and lenders. (Sound familiar?) Credit became tighter and more expensive as risk premiums increased. More than 1,000 thrifts failed, and it cost the government (a.k.a. taxpayers) $129 billion to fix it. (As of this writing, seventeen banks have failed in 2008, with another 100 expected to go down in 2009. However, today's banks are much larger, so the financial impact of their failures may yet equal that of the S&L crisis.) **Still, within just two years, our memories of this time began to fade.** Banks filled in where the S&Ls left off. Values corrected to where they belonged and began to rise again, and the bull market was back in control.

By the way, I bought my first house, the 620-square-foot junker that yielded $7,000 in profit, back in 1986. Then I took that money and started on my next deal. And my next. The houses we did on Bankers Row in Delray Beach were renovated in the midst of the S&L crisis and turned a healthy profit. That's because I didn't depend on the S&Ls or the media to make my business flourish. **My constant focus: buy right, improve for maximum value, and market like no one else.** To be honest, and at the risk of sounding a little naïve, I wasn't aware of the severity of the credit issues back then until years after. I didn't pay much attention to the problems of the financial institutions because I was too busy making a market.

The Asian Market Crisis

The Japanese housing bubble burst in 1996, and the Asian market crisis was from 1997 to 1999. I looked at data from that period and, although our stock market suffered, I found no significant impact on U.S. real estate. (I did find this outrageous fact: the land under the Imperial Palace in Tokyo was worth more than all the real estate in Canada at one point.) The reason I included this crisis in my study is that I distinctly remember the barrage of negativity surrounding it; in particular, I remember seeing an Asian guy on the cover of *Forbes*, pulling his hair out because things were so horrible, while I was posed a few pages later in the same publication in front of a $12 million home we had recently sold, and my hair was just fine. **The lesson here: not every economic crisis translates to real estate, especially when it's on foreign soil.**

The Internet Bubble Burst

The Internet bubble spans 1995 to 2001. It burst in 2001, so I looked primarily at statistics from 2001 to 2002 to see how the burst affected real estate markets. Aside from housing in Silicon Valley and the surrounding areas, where dot-com gajillionaires had been overpaying for nice but, by most standards, average homes, the impact on national real estate was minimal. Those of us at the higher end, however, were suffering from inaction on the part of our buyers. One thing the ultrawealthy disdain is uncertainty. Once that uncertainty was cleared up and we knew we were heading into a recession, buyers returned. (That's counterintuitive, I know, but all they needed was to be sure in which direction the economy was headed. They weren't worried about the recession itself but about *not knowing for sure*.) Meanwhile, the Fed got proactive and dropped interest rates, so that offset the expected drop in demand for housing caused by a major economic event. At that time, the rate of inflation was particularly low, between 1 and 2 percent. (Remember that during our perfect storm, it was up to almost 15 percent.) We had our best year up to that point, selling one home for $30 million.

Yes, of course, I kept an eye on the financial news because my buyers cared about it. **But still, my focus was constant: buy right, improve for maximum value, and market like no one else.** I didn't pay that much attention to stock-market fluctuations, because I was too busy making a market. Again.

The Great Real Estate Depression of '08 and '09

As of this writing, the most recent boom began in the early 2000s, fueled by subprime mortgage loans and other esoteric money products. Everyone from Main Street to Wall Street to Skid Row was in on the money magic. Anyone with a pulse, and even a few who had none, could obtain the 125 percent loan-to-value (LTV), negative amortization mortgage at a 1 percent starter rate on a home that was priced $500,000 beyond their means, with no documentation or verification of income. And for good measure, those same people went out and financed new fancy cars when they should have been driving nothing more than a Yugo, for goodness sake.

Credit whores, all of them.

For a while, it looked as if you'd have to be an idiot not to make a profit investing in real estate—no, wait, any idiot *could* make a profit. Plenty did. And the mania ratcheted up housing prices beyond a sustainable level as people eagerly overextended themselves with questionable credit to buy, buy, buy—wait, let me correct myself again: it was actually charge, charge, charge. "Charge it today and pay for it never" was the lifestyle. (And if that describes your lifestyle today, heed my warning.)

Then the market corrected, big time in many places. Housing prices fell 50 percent in some areas. Home buyers defaulted on their loans. Despite being "too big to fail," Bear Stearns and IndyMac Bank went belly-up, and Lehman Brothers wasn't far behind. Merrill Lynch succumbed to a pressure-filled takeover by Bank of America. Fannie Mae and Freddie Mac, the two largest housing lenders in the country, had to be bailed out. AIG got its $80 billion so that there wouldn't be even wider-spread collapse. Wachovia got in so much trouble that Wells Fargo came to the rescue by merging with it for pennies on the dollar. The same happened to Washington Mutual, which ran into JPMorgan Chase's open arms for a pittance. (Shades of the S&L crisis, right?) The sky was falling, the sky was falling!

And then a new day dawned. Eventually, the sun came out. Returns didn't jump back to previous levels of 12, 15, or 30 percent, but they did become respectable again, as defined by the historical 6.5 percent—a comfortable return in many places. The blue chip investment of real estate reclaimed its historical earnings and proved its proper valuation. We survived it, just as we survived the previous cycles, and just as you'll survive the next ones.

I gotta admit, the fear-feeding frenzy that has surrounded this recent period has been hard to ignore. I've had to rethink some of my own funding strategies. Early on, the pundits burrowed under my skin and irritated the heck out of me. I wanted to burst or bust some talking heads. Obviously, they irked me enough to address them in *Burst This!* **But as you're now well aware, it's quite possible to see through the smoke and mirrors and refocus on what's important: buy right, improve for maximum value, and market like no one else.**

Back to the Fundamentals

Of the information I reviewed, I found the following statistics to be most telling—and the ones I counsel you to watch:

- **Interest rates.** You're smart to recognize when rates are rising so you can lock in reasonable rates and also avoid overleveraging yourself with debt. Also, rising interest rates will make it more difficult for your buyers to obtain financing.
- **Unemployment rates and inflation.** Whenever we've been above 8 percent for both, it has spelled trouble for real estate— and the entire economy, as well. Consumer confidence falls along with demand for new houses in regional markets where job loss is most prevalent, and the cost of your grocery bills pinches the purse. While I don't see either returning to 8 percent anytime soon, particularly with our productivity levels in this country, if we were to attain either of those levels, it would be cause for serious concern.
- **Time on market.** As the number of days to sell a house increases, you need to factor that into your investment formula. (More on that in Chapter 6, I promise.)
- **Consumer confidence.** Keep an eye on this number, an index released each month by the Conference Board, which is a good barometer of Americans' sentiments and predisposition to buy. The survey covers how people are feeling about everything from personal earnings to inflation to general business conditions.

As for the rest of the background noise? You can pretty much tune it out. Focus on making your market, instead. Sure, you're not going to stand in the rain if you can help it, but neither should you rearrange your whole life. Pay attention to periodic updates, but you don't have to stay glued to a financial channel all day. Go on about your business. The truth is we've been through it all before—an oil crisis, a credit crisis, an inflation crisis, an unemployment crisis—and we survived. Some people thrived. The next part of this book will help you ensure that you're among this select group, no matter what the economic climate.

Your Chapter 4
BURST OF INSPIRATION

- **Know that it has happened before and will happen again. During any of the up cycles, did you or anyone you know get caught up in the excitement? Did you or the other person make or lose money, and why? What would you do differently or the same today?**

PART TWO

THE MARKET MAKER

Take the "Lunch Pail" approach: do your job,
do it well, and do it every day.

O ne of the primary takeaways from this book should be the recognition that you choose whether to be a bubble-head or not. You decide whether to follow the fear and excitement of the masses, to live and die on the ups and downs of other investors, to stand still or jump headlong in response to the pundits—or to go the other way as a confident contrarian making your own markets.

In real estate, risk isn't only about the money you have on the line. It's also about your willingness to be a maverick, to challenge the status quo with a *Burst This!* mindset. It's about the responsibility associated with taking larger and larger chances to do something different from anything that has been done before, to venture where others are too lazy or too scared to tread, to bank on your own judgment and skill and determination, to step out of the comfort corridor and strike off in a new direction.

What you've read so far in this book has been intended to influence how you think in general, and ultimately how you think about real estate. What's important and what's not. What's real and what's not. What endures and what doesn't. My hope is that it saves you not only from the common path of getting caught up in other people's ideas and emotions and analyses, but also from the real estate-junkie mentality. If you want to succeed, you can't always be looking for your next fix(er); you have to find The One and then follow it through all the way. Close the loop; get it done.

But let me emphasize that you don't close the loop 90 percent: that wouldn't be closing the loop; that would be leaving it undone, and that's where most others fail. Be sure you *completely* close the loop. It's not enough to just be in the game, scoring the next great deal. After the handshake and the party to celebrate your great find, you've got to follow it out to the end. You've got to *execute*.

That may sound glaringly obvious, but it's rare for me to meet someone who takes this part of the process as seriously as I do, and I'm convinced that's why it's even more rare for me to meet someone who has a reliably successful twenty-five-year track record like mine. I'm not talking about the size of the homes I build or the net return on their sale. I'm talking about *consistent return on investment*, year after year, project after project, which should be your goal as a real estate investor. I'm talking about significant profit margins not just once in a while, but nearly *every* time you do a deal.

It all comes down to execution, taking what I call the "Lunch Pail" approach with every deal, every day. This is where the rubber meets the road, where those who are satisfied with unpredictable returns (lucky and up big one deal, losing money on the next few) part company with those who are in it for serious money. It's where you pave the way for a future with either a long, costly wait for your buyers or a lucrative, reasonably quick sale.

In the next four chapters, you'll be reading the precise steps I take on every project. This part of the book is about solid practices you can apply to any real estate investment at any price point, whether you're planning to renovate or build from scratch, whether you're interested in single-family dwellings or multiple-unit buildings, whether you're buying your first investment property and hope to move up someday or looking to increase your margins on your one-hundredth deal.

- Chapter 5, "Create Your Own Market, Not Your Own Bubble," begins by clearly defining what it means to make a market and then gives you specific ways to do it: where to find the best opportunities, how to get to know and serve your potential buyers, and how you can capitalize on the same trend I'm pioneering right now.
- Chapter 6, "Once You've Bubble-Proofed, You'll Celebrate your 'Buy' Day more than your 'Sell' Day," will show you that you make almost all of your money the day you buy, not the day you sell. This chapter delivers the exact formula you need to ensure that whatever opportunity you buy insures a profitable margin (and the only conditions under which you should vary that formula). This is the same formula I've used before purchasing every single property since I began in this business in the

mid-1980s, from that first $50,000 transaction on up to my most recent multimillion-dollar deal. This is the formula that's made certain I've profited very well on nearly every deal I've ever done.

- Chapter 7, "The Other Holy Trinity," covers the all-important three elements of scheduling, budgeting, and quality considerations of improvements, which can make or break your ability to sell quickly (or at all) and secure your desired profit margin. It shares what I've learned about how to create a realistic time frame for every real estate project, how to work with contractors, the virtues of overimproving rather than underimproving, and the best places to put your improvement dollars for maximum return.

- Chapter 8, "The Most Obscene Four-Letter Word," gives you straight talk about the often dirty business of debt. You need to look no further than the U.S. economy in late 2008/early 2009 to see the effects of irresponsible debt. Handled responsibly, however, debt can enable you to seize opportunities others miss. Misused, debt can turn into a sinkhole for your profits, sucking them right out from under you and possibly taking you and your investment along with them. In this chapter, you learn fail-safe methods for monitoring and managing any loans you secure, as well as setting up your personal finances to support a healthy return on your business interests.

If you're ready to get to work—to do the job, do it well, and do it every day—read on. This part of the book is about showing up, taking care, paying attention, following through. It's not as much about how-to (although you'll get plenty of that) as it is about how to *stick with it*, how to *thrive*, and how to *insure generational success*.

Now let's make some markets!

5

CREATE YOUR OWN MARKET, NOT YOUR OWN BUBBLE

At the beginning of *Burst This!*, I shared with you the exact conditions that would cause you to create your own bubble: overpaying for an opportunity, overextending yourself with too many projects, overleveraging yourself with too much or too costly debt, over- or underimproving the home, getting overexcited, and under-marketing.

Clearly, that's what not to do.

Now it's time to closely examine what you *do* want to do. The cornerstone of your bubble-proofing strategy has to be a commitment to making new markets. You achieve this through *differentiation*, making your home stand out and appeal to a specific group of people that you've gotten to know very well—also known as potential buyers. (Remember, while most of the examples in *Burst This!* are aimed toward real estate investors who buy, add value, and then sell single-family homes, every strategy also applies to buy-and-hold investors, otherwise known as *landlords*, and people who purchase multiple-family dwellings or apartment buildings. Even if you're in the market to buy a home for yourself with the idea of living in it for several years, eventually you or your heirs are going to sell that home, and if you or they want top dollar, you'll need to buy right, create value, and make your market by differentiating your property from the others on your street or in your neighborhood.)

There are two surefire ways of making a market, by creating value and by creating a masterpiece:

- **Create value in undervalued, undiscovered, or overlooked locations.** Reclaim a "lost" neighborhood—an area of town that used to be good, has depreciated a bit, but is on the cusp (or has the potential) to turn around in the next two to three years, as I did with the foreclosure homes I bought and rehabbed in my early days of investing.

  You also can find an up-and-coming area that's near a neighborhood with cachet and improve properties there so they resemble (or outdo) the ones in the areas with greater name value. For instance, even though Manalapan is right next to Palm Beach, Palm Beach oceanfront property values are $150,000 to $200,000 per front foot while Manalapan's are closer to $75,000. Why? To my real estate contrarian's eyes, the only reason is Palm Beach's 100-year name recognition. Manalapan's natural advantages outweigh Palm Beach's on almost every point. Every single high-end home in Manalapan is on a body of water—either the Intracoastal Waterway, the Atlantic Ocean, or both. Palm Beach can't say that. Most Palm Beach oceanfront properties have a road that runs in front of them. Manalapan oceanfront properties go from the ocean to the Intracoastal Waterway. You can put a boat at your back door and walk on your private beach out your front door. No Palm Beach property has that degree of water access. So when we looked at Manalapan, we said, "Manalapan has everything high-end buyers are looking for in Palm Beach, and then some! The only thing missing is name recognition—cachet. And we're experts at creating cachet." Today the properties we're building in Manalapan are raising the bar for luxury and desirability. In the next few years, these properties are going to have the same name recognition and cachet as Palm Beach used to have for our target market, the discriminating buyer who wants the best and is willing to pay for it. I can anticipate Manalapan's oceanfront prices equaling or exceeding Palm Beach values in the next decade.

If this seems like pie in the sky given our current real estate market, all I can say is that we did the exact same thing in Delray Beach, starting fifteen years ago right after the last "credit crisis." I've had plenty of experience creating cachet, and knowing my market as I do, it's not brag, just fact. When you begin your own bubble-proof investing, getting to know the areas where you're buying and your target buyer intimately, you'll gain the same degree of confidence that I have in your power to make the market.

• **Create a masterpiece.** Establish unique architectural appeal and give buyers the chance to own a home that reflects their personality and your unique artistic expression. Create or renovate an existing home with improvements you know a future buyer will love. One of the key trends in features that will help you make your market is building or renovating "green." You'll also hear a lot more about the advantages of going green in Chapter 7.

If you're reading this book so that you can make a smart purchase on your first or next family home, this may not seem as important to you. However, if you care at all about resale value—and you should—then the following points must be kept at the forefront of your mind. If you're reading *Burst This!* because you love real estate and want to make it your career, or you want to take your career and properties to the next level, I suggest you pay close attention, get out your highlighter, mark the most important parts, and dog-ear the first page. I suspect you'll want to re-read this part of the book more than once. I've made a habit of reading every good book from cover to cover twice, because it's amazing what I learn the second time through.

SEE VALUE WHERE OTHERS DON'T

They say the three keys to real estate are location, location, and location. In most people's minds, this means you really need to find a great neighborhood, a place where properties are highly prized, and sell quickly. But when I was asked by Martin Bashir from the TV show *20/20* if "location, location, location" was the key to success, I said, "I don't buy it!"

I think the reason "they" repeat the word *location* three times isn't to drive the point home but to give you the *real* secret to maximizing your return on your real estate investments: **the first person to get to the location makes the money.** The other two are followers, and their profits are much less in comparison. It's like the California gold rush: the first people on-site mined a fortune, and the poor folks who arrived later had to try and eke out a living by sifting through the pyrite (fool's gold) that the early comers had left behind.

You need to be the first to establish *the* location, then you'll make *the* profit, then you'll make *the* market, and then you'll have followers, just as in the gold rush.

Every location with cachet didn't start out as prime property. Malibu was a hick beach community until celebrities started buying properties for their weekend getaways. Beverly Hills, Palm Beach, Boca Raton, Aspen—all of the most expensive zip codes in the United States at one time were far less attractive, less expensive, and had no name recognition. The people who bought into these communities *before* property values went through the roof were the ones who profited the most. And I would argue that as a smart contrarian investor, with a little research and even more vision, you too can find the "undiscovered gems" in your area and benefit from the next real estate gold rush. After all, isn't that the ultimate in bubble-proofing?

There is one circumstance, however, in which location, location, location applies, and that's when you buy your own residence or vacation home, and you care about your neighborhood more than the potential upside. Most people have a clear idea of the kind of neighborhood in which they want to live—the school district, the local amenities, proximity to work, and so on—and they don't want to wait more than three years until the schools improve or the run-down business district is renewed. The same is true of a vacation home purchase. In both circumstances, people are usually looking at their property as lifestyle choices first and investments second. Therefore, if you want to live in a nice, already established neighborhood or vacation destination and you're willing to limit your upside when you sell, go ahead and look for location first and appreciation potential second. (Always remember, however, that even if you find the house where you plan to live for the rest of your life, you won't own it forever. So why not take the *Burst This!* approach to making sure you're creating value in whatever you buy?)

Instead, be willing to make the location and make the market, using the ideas in this book. When I look back over my own career, the times where I've made the most money were the occasions where I went against the conventional location wisdom. With a *Burst This!* approach, you know a property can make the location, instead of the other way around. You can find properties at the right price and then improve them to the point where they set new benchmarks for the whole neighborhood. Your job is to go where others don't or won't, because you can see potential value where they can't. **You, and not the location, are the ultimate determiner of a property's value.** Remember, there are often markets to be made within walking distance of your own home. You don't need to canvass the country looking for deals. I've always stayed close, starting to look within a five-mile radius, and if I couldn't find something there, then I'd move on to a ten-mile radius, and so on, up to a maximum of about fifty miles away. I have made an entire career without leaving that radius! Certainly, your town or city will have neighborhoods that fit your criteria for investment within those limits.

Remember what I've said about the homes I bought to renovate in communities where other people were too scared to go: questionable neighborhoods, burnt-out buildings, properties where poachers had stolen the copper pipes right out from under the building. Other investors were nervous about putting money and time into places they were sure would be vandalized or ransacked by someone who needed scrap metal to sell for a few bucks. To avoid that problem, I found a simple solution: I hired local folks to work on the project, and I let them know what we'd be doing around the neighborhood, too. For the most part, I was working the outer edges of the worst parts of town, what they call transitional neighborhoods and fringe areas. I also looked for neighborhoods that were near public or cultural renaissance areas, where public improvement dollars were paving the way for private investment—places like new schools, cultural arts centers, courthouses, community centers, fire stations, police stations, etc. So we had a mix of people, both the criminal element that could make it seem dicey, and also the solid wage earners and home owners who were saddened by the decline of the area and would love to see their own property values raised. I expect this is exactly what you'd find in similar areas near you—and the latter group will not only help you get the job done but will often go so far as to protect your investment. Even in the most dangerous neighborhoods, rarely did I ever have a problem with damage.

The underlying principle here is to **look for undervalued neighborhoods where home prices or general price appreciation hasn't kept pace with others in the area, but isn't too far behind either.** Visit a respectable broker and ask, "Where *shouldn't* I be? Where should I stay away from?" Then go there, take a walk around, find that less-desirable neighborhood, and begin your research.

- **What are the trends in violence and crime?** If the trend is spiking upward, this may be a reason to stay away, but if the crime level is flat or declining, the neighborhood could present an excellent opportunity for you. Pull police statistics on violence, robberies, drug busts, and so on. Look at the trend and then ask to see the police chief or a higher-ranking officer who can help you interpret what you see.

- **What's your gut feeling?** When you're walking around, what does your gut tell you about how long it might take for the neighborhood to turn around? Two years? Five? Ten? I always thought that if it could come around in two or three years, I'd consider investing, and if it was more than that, I'd pass.
- **What's coming soon?** Find out if there are any events on the horizon—municipal rebuilding, private business investment, rezoning, infrastructure changes, bond issues, and so on—that might increase the value of the neighborhood in the next few years. One of the smartest moves and easiest money you can make is to learn about the long-range revitalization plans for your town or city. There's almost always something in the works for marginal neighborhoods, and efforts usually start on the fringes, right where you're looking to buy. If you know the target areas for revitalization, you can cooperate and collaborate with the city or town. This is what I'm talking about when I say that you can not only set a new benchmark for housing values, but you also can help improve the neighborhood in other ways.

The answers to these questions will tell you whether this is a place to continue to focus your search for the right opportunity or to abandon it and extend your radius.

Nowadays, I'm still going where others aren't. I've never done an oceanfront project in Boca Raton or Palm Beach, where undervalued properties are all but nonexistent, but as I mentioned earlier, I've done plenty in Delray Beach, Ocean Ridge, Gulf Stream, and Manalapan because I recognized that these other oceanfront communities had most or all of the same amenities—but not the cachet—of Boca Raton and Palm Beach. Not the price tags of Boca Raton or Palm Beach, either. At least, not until after I got there and raised property values. Now these cities have some of the most valuable real estate in the world, and we contributed to that stellar rise by making them the markets they are today. For example, when I first started on the ocean in Delray Beach close to twenty years ago, the cost of an oceanfront lot was $7,500 per front foot, so a 100-foot lot was $750,000, a price that I thought reflected undervaluation. Today, that same lot is nearly $100,000 per front foot, or $10 million for the same 100-foot lot! In fifteen years, that represents a 1,334 percent increase! That's the kind of appreciation that comes from moving from undervaluation to full valuation of properties. Why are they fully valued now? In large part, it's due to what we created there, and the cachet that came with it.

To see whether the area you're considering is undervalued and a viable place for investment, check into the following:

• **What are the high and low home prices?** You need a comparative market analysis for the previous two to three years. This means you'll research both the entry-level/lowest price homes and the highest price comparable homes sold in that area. You can get help with these numbers by visiting local realtors, the county property appraiser's office or website, private appraisers, county assessor's office or website—and sometimes by checking your local newspaper. Depending on where you live, you should be able to find all this information online. Over the three-year span, look for prices that have held steady, appreciated very slightly, or even depreciated a little, which indicates stagnation.

- **What's selling, what's not, and why?** Familiarize yourself with the inventory in the area: What's the average time a property stays on the market, and at what price point? How many sales have there been per year for the last three years? Neighborhoods with slow turnover can indicate that it's 1) fully valued and people aren't selling (limited opportunity for you), or 2) undervalued and people are afraid to buy (opportunity). You'll be able to tell which it is if values are escalating at an average of greater than 8 percent year over year for the last three years. If so, then those neighborhoods could be fully valued—generally, you will want to avoid these. In addition, be sure to look up the average asking price compared to average selling price, size of the average house in the area so you can learn what the homes are selling for on a dollar-per-square-foot ratio, number of bedrooms, bathrooms, and so on—and compare that with what's moving and what's been sitting there for a while. This will give you a sense of what people *want.*

- **Are there political or zoning considerations?** Attend meetings of local government and various neighborhood associations or set up a private meeting with a community-improvement director in your target city to keep tabs on their activities. You want to ask about everything from park upgrades to traffic management to crime-reduction efforts to what's being built down the road, whether it's a big-box store or a residential-treatment center. In other words, if it affects property values, you want to know about it. You can also stay current with this by joining the chamber of commerce and a social- or service-oriented group. I was on the board of directors of the Delray Beach Chamber of Commerce starting in my late twenties, and

I stayed there for fifteen years. The information I gathered was invaluable.

- **What are the local building codes or restrictions?** Each municipality and, in some cases, each neighborhood can have distinct rules and regulations about what can and can't be built in the area, so you need to investigate thoroughly. You'll want to find out if there are different codes for new construction and renovation, what limits may be put on architectural style or height, whether outbuildings are permissible, and so on. Beware of architectural commissions, or "pretty committees" as they are often called. Many of their decisions are not guided by a code or other mandate; they often can be quite subjective. It is nearly inevitable that you will need to make a presentation in front of one someday. Be sure to come fully prepared to show why your home will improve the community. If you're building near the ocean or other bodies of water, you may find strict regulation on both design and environmental impact. Make sure you know the rules and who will approve your plans, as both will affect your ability to improve your investment purchase. Most land development regulations or codes of ordinance are posted on your municipality's website. I read them regularly, even today, because the last thing I want is a surprise when it comes to my construction and improvement plans.

After you've identified your target neighborhood(s), familiarized yourself with the pricing and sales history, understood local building restrictions, researched upcoming developments, and know what you're looking for—only after you've done all that—you're ready to consider specific investment purchases. **A good place to begin is with**

the REO (Real Estate Owned) or loss mitigation officers at local banks. These people handle any properties that have been taken over by the bank due to receiving a deed in lieu of foreclosure, as well as properties owned by the bank as a result of a completed foreclosure. While REO officers won't be the ones who sign off on the deal, they are your first point of contact. In the current market, as in every other market in the boom-and-bust-and-boom cycles of real estate, buying properties taken over by banks can provide you with some of the sweetest deals around, and today there are plenty to be had. Banks are lending institutions; they don't want to be property owners or landlords. Every piece of property they own represents a drag on their books and a decrease in the amount of available capital. Even if the financial relief package of 2008 or any subsequent stimulus, or "bailouts" as they now call them, result in the buying up of delinquent real estate loans—getting them off the banks' books— there is no government agency offering to take over the foreclosed properties themselves at this time. If one is established as a clearing house (as after the S&L crisis), they will still need to dispose of the properties en masse. The banks and the government may breathe a sigh of relief that the worst of the mortgage loan portfolios are covered, but they will still have to figure out what to do with the property itself—the actual real estate—that they've taken over. I'm sure many banks are sitting down with their REO/loss mitigation officers and saying, "Get this stuff off our books *now!*"

And that's where you come in. As a real estate investor, you're in a position to take the property off the banks' hands, lightening their load by reducing inventory that banks really don't want to hold. You can be the equivalent of the U.S. Treasury for the property! Of course, I'm not talking about $700 billion—just the one or two properties that meet your requirements for good investments. And on your side, you'll be able to get an excellent deal on the properties you acquire—as long as you do your homework and are smart about your offers.

Do you see why REO/loss mitigation officers should be your first stop when looking for properties?

(By the way, even as the government steps in to stop the tide of foreclosures in this country, there are still so many properties in the pipeline—in default, or in some stage of the foreclosure process—that you will have ten times the properties to choose from than I did when I first started bidding on real estate on the courthouse steps. And yes, that's a real number: *ten* times as many as I had to choose from. As with every cycle, the worst of times for some can represent the greatest opportunities for the contrarian who is quick enough, smart enough, and liquid enough to take advantage of them.)

The other kinds of deals you will find more frequently in downward-trending markets are short sales. In a short sale, the bank agrees to sell you the property for less than the face value of the mortgage. Now, short sales can be more difficult than simply buying a foreclosure, because the banks are very shortsighted (pun intended) when it comes to the virtue of getting the property off their books versus getting back what they loaned on it. Banks often will hold onto properties until the last minute, until the owner defaults and the house goes into foreclosure, and they price the real estate too high for current market conditions, just because they hope to recoup as much of their money as possible. That's the kind of shortsighted vision that has repeatedly gotten banks into a real mess.

But there are a growing number of great opportunities to be had in short sales. All you need is patience and a willingness to negotiate hard with the parties involved, including both the bank and the owner. With a foreclosure, you're dealing only with the bank, because it has taken over the property. With a short sale, the owner may be in the process of foreclosure but still holds the mortgage and the property. And that fact represents opportunity for you. As an investor, your greatest ally in pursuing a short sale isn't the bank; you need to deal with the owner of the property. Imagine this: You're so behind in your mortgage payments that the bank is either threatening you with foreclosure or has actually started the process. Then you get a call from Susie Investor, who says, "I want to help you save your credit and avoid foreclosure. Let's go to the bank together. I'm going to offer the bank X dollars (at least 30 to 50 percent below the loan's value) to pay off your mortgage, and I'll give you Y dollars, as well. You end up with some cash and your credit is intact." How many struggling homeowners would see Susie as the answer to their prayers if the offer was presented in the right way?

Realize, however, that a short sale often can take longer and be a tougher sell to the banks. Be patient and be willing to walk away from the deal if it doesn't meet your financial criteria. Keep in mind that, even if the banks don't want to acknowledge it, you're doing them a favor. Foreclosures are costly to banks and often messy. By stepping in with a short sale, you head off the bank's need to fore-close; that should be worth the discount you receive. Although I know a bit about short sales, I'm no expert. I recommend a book by Dwan Bent-Twyford and Sharon Restrepo titled *Short-Sale Pre-Foreclosure Investing*. It goes into much greater detail.

In good times and bad, banks are going to be your best sources for possible investment properties. That's where I went for the best deals twenty years ago; the only difference is that back then I had only 50 properties to choose from; now you may have 500 and up. I believe we are in the midst of a 100-year "storm" in the real estate market. But just like the hurricanes that wash the coast of Florida where I live, when the storm blows through, you'll find some of the most beautiful shells washed up on the beach. As a *Burst This!* investor, you now have more opportunity than at any other time in the last 100 years to pick up the beautiful "shells" of undervalued property. You simply must keep your head out of the sand, keep your eyes open, and be ready to take advantage of the deals you find and, yes, take the risk.

While banks are your best resource for leads on investment property, you also should check with the county and the IRS for property sold to pay back real estate or income taxes, and sheriff sales for property seized due to illegal activities. "Distress" sales of properties are common all over the United States, and you're wise to see if you can avail yourself of these opportunities. When I got started in this business, my very first deals were made on the courthouse steps. (This was before I found out about REO officers.) I'd pick up the paper and comb through about four dozen foreclosed properties being auctioned off the next week. In my first six months, I went to the auctions whenever they were held and bid on properties in my head, but I never actually raised my hand, as I was too scared. This was my version of the back-testing I recommended to you in Chapter 2. I learned the process, the area, the kinds of things to look for in foreclosures, which banks were dealing in these kinds of properties, and so on.

In bidding on these properties, I averaged about one deal for every forty properties that made the cut to my short list. The "long list" would yield one property for every 4,000 that went into foreclosure! Keep in mind that I drove by every one of those forty short-listed properties, inspected it, figured my margins, and only if it penciled out did my hand go up at auction. As I mentioned, the number of properties being foreclosed on in any given week might be close to ten times what I saw go across the courthouse steps. That's why dealing with the banks is your best bet for a great deal.

In time, I started dealing directly with the banks' REO or loss mitigation officers, bypassing the competition at auction. As always, the trick is to get there first. You can drive through your target neighborhoods and look for signs of a distressed property: the lawn that hasn't been mowed in ages, mail falling out of the mail box, broken windows, torn screen doors, trash in the yard, general dilapidation.

Better still is to reach the owner of the house before the banks get their lawyers involved, and long before the house goes for auction on the courthouse steps. This is where the real money is made. This takes knowing the people in your target neighborhood, talking with them about whose circumstances may have changed and who might entertain the right offer, writing letters that let owners know you're looking to buy, joining the neighborhood associations, and so on. You want to walk or drive the neighborhood regularly and notice if any house is starting to look worse for wear. Talk with the owners, and even the neighbors of homes that aren't looking troubled. See what you can learn. Ask, ask, ask. Let them know you're looking for properties in the area.

Create a Masterpiece Your Buyers Will Love

To find the right property, you'll be talking to a lot of people and looking at a lot of homes. A huge number of such conversations will never lead to a deal, but all of them are essential to your ability to acquire the knowledge to obtain the right place at the right price. Nothing beats personal contact and establishing genuine relationships in the community for getting to know not only what houses might be available to you, but also for getting to know the taste, preferences, and personalities of people who are like the buyers who will be drawn to your finished masterpiece. *You must understand the psychology of your buyer*, the characteristics they possess, and what they consider most important when it comes to their home. After all, a home is the largest purchase most people make in a lifetime. It is a daily, visible reminder not only of our level of success but more important, who we are. For instance, a hip, young entrepreneur with cash and unlimited prospects probably won't be interested in a home with tiny, cozy, old-fashioned rooms; he or she will want big rooms for entertaining, the latest home automation gadgets, a huge pool, "green" features like solar, and minimal upkeep. On the other hand, Mr. and Mrs. Middle Class who have saved to scrape together a down payment (which more people will have to do again) for their first house may look for things like the white picket fence, new appliances, and a nice backyard where they can barbecue and entertain.

Whatever your market or price point for your properties, you must get to know the tastes, personalities, and preferences of the buyers who will be drawn to your finished masterpiece, because you must build *for them*. There are two big mistakes I see real estate investors make. The first is overimproving aspects that don't mean much to their potential buyers and underimproving elements that make or break the deal. For example, if your target buyer is Mr. and Mrs. Main Street looking for their first starter house, don't spend a mint on exquisite light fixtures or gourmet-grade appliances.

Instead, put in nice enough lighting and appliances, and spend your money to fix up the backyard, put in that barbecue, and put a picket fence around the front.

The second mistake is building or improving to suit your taste rather than the taste of your target buyer. You may feel that 1950s postmodern homes with huge windows and Danish wood are the ultimate in style, but if you're investing in the Northeast where the cold winters make huge windows and drafty, open interiors incredibly expensive to heat, and all the other properties in the neighborhood are more in the style of Cape Cod cottages, you may get one buyer in 100 who likes to stand out from the crowd, but you'll miss 99 others who would love to live in your updated version of a Cape Cod, with clean lines, warm woods, a kitchen that opens onto the family room, double-paned windows, heated floors, and an energy-efficient furnace. **You must get inside the heads of your target buyers and create their perfect home, not yours.**

I've said more than once that although I'm an artist, I have no interest in starving. If the artistic expression doesn't make sense, then it stays unexpressed. I'm a businessman first. And as anyone who succeeds in business will tell you, the first rule is to understand your customers. My customers are the reason I decided to paint some of our early fixer-upper houses sky blue and pink and mint green. Pastels don't reflect my personal taste, but I knew that a lot of the people who would be interested in buying in the neighborhood where I was renovating homes were interested in bright, clean colors. I didn't do it because other people were doing it—no one else was—but because I learned a lot from those who lived in the neighborhoods, I knew that the area residents liked it, and so would my potential buyers.

Even if you plan to live in your investment property for a couple of years while you renovate and the neighborhood improves, you'd be smart to buy according to one and only one criteria: the perceived value of the home in the marketplace. The goal is to make a profit, not to be "in the game." Choose properties and renovate or build them based on how you believe your buyers would like to live, not how you would, although in some cases this may be the same.

Ideally, you'll know what your buyers will appreciate even before they do. Right now, I'm deeply involved in the creation and sale of two estates that differ drastically from comparable properties in my area. First, they both reflect what I like to call "ian" architecture—a style influenced by many trips to the South Pacific—based on Balinesian, Tahitian, Fijian, and Polynesian homes with their thatched roofs and open-air feel, the stunning teak and coconut woods, and gorgeous views of the water. Again, I didn't undertake these projects because I saw other people doing it—no one else is—but because I know my ultrawealthy buyers, and I can tell you what they desire before they've ever even seen it. Let me repeat that: *One of the keys to making a market is to have a subliminal sense of knowing what your buyers want before even they know it.* Yes it's risky, but so is pulling the machete out and being the first to clear your way to that ancient temple buried deep in the rain forest that contains the prized treasure. Christopher Columbus sailed west even though most of the "civilized" people in Europe thought he would sail off the edge of the world. But he knew in his heart that something awaited him in the unknown reaches of the ocean, and he took the risk and garnered the glory (and the profits for Spain) of discovering the New World.

At my price point, differentiation remains crucially important: it doesn't make sense for me to keep going with the same architecture or building practices when there are more exciting possibilities in a new direction. I'll admit, today I'm taking a gamble both with the "green" aspects of these estates (they will be the largest and most expensive "green" homes in the world) and in the architecture (many homes in South Florida follow the Mediterranean styles). But, as you read at the beginning of this chapter, that's the calculated risk of the market maker: to create something unique, to know you'll be able to captivate at least one buyer who will love what you've done, and to move forward with pride and passion.

As far as architecture is concerned, I have consistently made my market by either choosing a style that no one else in the area was producing, or by amping up the prevailing style so that it was bigger, better, and more luxurious than anyone had done before. My first built-from-scratch spec house, La Marceaux, was inspired by the French architecture found in the Loire Valley. At the time, most oceanfront homes in the area were versions of the vaguely Mediterranean "Florida" style: light colors, smaller windows, barrel tile roofs—think heavy Italian architecture. In contrast, La Marceaux featured steeply pitched, French slate roofs, two turrets, a two-story-high living room, a movie theatre, a game room, and a replica of the Oval Office. When it came to an estate I sold in Manalapan a few years back, I took the kinds of luxurious touches my target buyers had come to expect in their homes and made them significantly more spectacular. The home had a seventy-five-foot-long disappearing edge pool that looked like it was flowing into the ocean, a two-story master suite, an aquarium with a replica of the sunken Spanish galleon the *Atocha* half-buried in the sand and coral with gold dubloons strewn about, and a two-story guesthouse next to a hand-built rock wall, over which cascaded a waterfall that splashed directly into a second swimming pool.

I go the extra mile because I know that my target buyer is looking for two main things. First, they need something that adequately represents the "lifetime achievement" award they so deserve. They've been exposed to so many different, incredibly beautiful places that they're often somewhat jaded. Instead of just a home, they want a new experience, something that's different from the other properties they've seen. They've worked their entire lives to put themselves in the position to purchase our artistry. And second, they want (and expect) the ultimate in luxury. So what I create either must be markedly different from the other properties they investigate, or so much more luxuriously spectacular, that nothing else could compare. Using those two rules as my artistic guidelines, my properties are snapped up in days rather than years.

With all that going for the estates, why do the green thing at all? Many reasons—the main one being that I know my buyers' desires even before they're aware of them. The cachet of an "all-green" home will appeal to many people who perhaps never thought about building green, but who would be delighted to be able to brag to their friends about how they are fighting global warming with their new estate. It's especially appealing when they see that an all-green home requires absolutely no sacrifice in luxury, beauty, or amenities on their part. (It's the ultimate version of having their all-green cake and eating it, too.)

On my side, going green means that we get to redefine the Frank McKinney brand yet again. I'm the new "Jolly Green Giant," creating the most opulent oceanfront homes and leading the charge for environmentally responsible luxury construction practices. I don't eat granola every morning, nor do I go out and give my strangler fig tree a big bear hug every night after work, although trees are a hobby of mine, and I love my 2002 Honda Insight 60 mile-per-gallon hybrid. But I'm not a hypocrite, either. I was driving that hybrid long before we started building green. I walk my daughter, Laura, to school every day instead of driving. (We've made more than a thousand adventure-filled treks since she was in prekindergarten, and just this year turned those adventures into a young-reader fantasy novel titled *Dead Fred, Flying Lunchboxes, and the Good Luck Circle*.) I turn off the tap while I'm brushing my teeth. I'm more worried about the rising sea levels than I am about the current state of the economy, which I've already told you looks fairly grim at the moment. So, yes, I care about the environment. But I'm far from the purist who thinks *green mansion* is an oxymoron or a blasphemy, as my large green homes have been called by some. As George Bernard Shaw wrote, "All great truths begin as blasphemies." So I say to the eco-purists, get real—homes are getting bigger, not smaller. The average American home has increased in size by 40 percent since 1970. Instead of trying to swim against that forty-year tide, why not do what we can to decrease the energy use and carbon footprint of those bigger homes? Wouldn't it be better for the planet if we were to build and live green in every house, at every size, in every neighborhood?

Truth be told, I see green building as an extraordinary opportunity. We're making a market, setting and pushing a trend. At Acqua Liana and Crystalina, we're implementing the rigorous standards as prescribed by the U.S. Green Building Council's (USGBC) LEED-H program (Leadership in Energy and Environmental Design for Homes). Understand that there are homes with green intentions, and then there are the very few that meet or exceed the exacting standards established by the LEED-H program. By pursuing the certification and rating—which is conducted and verified by no less than five different third parties, and runs the entire tenure of the eighteen-month construction process—we're doing something no one else is doing, and doing it while bearing a huge amount of risk.

Right now, the green trend is at the earliest stages in the marketplace. Often we hear "the credit crisis is in the seventh inning . . ." or "the real estate market rebound is in the third inning . . ." Well, using the same baseball analogy, when it comes to green building they're still playing the national anthem. The game hasn't even started yet. **According to the National Association of Realtors, 46 percent of people are interested in owning a green home.** However, as of 2008, there have been only 1,434 homes (1,240 new construction, 98 existing buildings, and 96 "core and shell") certified by the LEED-H program as green. When you compare that number with the total number of housing units in the United States— 129,871,000 in the second quarter of 2008, according to the U.S. Census—only .000011 percent (1.1 *thousandth* of 1 percent) of existing homes are green. While this is obviously a minuscule fraction, it represents a 2,000 percent increase in the number of LEED-H certified homes in just one year (from 2007 to 2008).

As an investor, these numbers should make two things very clear to you. First, the average American homebuyer is receptive to green products and practices, and that trend will only increase as we continue to hear about the climate challenges facing our environment and rising prices for fuel. Going green will be a huge point in your property's favor, as you show potential buyers how they can reduce their heating and cooling bills while reducing their carbon footprint.

Second, we are in the extreme early phases of the "greening" of America, and if you're smart, you'll make it part of your business plan now. **This is the cutting edge of what I believe will be the most** significant wave of the future in real estate. **This single element, implemented properly, could lift national sales of real estate out of the depths of despair.** I realize that's a bold statement. Is it true? Come back to this in five years and see if the crystal ball was accurate. **Green is the next killer app in real estate.** Not only because more consumers are interested in going green, but also because the government, at all levels, is likely to support the trend. For several years we've been seeing green practices, like installing solar panels or driving a hybrid car, supported by tax breaks; heck, in Las Vegas, the city was paying property owners to rip out their lawns to cut down on water usage. And with Acqua Liana we received a $40,000 check from the government because we used solar. But I believe the time is coming when we'll be required *by law* to build green and reduce energy usage, water consumption, and the pollution we create in our homes. So if you build or renovate "green," you can demonstrate to your buyer that you're not just saving them thousands of dollars year after year with the energy- and water-efficient appliances, watering systems, low-flush toilets, zone air-conditioning and heating, and so on, but you've also saved them the inconvenience and bother of putting in those upgrades themselves when they're required by law. I can guarantee that you will recoup and profit from the cost of the green improvements you make to your properties. Can you see that it makes sense to renovate or build new with green in mind?

Whether you're renovating or starting from the ground up, you can implement numerous green features that won't cost much more than what you're already spending—and you get an immediate increase in perceived value, plus you get to pat yourself on the back for doing something good for kids, families, and communities all over the world. That's what caring for the environment means: being responsible with our resources so that there's enough clean air and water to go around, including enough for the generations to come, and doing our part to balance the scales of climate change. You'll read more about ways to go green in Chapter 7.

Look, it's natural to resist change. We all do it. I still grumble when I have to unlearn the old ways and relearn the new ways. Sometimes, going green is a pain in my ascot. But it has given me a whole new lease on a career that's probably closer to its end than its beginning—and it's probably even pushed the end back a little farther because I have renewed interest in my profession. It's engaging and rewarding for me to be contributing to the mandate, to be setting new standards, creating new criteria. I get to be the voice of reason, a counterpoint to those who get bogged down in the maniacal minutiae, the ones who aren't willing to say yes! It's a step forward when the most magnificent homes in the country help their owners reduce their carbon footprint instead of enlarging it.

To make a market, you don't have to completely reinvent the wheel. Take what you've learned here and add your own unique spin. Will you be the first one in your area to introduce a new architectural style? To raise a sagging neighborhood to new standards? To help your buyers reduce their carbon footprint just by putting them into a house they love? Don't be afraid to be early to make a market. Be willing to step out and take a chance. Remember, it is the market makers who make the big money. The visionaries who execute on the vision—not the idea guys who dream all day—make the big money. The risk must be taken for the big money reward to be realized. There are many more talented real estate investors out there than me, and you are probably one of them. The primary difference between me and them, or you, is my understanding that I must venture into areas that others can't imagine to leave that real estate legacy, and make millions in the process. Join me; I know you can.

Your Chapter 5
BURST OF INSPIRATION

- With the greening of America still in the national-anthem stage, start thinking about how you might capitalize on it in your current or next property. Begin your research now: visit the USGBC website for more information on LEED-H, find out what groups may already exist in your area that support green building practices or have green interests (a possible market for your properties), suggest a green initiative at your real estate investment group, and so on. *Get involved.* Go on, green your business plan and your bottom line.

6

ONCE YOU'VE BUBBLE-PROOFED, YOU'LL CELEBRATE YOUR "BUY" DAY MORE THAN YOUR "SELL" DAY

When a property makes it through the gauntlet of worthy suitors, and we've met at the closing table together, with my pen in one hand and my check to buy the property in the other, I always walk out with a big smile and Pizza Hut on speed dial. Every time we close on a big purchase, Nilsa, Laura, and I order a large pie with mushrooms and two liters of root beer to celebrate on-site at our new acquisition, either on the front steps, in the living room, in the pool, or on the sand of the vacant lot of the new project. Nilsa and I started this tradition with Driftwood Dunes in 1991 (our daughter came along in 1998), and as recently as last year, we did the same on the sites for Acqua Liana and Crystalina.

You may be wondering if this isn't backwards. *Shouldn't the selling date be more of a party? And shouldn't there be some champagne involved?* To the contrary; I expect to make a profit by following my system, and it's a day filled with possibility and opportunity. (Sell days tend to be filled with relief.) Sure, we celebrate the day we get paid, as well, and I've been known to break out the champagne for Nilsa then (sparkling apple juice for me and Laura, thank you), but there's nothing like enjoying the creation of that opportunity where you know, based upon your research and your ability to execute and "close the loop," that you just made a great deal.

In this chapter, I give you the exact—and surprisingly simple— formula to calculate whether any specific property warrants the attendant risk. It's a formula I've followed for almost twenty-five years, through all kinds of market conditions. It will help you answer the question, "Is this The One for me?" Since we're focusing on real estate and not romance, figuring this out is a lot less angst-filled than you might imagine.

You could call this the bottom line of bubble-proofing; one of the key reasons I've never lost money on a for-profit deal. You can also credit the close attention I've always paid to the buy side of the transaction. Throughout my career, buying properties at extremely good prices has been the cornerstone of my success.

There is room for error: you could mess up a little on the acquisition side and then recover by creating a magnificent home and selling it with ingenious marketing. I've done it myself, but it's nothing you want to do intentionally. Instead, *buy right*. With a solid purchase up front, you all but guarantee your margin and can count on your property like an annuity: an investment that will provide you deferred and nearly assured profit. It's only a matter of time before you cash in and realize the handsome profit you actually created the day you bought the opportunity.

When you buy right, you've completed the first step in bubble-proofing your real estate investment portfolio. One more time: we are in this to make money, and your likelihood of doing so approaches triple digits in terms of percent if you pay hyperattention to what you pay for your opportunity.

Acquisition + Improvement = Not More Than 65 Percent of Retail Price

Acquisition **is the cost** of the property, what you'll pay to the seller for the home, property, or vacant land. That's it.

Improvement represents the cost of whatever you plan to do to make the house or land ready for market—the additions, rehabilitation, restoration, or new construction you'll complete to add value to the property. This could be as minimal as clearing out the uncollected junk mail from the mail box and mowing the grass once, or as extensive as building a $30-million mansion from the ground up. It would include everything, top to bottom, inside and out, from a new roof to reconditioned hardwood floors, from freshly painted fencing to fluffy new towels and a fragrant bouquet in the kitchen—or, for that matter, everything from solid-gold, low-flow water fixtures to a 24-foot oceanfront sheeting water wall.

That's it. Really. Those numbers will take some time to figure (and the next chapter will help you to spend your improvement dollars wisely and for maximum buyer appeal), but still, it seems almost too quick to compute, doesn't it?

Can it really be so simple to determine whether your property is a good deal or not? It really can. I don't believe in overanalyzing, as you know. I've watched plenty of people lose out because they spend too much time calculating their returns, using lots of figures to talk themselves out of a good deal or, even worse, to convince themselves that a poor investment was actually a good one. Don't make either mistake. Stick to this simple formula, and then seize the best opportunities.

Of course, you're not using this formula haphazardly and throwing out everything else you've learned. By the time you're running these numbers, you've already carefully researched the neighborhood. You've reviewed historical rates of property-value appreciation and time on market, you know the high and low prices in the area, you've compared asking to selling prices, you've checked crime rates and learned what municipal improvements are coming, and you're familiar with the current inventory's asking prices, sizes, and amenities.

You've also examined this particular property's condition and quite possibly already had it inspected. (Absolutely, do this if you can. The fees for an inspection may be the best money you ever spend, as it gives you a clear view of the kind of improvements you need to include in your budget, and it may also provide you with leverage in your negotiations. Find a great inspector who you trust and respect to be on your team.)

So only one essential question remains: *how much will it cost to buy and improve this place, and can it be sold for close to a 50 percent profit?*

Wait a minute. Am I really saying that you could make over 50 percent profit on your investment? Yes, exactly. In a hot market or the early stages of a boom trend, that projected number should be very close to 50 percent (e.g., $100,000 retail sale with 65 percent, or $65,000 into the deal = $35,000 profit on $65,000 investment = a little more than 50 percent return). In more uncertain or challenging times, that projected number should be higher, up to 100 percent return ($100,000 retail sale with $50,000 into the deal = $50,000 profit on $50,000 investment = 100 percent return). That may seem counterintuitive, but this greater margin accounts for times when the economy contracts, strains in the credit markets (which make it harder to get financing), a smaller pool of buyers, unforeseen delays, greater carrying costs, and so on, all of which are associated with a slow market.

For the sake of round numbers, and using the midpoint of the examples above, let's imagine you've identified a house you want, priced by the seller at $100,000. You believe, based on your market research and your ability to market the property, this house has a repaired or "after-market" value of $125,000. (I know, locating a house for $100,000 is difficult in many places around the country, but this is just an example chosen for easy math.) Given the poor condition of the property, the state of the market and economy, the sellers' need to move the property, and your ability to represent these and other important factors to the seller and perhaps their bank, you feel confident that you can negotiate a purchase not to exceed $70,000, and you plan to put in $15,000 worth of improvements. According to the formula of *Acquisition + Improvement = Not More Than 65 Percent of Retail Price*, you must be able to ask around $129,000 when you sell ($85,000 into the deal divided by 65 percent (.65) = $130,769.23). Always list your property for sale with a nine in the numerical category before your zeros. (It's like selling a bag of chips for 99 cents—it's a psychological inducement to buy.)

Will you actually make that projected return? ($129,000 selling price less 85,000 into the deal = $44,000 profit. $44,000 divided by $85,000 in the deal = 50 percent +/- return.) Maybe not. Probably not. Rarely. There are many factors that will squeeze your margin.

Price negotiation, terms, buyer assistance, carrying costs, overimprovement (over budget), closing costs. (Are you glad I finally mentioned these? Were you anxious and saying to yourself, *Yeah, but...* when you read my formula and didn't see all these variables represented? Chill for a minute.)

This is exactly why you calculate the large spread you find in my formula. Any number of those variables will likely reduce your profit margin. That's the whole reason the spread is so large: to allow for unknowns that, at some point, will become knowns while also ensuring that you have enough room in the formula for the inevitable squeezes on the margin—and still give you an excellent idea of whether you're looking at a good deal or not. **The importance of the formula: it will allow you to act quickly without having to account for every possible margin-reducing scenario.** It's a decision-making tool, not a comprehensive budget for the project.

The *actual* deal would look something more like this: $129,000 asking price, $120,000 actual selling price (arrived at during negotiation), less $7,000 in closing costs, less $90,000 into the deal (including additional carrying costs and budget overrun) = $23,000 profit, or 25 percent return on investment. Not bad when you multiply that return by hundreds of deals over your career—and when you factor in that your margins improve with experience. How many deals like that would you have to do to exceed your current income? Less than you'd think, and you will get there sooner than you think if you stick with me. By the way, if you added two zeros to the above example, you would have profited $2.3 million. Add three zeros, and it's $23 million. That's bubble-proofing to the tenth power!

Using our example above (of course, you'll adjust by inserting your own actual numbers when you're considering a real deal), you need to answer two important questions in deciding whether to proceed or not:

- **Is the house a good value at $70,000?** Remember you're seeking undervalued properties, which means you want a purchase price that's 30 to 50 percent below current values in the neighborhood.
- **Is the $129,000 retail price viable?** Are there at least a few comparable houses for sale in the neighborhood listed for at least $120,000? In other words, will it make comparable sense for your retail sales price (RSP) to be about 10 percent above current prices in the neighborhood? You want to be within that range, thereby creating new highs in the marketplace at a reasonable pace.

If comparable houses are selling for much less than your RSP, and there isn't any wiggle room in the acquisition or improvement costs, then it's time to pass on the deal and move on to the next. But if the numbers work, you may have found your property—this may be The One.

If you think this is The One, your next step is to extrapolate one more possible scenario, so you have a sense of a worst case, to see if you can protect your capital. The acquisition formula gives you best case, and the above $23,000 profit example represents a mid-case scenario—the most likely outcome. In actual practice, I don't allow myself to dwell for long on the best cases, because I want to under promise and over deliver, even to myself, and besides they rarely ever materialize. If I make more money because someone paid my full price, or covered my closing costs, or I sold it the day it hit the market (reducing my calculated carrying costs), this is gravy, but I never,

never count on it. But I do always think and plan extensively about the worst case. What if I had to hold onto the property for a few years, paying for marketing, insurance, maintenance, the interest on the loan, and other unforeseen carrying costs? What if the two biggest mortgage lenders in the country went belly up? (You know that's possible.) What if the local market tanked, sentiment went south, and I could no longer imagine that people would pay the projected RSP?

Does the deal still provide a decent return?

Margins begin to shrink dramatically in your worst-case scenario, so you need to have viable exit strategies to protect your capital investment at worst, and at best, still profit from the deal. At various times early in my career, I was forced to institute one of three fallback plans when a property would not move and I needed it to. The first safety net is to lease-option it, where the lessor makes a nonrefundable deposit that would apply, either completely or in portion, to the selling price. They then pay an agreed-upon amount every month with a portion being credited to the selling price, and for that they are granted the option to buy the property at the end of the lease-option term. The second is to rent it, and the third option is to live there myself and rent out my primary residence. There are other possibilities, as well:

- Renovate for mixed-use if zoning allows.
- If you're holding a sizable piece of land, you can partition it into smaller lots and sell them.
- Take back a small second mortgage to get the deal done.
- In the extreme worst case, where survival becomes the primary focus, you may put "for sale" signs on both your own home and

the investment property, and see which one sells first. Hey—it's better than the alternative! You may be put in the position, again, of sacrificing today for a better tomorrow, and there's no shame in that. I had to take this unprecedented step as recently as last year.

The more "what if" options you have to implement in the event your worst case materializes, the better you'll sleep at night. The fear of those worst-case scenarios provides excellent motivation to move the house however you can, to find creative ways to sell. Don't let pride or pigeonholing your property into a particular kind of sale keep you from doing what's necessary, including lowering the price. Maybe price reduction is a no-brainer, but I've seen people go down with the ship just because they won't shave a percentage point or two off their anticipated profit margin. You must constantly prepare yourself to do whatever's necessary to find a buyer for the home. That's the name of the game, always: *move the property, make your money, and move on.*

So either establish how you'll ensure that this investment will pay out in almost any case, or recognize that it's not The One for you. Some of the best deals I've made are the ones I walked away from. Not all are meant to work out. Remember, bubble-proofing is about maximizing opportunities and minimizing hazards. Focusing only on one scenario would be a huge mistake, and it's one you can easily avoid with some foresight.

Again, let me suggest that when you first begin using a *Burst This!* approach, you rehearse on potential properties by generating numbers simply for practice. You'll learn a great deal by testing the formula on various properties at different price points. But even if you practice, even if you run all the scenarios, even if you think you have a sure thing, can you still fall short of your profit goals? Of course. To state the obvious, life is uncertain. As you learned, real estate cycles are fairly predictable, but circumstances can change quickly. Appropriately, the acquisition formula is designed with enough profit potential to handle most situations and still net you a nice return, boom or bust, up or down, bear or bull. It's bubble-proof—as long as you do your homework.

Negotiating With Sellers— Acquiring the Property

Believe it or not, in addition to money, other factors can be quite important to sellers. Additional needs, desires, and wants usually come into play, and if you can craft your offer in a way that fulfills those, too, you have a much better chance of acquiring the property at a price that works for you and the seller both.

As a potential buyer, your job is to accurately understand the sellers' psychology so you can negotiate an excellent price with them. You need to learn why they might be willing to sell to you at a discount. Are they facing a financial crisis? Have their mortgage payments become a challenge? Has the house been on the market so long that they're scared of being stuck with it forever? Are they already in foreclosure? Are rising property taxes and insurance rates pushing them out of their house? Maybe it's none of those things, but there might be other reasons. What stage of life are they in? How old are they? What's their level of health? Are they working for someone else or in business for themselves? Are they retired and looking to move somewhere with lower taxes and maintenance, or to an assisted-care facility? Is their family outgrowing the current residence? Has one of the owners been transferred to another city? What's their history with the property? How long has it been in the family? How long has it been on the market? Have there been any price reductions? What did the seller pay for the house? How much debt remains on the property? Are there any outstanding liens, loans, or tax bills?

You can find a great deal of this information online by visiting the websites of your local property appraiser and clerk of the circuit court. It's amazing what you can discover from those two sources: who owns a particular house, where the owner lives (in that house or not), what the owner paid for the house, what the mortgage is, if the taxes have been paid, previous sales history, and whether there are liens on the property. In a few pages, you'll see a note I sent to "Fred," who I'd discovered was likely to sell his oceanfront home to me at a discount; although I knew he had a tax lien on the property, as well as three mortgages, two of which were late, I didn't mention those things right away. (I did talk to him about that later on the phone, however.) I knew more than the bank knew, and I'd learned most of it from the public records. This kind of information can prove invaluable in bubble-proofing your real estate investments.

The owner's real estate agent can also fill you in on any details likely to affect the sale of the property. Your best bet, though, is to go directly to the source, to the owners, and get to know them personally. (I knew Fred quite well, as I'd sold him the same home I was looking to acquire from him.) You need to build rapport with them, and then listen to what they have to say. Their answers to all of the questions I listed above reflect what they really want from the deal.

For example, in cases where the owners are in distress, often the best offer you can make is to assume the loan or approach the bank for a short sale, which might give the owner some much-needed cash, give you an excellent price on the house, and give the mortgage lender most of its money without it having to take possession of the house. If the house is being sold by someone who is elderly, you may need to contact the heirs or others who have a financial interest in the property—and heirs usually want cash, so their greatest interest may be in selling the property quickly. If someone decides to move, if they're retiring and just want something different, or even if you come across as personable and sincere and they really like you—all of these circumstances can provide opportunities. Most great deals, however, will involve some form of distress.

Once you decide on a purchase price that meets your acquisition formula, make your offer to the owner in person and in writing. I used to carry blank contracts with me whenever I went to meet with owners so that I could move on a property immediately if it was a great opportunity. If the owner is ready to sell, sign the contract as soon as practical so the seller doesn't have the chance to suffer from seller's remorse, which is far worse than buyer's remorse—if you allow it to fester, it could cancel your call to Pizza Hut.

Make your offers and contracts so straightforward that even a person distracted by financial stresses, a health crisis, or any other major life pressures will have no trouble reading and responding quickly. When I first started acquiring properties, I assumed that sellers would respond best to detailed offers with everything spelled out, every light bulb accounted for. However, I came to realize the opposite: the more concise and direct my offer, the greater the chance of the owner accepting my terms with less haggling. This holds true even, perhaps especially, with the multimillion-dollar properties I buy today. Below is what I call a "talking paper" that I used to buy a promising oceanfront property for $20 million. This document isn't a contract but instead an outline designed to get right to the point so we can determine if we could get right to contract. The name and addresses have been changed for privacy, yet the rest is exactly how the deal was communicated. Notice how simple it is:

Fred,

You certainly have one of the nicest homes along the coast, yet, per our discussion, if you can wait closer to a year to sell it, you could do far better than if you sold this winter.

Comps at 2340 (your neighbor, sold for $39,400 per front foot), 2260 (sold for $43,860 pff), and 2180 (sold for $47,500 pff), all sold within the last six months, indicate that waiting would be in your property's best interest. If you multiply your land by the average of the three above = $13MM. Of course, you must add back the value of your improvements, which is subjective.

Given the severe risks associated with the current marketplace and our inventory level, I can offer the terms below. If this does not work for you and you want to sell your beautiful home for more, you probably will. I completely understand. Keep me in mind in the event you change your mind. Should we sell some inventory, I may be back if you still have the home.

1) $20,000,000

I will close as quickly as possible. We are fine with you taking all or part of the furniture from the home. Our closing costs would be limited to the standard buyer's closing costs such as our own attorney's fees, state taxes and recording fees on the note and mortgage (if any), recording fees on the deed statement, lender's title policy (if any), and survey. Your closing costs would be limited to the standard seller's costs, such as your own attorney's fees and documentary stamps on the deed.

2) No brokerage commission

3) As-Is, with right to inspect

4) 30-day close or sooner

5) Financing contingency

6) Confidentiality clause

If this works for you, I will have my attorney draft the contract at once. Title work is fairly new and all involved (Bank of America) are familiar with the property.

All the best,

Frank McKinney

Don't let the simplicity of this note fool you: I took my time writing it over a few days, because I wanted to hit just the right notes—and nothing more. There are plenty of subliminal messages in it, from the salutation (the use of his first name is familiar and friendly), to the compliments I paid to his home and honest assessment that he'd be better off if he could wait to sell it (counseling him that he could make more money another way), to the comps I included (which were, of course, some of the worst comps in the neighborhood, but they also happened to be near him—and they reinforced my position as the expert).

By focusing him on the value of the land, a modest estimate of $13 million based on those comps, then offhandedly tossing in some undetermined value for the "improvements," I allowed him to focus on the known (land value), while depreciating his improvements. The land had a beautiful 30,000-square-foot house on it, but I wasn't concerning either of us with accurately assessing its value, which easily exceeded the $20 million I was offering. Because I was drawing attention to the land value only, my offer of $20 million sounded like a good deal for him. I also let him know that I was carrying a lot of inventory and wouldn't be in a position to offer more until some of it sold—much later. But I knew he'd want to sell his own home as soon as possible, if he could.

I also stipulated no closing costs, no broker, and a thirty-day turnaround on the property. He would save the commission (at least $1.5 million) and get money out of the property within a month. Equally important was what I didn't say. As I mentioned above, I knew that this owner was in financial distress, but putting that in a letter probably would have made him defensive or embarrassed—not the reaction I wanted, and the kind of thing that can quickly leave your deal for dead. Fred needed to feel as if I was on his side, and only then could I let him know what I knew—that's the kind of thing you can say only in person, with some compassion, a little sugar delivered with the necessary medicine.

Fairly quickly, he took the deal. The "talking paper" was converted to a binding contract, and we bought the property, renovated it, and later resold it with an asking price of $50 million.

Strive to wrap up your deals within a day or two. (Who knows what unforeseen meteor showers might drop an asteroid on your deal? If you'd been in a protracted closing during the financial meltdown in late 2008, imagine what might have happened. Much simpler, less sweeping, but equally unforeseen circumstances can come to pass, killing a deal without any warning.) Ideally, the response from the owner will come the day after you've submitted your initial offer. To facilitate this quick turnaround, be sure to streamline an initial purchase offer as I did in the example above, including only key elements:

1. **The purchase price.** The seller's eyes will go to this dollar amount first.

2. **Cash terms.** Make a cash offer, if possible, with limited financing contingency, which means you've already secured whatever loan you'll need to purchase the property, and the seller won't have to wait for you to get approval. (You're *providing* cash, although some of it may have come from a lending source.)

3. **The deposit amount.** If you can, include a respectable deposit; this shows the seller you're serious and provides the incentive of quick cash.

4. **The closing date.** If at all possible, make it a thirty-day (or less) close. Typical transactions can stretch sixty to ninety days, but it is in your control to shorten the time. Even if this means allowing them to stay for an extra month for a dollar, your job is to make the buy of the century. The closing and the move-out date don't have to coincide; they don't even have to be close. When you've found the right property at the right price, it's worth giving the current owners as much latitude as practical, making it very difficult for them to say no. When we bought our own home, we allowed the prior owners to stay put for six months after closing, just so we could get the deal signed, sealed, and delivered. Even in the current challenging

real estate market as I write this, our house is worth 650 percent more than we paid for it ten years ago.

5. **"As is" provision.** Specifically state that you intend to purchase the property "as is with right to inspect" and/or "subject to a satisfactory survey." Both provisions allow you to do a personal inspection of the house and grounds and to get out of the deal if there are any problems with encroachment, property easement, or other unexpected findings that make the property no longer feasible for you. It gives you a way out if you were to discover something serious enough to make you reconsider the deal.

6. **No brokers.** Save your seller the expense of commissions if you can. But remember, you're not looking for a way out.

7. **Confidentiality clause.** Include this if you feel it's warranted. It often makes a seller feel more comfortable to know their current financial situation won't be disclosed.

Upon acceptance of your offer, go ahead and bring in the lawyers to draft the paperwork. Be sure you continue to work directly with the owners on any major deal points, however. You and the owners should make the terms, not the lawyers. Agree on the big things and sign the contract; leave only the minor details to your attorneys, if any at all. Bad attorneys have a tendency to drag out negotiations or even alienate your seller in an effort to validate their fee. Your mindset will be decidedly different than that of an attorney. Sure, you want to create a win for yourself, but it's equally important (actually more important) that the seller feels that he or she has won, too.

Bubble-proofing means you must grow accustomed to accepting a great number of paradoxes. You're required to intently study your market and potential properties—but not get so bogged down in research that you talk yourself out of buying anything. To be willing to look at many, many properties in search of The One. To be patient in finding the right property at the right price—but to think and act fast when you do. To grasp the complexities and nuances of human psychology—but to keep your proposals simple and straight-forward. To guard against being greedy (the great deal-killer) but also to be willing to walk away if you can't get the terms you want. To apply the formula religiously—but be willing to stretch a per-cent or two to make the deal. To be aware of the larger economic cli-mate—but not get caught up in the mass greed and fear that drives it. To make well-reasoned decisions—but to operate outside of the "comfort corridor." To celebrate the day you *spend* money on a prop-erty—the "buy" day—more than the day you pocket your profit. And a few more seemingly contradictory behaviors that you'll be learn-ing about in the next couple of chapters, such as overimproving a home without actually overdoing it, and being a daredevil when it comes to making new markets—but being as unexciting as possible when it comes to the use of debt.

Stick with this, practice what you're learning here, and you'll not only bubble-proof your real estate investments, but you'll earn your Ph.D. in "paradoxicology," too.

You want that bubble to turn into a force field for you? Apply the acquisition formula like the paradoxical doctor you now are . . . And save a slice with extra cheese for me—I'm celebrating with you!

Your Chapter 6
BURST OF INSPIRATION

• Remember: *Acquisition + Improvement = Not More Than 65 Percent of Retail Price.* Can you picture your next "buy" day, what it will be like to know you have purchased your property with the annuitylike surety of the acquisition formula you've learned here? How will you celebrate?

7

THE OTHER HOLY TRINITY: Time, Budget, Quality

The fast/cheap/good triangle presents a false dichotomy, especially for real estate investors. You know what I'm talking about? The business axiom that you can have only two of the three, and that one of these conditions must be sacrificed to deliver the other two?

When I first heard about this, I dismissed it as ludicrous. You mean I can have a cheap and fast cherry Slurpee, but then it won't be any good? Or a good and cheap cherry Slurpee, but it'll take forever? Or a fast and good cherry Slurpee, but it'll cost a lot? Hmmm. When I go to 7-Eleven for that ice-cold treat, I want them to take enough time to mix it right, charge me a reasonable price, and deliver something that tastes great. I don't even know why you'd want a fast, cheap, or merely good cherry Slurpee in the first place.

Then, when someone told me that they teach this triangle in marketing classes and that it's considered a useful engineering model for product development, I started to understand why it's so common to find second-rate goods, like hairdryers you have to replace every two years, and why something like my dad's old Army shirt from his Pentagon days or the towels I use every morning are so extraordinary. I've cut the sleeves off the shirt and wear it all the time as a tribute to my dad and all who have served in the military. It's nearly forty-five years old, and it's a little bit rough, but the seams are tight and I wouldn't be surprised if it outlasts me. The towels are from my dad, too. They say "1956 U.S. Olympic Team" on them, and he brought them home from Melbourne, Australia, where he competed as part of the U.S. swim team and won his gold medal for the backstroke. I'm proud that my dad won one of each, a gold, silver, and bronze medal, from the 1956 and 1960 Olympics, and the towels are a wonderful memento. Meanwhile, newer towels that we bought a little over a year ago are in tatters, yet these that are more than half a century old still look and feel great. Granted, my dad's towels were packed up for a few years before I got them, but I've used them every day for about five years! That shirt and those towels were definitely engineered and manufactured under something other than the laughable "project triangle."

Here's why no self-respecting bubble-proofer would even consider following that half-baked fast/cheap/good recipe for success, either:

- First of all, getting it done "fast" isn't usually ideal, although getting it done *on time* can mean the difference between squeezing your margin and crushing it.
- Second, while you definitely want to forecast and then manage your *budget* carefully, being cheap *never* maximizes ROI (return on investment) and will ruin your brand and, in turn, your reputation.

- As for "good"? You don't want your project to be "good"; to minimize days on market and sell at a premium price, it must be *magnificent*.

As someone once said, "Beware the lollipop of mediocrity. Lick it once, and you suck forever." Or at least until you've learned the lesson and done it right the next time. So ditch the fast/cheap/good triangle, because everything about it is average, unspectacular, ordinary, and will never contribute to the creation of a market or a masterpiece.

Bubble-proofing demands that you commit yourself to rising far, far above mediocrity, that the improvements you make to any property are not only unique, stunning, and compelling, but also cost-effective and done on time. The acquisition formula and your decision to invest in the first place depended upon it. Now, you must be artist, investor, and boss, all conspiring to create a market and masterpiece at the same time. To realize the potential of your investment and maximize your profit, you must:

- Plan the schedule and then keep an eagle eye on workers' productivity so that everything can be completed on *time*.
- Stay laser-focused on the bottom line by developing and managing a realistic, flexible *budget*.
- Train, then allow your imagination and vision to drive the project so that it becomes magnificent, insisting on above-average *quality* at every turn.

For the last ten years at Frank McKinney & Co., we've called this three-in-one improvement strategy **the holy trinity of *time* (schedule)**, ***budget*, and *quality***. Each of the three depends on the others; none is more important than the next. If scheduling were to take a back seat, and the job were to run long, it would delay the ultimate sale and increase carrying costs. Significant budget overruns would cut sharply into the margin, so decisions to spend more than anticipated have to be carefully weighed against any benefit that might be gained, such as increases in quality that could be reflected in the asking price. Indeed, every decision about quality (especially overimproving, meaning doing more than you'd originally budgeted in time or money) has to be checked against the bottom line.

Keep this holy trinity of time, budget, and quality always at the forefront of your mind in order to see the acquisition formula—and therefore the *Burst This!* approach—pay off. Each element must always be checked against how it will impact the other. Every decision must be put through the filter of the holy trinity.

Deciding on the level of quality you'll be implementing in the home, detailing your schedule, and establishing a budget aren't discrete tasks. Because each influences the other, it's not a 1-2-3 job, but instead a process of setting initial expectations and then revising regularly. At Frank McKinney & Co., we review and update the budget and construction timeline weekly, with a thorough review of what we call our "cost-to-complete" on a monthly basis. Our quality control checklist gets constant and ongoing attention. (You'll see more on this in Chapter 10.)

Often, the primary focus of the novice is on time and budget, skimping on quality or neglecting it altogether. Even at the highest levels, I still occasionally see someone who blasts through a house, forgetting entirely that the ability to *sell* the house (and isn't that the point?!) will depend solely on the ability to move the buyer from need to desire. That takes more than just money. It takes time and careful consideration, along with intense attention to detail. To command a price at least 10 percent higher than neighborhood comps, and to sell quickly, you need to create a home that sends a message.

That message cannot be, "I did what I could with the time and money I had," or "You can't have it all." Instead, a home into which you invest your time, money, artistic vision, passion, and hopes for a handsome return should confidently assure your buyers, "You can have so much more than you ever imagined!"

Complete all of the initial planning for time, budget, and quality during the first two or three months—while you're designing and going through the permitting process for your new home or large-scale improvements, or the first two or three days if it is a smaller renovation. **This is when you first adopt the identity not just of an opportunist, but of an artist, too.** You'll be balancing quality and cost constantly. You'll be making decisions about whether certain improvements will add value in a way your buyers will appreciate, or whether those upgrades should be abandoned or just shelved for another project where it makes more sense. You'll put together a budget and timelines for completion based on your design. This chapter will help you make those decisions and get the help you need.

For starters, let me mention real estate investment clubs again. In so many ways, they prove to be a great resource. Find a club that will not only help you when you're looking for The One, meaning the property you'll focus on until you sell it, then move on to your next; for more advanced investors, this may actually be The Two or The Three or even The Twenty, but each should be treated as The One, which is what your buyers would want, isn't it? But find a club that can also advise you about improvements after you've acquired The One. Members may have recommendations for reliable subcontractors, as well as for those to avoid. They can tell you how long it usually takes to complete each type of improvement, and how long your house may take to sell. You may even get to know someone at the club who would be a great partner for you. I'm not a partnering kind of guy myself, but if that's what you're looking for, a club can be the perfect place to meet someone to work with. (If you do partner with someone, I suggest you get them a copy of this book.)

What a real estate investment club *can't* do is help you with the quality part of the equation. This will rest with you and your team, and it starts with your vision and passion. At Frank McKinney & Co., we always codify this vision and passion into a statement describing the project and what it will represent for us, why we've acquired it, and what we're going to do with it. This document, which can evolve as the project unfolds, shapes every action we take toward completion, plus the marketing and selling of the property, the experience of our buyer, and ultimately the deal we're able to make.

Similarly, when I decide to write a book, I always come up with the title first. As bestselling author Stephen Covey advises, I "begin with the end in mind." *Burst This! Frank McKinney's Bubble-Proof Real Estate Strategies; The Tap; Dead Fred, Flying Lunchboxes, and the Good Luck Circle; Frank McKinney's Maverick Approach to Real Estate Success;* and *Make it BIG!* had titles long before I knew exactly what I'd include on their pages. Sometimes it would take weeks to come up with that perfect title that would drive every word. The title is the core concept, and then that gets fleshed out into a "blurb," which is a lot like the vision and passion statement for a property. (You can see what the *Burst This!* blurb evolved into by looking at the back cover of the book you're holding in your hands right now or by visiting Burst-This.com.) The book's table of contents, and later a detailed outline, develop from the title and the blurb. Once we establish a cover design, every word of the manuscript is written with that title and cover in mind, never straying. When I get stuck, I refer to that image and those words and break right through any "writer's block."

Another, simpler example is cooking. Sure, you might produce something edible by throwing a random bunch of food into a pot, but if you want to create a truly delicious meal and present it beautifully, you need to have an idea of what you're going to make. As I've learned from my father-in-law, even five-star chefs plan their creations before they pick up a knife or turn on the gas. Of course, they improvise—some fresh basil here, a little truffle oil there—that's part of the artistry. Still, they begin with the end in mind.

Our vision and passion statements at Frank McKinney & Co. help keep everyone focused together on the end result we're creating. My employees post the statement next to their work stations so that whatever they're doing—from talking with vendors and subcontractors to filing paperwork—they're guided by the vision and passion for the project. It shapes our company culture. So pull out that sheet of paper before you undertake your next or first project and create your own vision of what will move your project from house to home, your buyer from need to desire, your brand from unknown to household name. Using my example above, how do you want your buyers to perceive your artistry? Take your time, and don't start your next project until you have completed this exercise. Keep it simple, making it no longer than a few paragraphs.

Here's an example, a vision and passion statement created for Acqua Liana that took a few weeks to write with the input of many key players on my team.

Acqua Liana
620 South Ocean
Our Vision & Passion Statement

Acqua Liana ("water flower") will redefine a world marketplace we continue to create and dominate. Acqua Liana will showcase our artistry at its absolute finest, a blooming representation beyond comprehension.

Prior Frank McKinney creations have been magnificent; however, the upward spiral associated with striving to better our previous best is what life is all about. This is what we will accomplish with Acqua Liana.

Acqua Liana will establish a higher standard than has yet been experienced by our market. This will be accomplished in two distinct ways. First, we will combine Tahitian, Fijian, Balinese, and Polynesian styles. South Florida coastal architecture is long overdue for such a fresh, tranquil, and tropical design. Next we will undertake a dual "green" certification process that will make Acqua Liana the world's largest and most opulent certified green home.

Innovation will be found in all aspects of Acqua Liana: in the design, amenities, finishes, and the creation of environmentally responsible, luxury-construction practices where our influence will be felt around the globe.

By combining the experience gained from nearly twenty-five years of making markets with the creativity and total sensory immersion afforded the fortunate few, our eventual owner will experience a lifestyle where, upon arrival at Acqua Liana, all five senses are heightened to a state of subliminal euphoria. Intoxication with the majesty of our artistry will overwhelm.

Time: You're the Boss

The sooner you get the property finished, the sooner you can sell it. That's a given. Most homes don't sell pre-completion; in my oceanfront career dating back to 1991, I've sold only two before they were done. (This doesn't mean you won't start marketing and making the place attractive to potential buyers the minute you own it, but we'll get to that later.) Generally, buyers don't have the imagination, the vision, or the foresight to do what you do. You're the expert in your field, and they in theirs. Nor do they generally possess the skills that you'll have (or hire) to see that house finished. They'll wait until it's completed before they purchase. Most buyers have no interest in a dusty, empty box, bustling with workers, which is what any house is before you improve it—or even a house that's 90 percent done. It's when that last 10 percent comes together that the home will really start to shine, when the beauty of what you've created becomes apparent to anyone who sees it.

That's when the fireworks start to fly, and you get to implement one of the most exciting parts of the *Burst This!* approach: showing your spectacular creation to the fortunate few. Why the fortunate few? Because if you follow the strategies outlined in this chapter, only a few will see your house before it is bought, and the rest will have to forever hold their peace, or at least until you create another.

Creating Your Schedule

So just how long, then, will it reasonably take to create a magnificent home to present to your target market?

On average, it takes one to one-and-a-half months to construct 1,000 square feet. (Acqua Liana hovered right around 1.2 months per 1,000 square feet.) Renovation is much less predictable because it depends on the level of improvements needed; sometimes it can go quite quickly, and sometimes it can take surprisingly long—even as long as new construction, but rarely longer. (Emphasis on *surprising*, as you never know exactly what you're getting into until you open up the walls, tear off the roof, pull up the carpet, and so on.) **So you can use the one-month-per-1,000-square-feet ratio for most major renovation projects, and one-and-a-half months per for new construction.** When you consult a contractor or other knowledgeable source, know these durations going into your first meeting with them.

Early on, I relied on a handyman, a guy who knew how to do a little of everything and could tell me anything I needed to know, including basic plumbing, electrical, which walls were load-bearing, and details from how long it would take to put down Spanish tile to how many people we'd need to hire and when I could expect the whole thing to be done. Unless you're a contractor yourself, you'll want someone with a good base of general knowledge on your team.

You'd do well to pretend you have a plus-sign on your forehead whenever you're talking with other people about milestones and deadlines. Things always take longer than they or you initially think. The schedule will slip. Count on it. Even if you or your contractor/consultant know your stuff, meaning you've completed a similar property before with similar improvements, add 20 to 25 percent to the estimated time for completion. Just do it. If you're a pro, remind yourself how important this is by thinking back: *do they ever finish on time?* If you're a novice (again, even with the help of a contractor/consultant), add 40 to 50 percent. Seriously. I can assure you that you won't finish in less time than you anticipate, and you need to give yourself ample latitude to deal with the unforeseen. I'm happy to be proven wrong with my supergenerous overtime estimate, but I suggest you always underpromise and overdeliver if you can. For example, you should assume that a 3,000-square-foot project, originally estimated at three months, will turn into a timeline of between four and four-and-a-half months, depending on your experience level. That's not unreasonable at all, but again, please prove me wrong. I'd be thrilled!

To account for this cushion in your schedule, add a day or two to smaller milestones that might give you trouble, such as plumbing (both rough/underground and top-out), carpet installation, and painting. Add more time to major milestones, such as demolition, foundation poured, roof dried in, electrical, windows installation or replacement, drywall completion, kitchen installation, and landscaping, as well as anything completely new to you, such as installing solar panels or geothermal heating. Adding a few days here and there will give you the desired cushion; this is a random practice, hardly scientific. Be sure you also give yourself a generous "fudge factor" at the end of the project. I often pad my final cleaning, furniture move-in, and white-glove inspection categories significantly to allow for final touches to be just perfect.

Although I've been in this business for a long time, we had to return somewhat to the beginner's approach when we introduced the new architectural style and green element with the creation of Acqua Liana. With this estate, we've done many things we've never done before. For the sister estate, Crystalina, the learning curve associated with the reproduction of many of those elements will be much less steep. For example, we'll be using the same poured solid concrete wall systems, with no wood whatsoever, and seven inches of insulation on the inside, so the house is extremely energy-efficient and quiet, not to mention hurricane-proof, which is a huge plus here on the beaches of South Florida. I anticipate I'll knock 10 percent or two months off my construction schedule for Crystalina, based on nothing more than the crucial amount of knowledge gained on Acqua Liana. Given the tens of thousands of dollars we must pay every month in interest, and how fast our properties move once they're on the market, that's significant. Already, I'm modifying the construction timeline for Crystalina based on our newly gained expertise on environmentally friendly, luxury building practices.

I've included an abbreviated construction timeline that we created for Acqua Liana as an Appendix for your reference. Here you'll see how many disciplines there are; for Acqua Liana, we had seventy-five different subcontractors and more than 300 workers during the eighteen-month process. You'll see the tenure associated with each phase. You'll see the milestones that usually challenge our schedule (as listed in the paragraph before last), where I added days.

Your improvement timeline for renovation or construction timeline for new homes can take the form of a flowchart or a spreadsheet. Regardless, this timeline starts from the first day the shovel goes into the ground, or the sledgehammer hits the wall, all the way through the day you're folding that last square of toilet paper into a diamond tip. (There's that commitment to quality, again.) It represents all significant milestones, which could include digging, grading, and compacting the dirt; demolition; laying the foundation; framing; all stages of plumbing for water and gas, as well as installing electrical and heating/air-conditioning; building any special outdoor features, like a fountain or a bridge or a pool; landscaping and laying sod; roofing; insulating, drywalling, and painting inside; installing new flooring;

adding indoor and outdoor lighting; putting in new fixtures, sinks, tubs, tile, and countertops; adding built-ins and other carpentry; paving; hanging window treatments, spot merchandising, and other decorating; giving the white-glove treatment before the first showing—and much more. Our long-version printout for Acqua Liana covers fifteen linear feet of wall in our construction trailer, and it's set in only twelve-point text, about the size you're reading here!

In compiling your timeline, you need to keep in mind any seasonal considerations. You may be the best scheduler in the world, but Mother Nature has her own clock—and rarely helps you save time. For example, you certainly don't want to leave roofing until hurricane season if you live where I do, because you're bound to experience significant water damage. You don't want to schedule drywall completion for the dead of winter if you live where temperatures drop below fifty-five degrees Fahrenheit, because the materials expand and are hard to work with when it gets that cold, and they can even lose their bonding qualities if they freeze before they're completely dry. Seasoned investors become completely familiar with how weather affects production, but if you're just starting out, you'll need to check, again, with your contractor/handyman to anticipate delays due to temperature or weather.

Always know there will be delays, no matter what they tell you.

Think about how your timeline dovetails with people's seasonal psychology, too. In regions where the leaves fall off the trees and the ground freezes or becomes muddy, winter is a more challenging time to show a home. But you can't wait until your front-yard snowman is no more than a puddle of water, a few pieces of coal, and a soggy carrot. You'll accentuate your buyer's experience by enhancing the beauty of the season inside your new creation. (We'll come back to this again in the marketing chapter, "The Grade School Compass Approach . . .") The market may go a little cold, both figuratively and literally. And during the winter holidays, no matter where you live, workers seem to be on a constant tryptophan drip—the slowdown is completely predictable, starting with that first taste of turkey at Thanksgiving and continuing all the way to January 2. You need to allow for all of this in your improvements timeline.

Dealing with Subcontractors

Without question, one of the most challenging aspects of this business is managing contractors and subcontractors, which starts with getting bids and then turns into months of babysitting to ensure that they finish their work on time. If you're not on top of their work flow, you can pretty much kiss your schedule good-bye. In all my years in the real estate business, this one issue—dealing with subcontractors—has been the only one that's made me seriously consider, on rare occasions, changing professions. Recall you are not on the Intel microprocessor assembly line here, where everyone is highly educated and wearing white cover suits with air masks. The only thing predictable is the unpredictability and unreliability of human nature. Follow these tips for getting the most and the best out of your subcontractors:

- **Ask around for recommendations.** If at all possible, don't choose someone from the yellow pages or other advertising. Referrals from satisfied customers are a much more valid source. Again, this is where a real estate investment club can be invaluable.
- **Walk around your own neighborhood** and find out who's doing

what. If you see something you like, ask to meet the person in charge, and then request that he or she walk you around the job site to show you quality of work. Again, if you like what you see, you can put this subcontractor on your short list for bids on your project.

- **Use only contractors who are licensed and have both liability and worker's compensation insurance if required.** There's no sense in putting your profits on the line or in supporting contractors who won't do what's necessary to protect workers. Every person on my projects is required to carry insurance.

- **Select reputable contractors and subcontractors,** and yes, it will cost a little more. They're simply more likely to show up for work and finish according to your schedule. Your neighbor's brother's friend "Hal" may be a talented plumber that you could hire on the cheap, but if he's not a good businessman—if he's not proven himself to be reliable in the marketplace—forget it. Saving the few extra dollars isn't worth the gamble.

- **Negotiate for your contractors' and subcontractors' warranties to begin the day the house sells,** rather than the day the work is completed. (Or, if they want something more definite, "when the house sells or two years from the issuance of the Certificate of Occupancy, whichever occurs first.") This will save you money in the long run if there are any repairs that are needed soon after you sell the home.

- **Set clear expectations.** Detail the work to be done and the completion date in your contract, and confirm the plan verbally. When you ask a subcontractor how long something will take, expect him or her to try to impress you with an underestimated amount of time—and then add the extra days and gain agreement. If, for example, the sub tells you it'll take a week to paint a house, you respond, "Okay, Jack. Can you do it in ten days?"

That's counter to what most people will say, and I guarantee you Jack will assure you he can. Look at the body language and assess the sub's response. Then confirm: "Great, Jack, you're going to be painting the exterior of the home, including trim, and you'll do that in ten days. Is that correct?"

Then, later, if there's significant schedule slippage, you can insist that Jack double up on manpower, put in some time on the weekends, do what's necessary: "Look, I gave you the benefit of the doubt and even added to your promised schedule, and you're coming close to screwing up. You need to step up the pace." It gives you an important point of leverage if (when) you need it.

- **Don't offer bonuses or penalties for beating or blowing your deadline.** The schedule is what it is, and the carrot-and-stick routine just opens the door to problems. If the work gets done late, then you've got an argument on your hands, as the contractor will blame you and insist that you either pay up the bonus or waive the penalty. You can destroy a positive working relationship in either case. If they did a good job, surprise them with some form of bonus, and it doesn't always have to be cash. Take their family to dinner, give them gift certificates to the local supermarket, etc. If they didn't do a good job, simply fire them or don't use them again.

Once your timeline is established, you'll need to watch it like a hawk. As I said, you're not in an assembly-line business, and you can't expect that everything will move like clockwork from one stage to the next. If the framer's late, then that affects the electrician, which affects the drywaller, which affects the painter, on down the line—which can also push your marketing milestones and ultimately delay your grand opening. You must treat every late delivery as one that could potentially affect the date you bring the home to market.

Meanwhile, you can't just find the right contractor and subs and then leave it up to them. You must be on-site regularly to oversee progress, make your presence known, build rapport, and establish your authority. You'll want to identify stars and underperformers, so you'll know who to rehire and, if necessary, who to fire. You'll also learn a little of each discipline to improve your own expertise, and you can perform constant quality reviews.

Being in the house as it's undergoing improvement should also spark finishing ideas, previously unplanned improvements, which can drive the schedule and the budget a little crazy—in my case, a floor-to-ceiling window here, an aquarium wet bar there—but it's justified by the upgrade in quality. During walk-throughs, you'll also get to develop and practice showing patterns, or the path you'll take as you walk potential buyers through the home. (Again, more on that in the marketing chapter.)

As part of your job as glorified babysitter, you must hold weekly sub meetings to help everyone manage their time well. I've also occasionally had to help them manage their money—if your sub isn't much of a businessperson and doesn't stay on top of his or her own books, and then doesn't pay suppliers, a lien can be put on your house because of it. (Believe me, I've been there—but only once, as the supplier was gone after that.) Mediocrity, human frailty, human failure. All are extremely disappointing and counterproductive to your goals as a real estate investor. Managing and mitigating these problems is a crucial element in any bubble-proofing strategy. Now you see why it can be so challenging.

Budget: Make Dollars and Sense

Indeed, I'm on the job site nearly every day. Years ago, it was because I wanted to help with the manual labor to both minimize costs and learn more about the construction business. I didn't attempt any of the skilled labor, though, because even today hammering a nail straight presents a challenge for me. So if we needed to put in a new roof, I tore off the old one myself. If we needed to redo the lawn, I ripped up the old grass. I had to pay somebody to do all of the skilled labor, but it was always clear that I was the boss. I was the one making decisions about the schedule, the budget, who got hired, and who got fired. I was in control, earning my stripes as the benevolent dictator, the compassionate capitalist, or (my favorite) the enlightened absolutist. I knew what was best for the project.

Nowadays, I can see a rip-off artist coming from miles away, and it's only because I cut my teeth on bids and budgeting on those smaller houses. That's one more reason I recommend that those who are just starting out in this business concentrate on The One in a low price range. Mistakes cost much less in a single starter home than they do in multiple properties or higher-priced homes.

Remember the acquisition formula: *Acquisition + Improvements = Not More Than 65 Percent of Retail Price.* By using this bubble-proof strategy, you're going to underpromise and overdeliver, again, even to yourself, and especially when it comes to estimating the cost of improvements. Just as you cover the unforeseen in the acquisition formula with that big margin that will inevitably get squeezed, you'll cover the unexpected in your budget with a significant reserve that will inevitably get used. Whenever we put together a spending plan for one of our megamansions, we always include a significant line item for "miscellaneous" to cover the what-if or the "this-home-just-has-to-have . . ." factor. I don't want to give away our Colonel Sanders' Secret Recipe as far as what we put into these houses (exactly how much money, I mean), but I will tell you that our miscellaneous line item is at least 5 percent of the total budget. If you're new to planning for these kinds of projects, I suggest your "fudge factor" be at least 10 percent. And it is often that extra 5 to 10 percent that means the difference between making a market (and a fortune) or making a colossal mistake.

In fact, if you've never budgeted construction or renovation (whichever is applicable to The One property you do next), be sure to consult someone who can create an all-inclusive budget with you, to the best of your combined abilities, before you commence your project. Don't concern yourself with every single item or possibility; you need to arrive at this number—with the "misc." line item included for the unknown—so you can determine if the project meets your acquisition formula. Call on that jack-of-all-trades who can tell you, "The roof's falling in, so we've gotta replace that. You want shingles, concrete, or barrel tile, cedar shake, standing seam metal, or what? . . . The plumbing is backed up, so we're gonna get the septic system cleaned out. The electric's shocking your hair stiff when you turn on the lights. Anything else you want to do?"

That's when the artist in you comes out: "Okay, I think we should also enlarge this master bedroom, and I know people appreciate a Jacuzzi tub in the master bath. We're going to have to gut the kitchen, blow out the pass-through, and make a much bigger pantry."

Novices regularly make two mistakes: 1) not starting with a realistic budget (making it too small), and 2) spending the money in the budget unwisely, usually on improvements that don't actually add value. To avoid the first error, remember that if you cut corners and diminish quality (do I hear someone taking the wrapper off a lollipop?), it doesn't matter what you've done with your schedule or whether you've met that skimpy budget, you won't be able to make a decent profit for your effort. If you do make money, it will happen only a few times before your reputation as a shi*%@ builder or renovater catches up with you, probably in less time than it takes you to unwrap another sucker. And that's just plain dumb.

As for the second error—improvements that don't add value— much of this chapter will show you exactly where it makes the most sense to put your money. Although I generally advocate overimproving, you don't want to go so far as, say, putting solid gold fixtures in a home when the neighborhood can only command prices reflective of brass-plating. Spending your money wisely means knowing not only what rooms should get the most attention and investment, but also what level of luxury will make sense to your buyers.

Remember, the primary psychological objective is to convert your buyer's need into desire. Start the process by putting yourself in your buyers' shoes, by understanding what's important to them when acquiring a home, and then create a budget that reflects those kinds of improvements. I'm not including a worksheet or some other list here because each property introduces so many variables along with unique opportunities. I suggest you use the following guidelines as you evaluate your project, and then develop a budget in consultation with an experienced contractor or handyman.

Outside the Home

The first thing buyers see is the exterior of the home, so you want to go for maximum curb appeal. To help your buyer fall in love at first sight, start from the top and work your way down.

- **Roof.** Ensure it is clean and in excellent repair. No leaves or dirt in the gutters, no missing material on the roof. Pressure-cleaning can remove moss, mildew, or dirt that may have accumulated, and some roofs can even be painted to look new. A new roof, while it could be costly, does considerably increase value.

- **Exterior walls.** Paint or replace the exterior finish of the house unless it's already spotless. Nothing says "new" like a fresh coat of paint.

- **Entryway.** Make a statement with the front door. This is one of the most important architectural details and one of the very first things your buyers will notice. You want the entry to the home to stand out, to draw the buyer in. At a minimum, paint the front door a different color than the rest of the house. Don't cover it with a screen or storm door unless it's absolutely necessary, and in that case, make the screen or storm door as attractive as the door behind it. The walkway leading to the front door should be inviting, too. You want the buyer to experience that "welcome home" feeling the first time they see the house and approach the front door.

- **Exterior fixtures.** Be sure your house number is attractive and visible from the street, and that you have new or like-new lighting fixtures on the front of the house. A beautiful new mailbox helps complete the picture. (Be sure you empty it every time you're on the property. An overstuffed mailbox tells buyers the house is neglected.) These small improvements cost little and speak volumes to your potential buyer.

- **Paved surfaces.** Your driveway and walkways need to be in good repair: no cement broken by root systems, no asphalt crumbling to rock. However, don't spend a lot of money resurfacing if you don't need to—patching and a fresh coat of blacktop is often enough to help the house look tidy and well-cared-for.

- **Landscaping.** The front and back yards frame the home, and money spent here can yield an excellent return. Lawns should be lush and mowed; laying new sod versus just dropping some grass seed is the way to go if you're turning a property around quickly or if you want it to stand out from the crowd. Any fencing should be attractive and in excellent repair. (You can give a starter home with chain link/other wire fencing a major facelift by replacing it with white pickets.) Define the boundaries of the property with a "staked survey" from a professional surveyor. Trim back any foliage at the boundary line and cut away any tree branches that are encroaching from neighboring property. You (and ultimately your buyer) pay for all of it, so show it all.

The front yard should say, "welcome," while the back yard should say, "come on in and stay awhile." It's part of the American Dream to sit in your own back yard, invite friends over, and have a barbecue while you play a game of Jarts and watch your kids and the dog run around together. You don't need to spend a lot of money on most places to ensure that the back yard is clean and any feature there (e.g., fountain, barbecue pit) is working and clean. Of course, if every other house in the neighborhood has a pool, and this one doesn't, you'll need to consider this major upgrade. Making a market means zigging while others are zagging, but it doesn't mean dispensing with amenities that everyone in the neighborhood obviously loves.

Inside the Home

The "moneymaker rooms" of any house—from $50,000 to $50 million—are the kitchen, the master bedroom, and the master bath. Plan to spend a large portion of your budget there. Compared to other parts of the home, you might spend as much as five times the dollars per square foot, as these rooms make the biggest impression on your buyer, particularly upon women. Pardon me for generalizing, but it's useful here: these are the "she" rooms in the house, the rooms women tend to care most about, the rooms women most want to reflect their taste and style, the rooms where they love to feel as if their every need has already been considered.

It's been my experience that, when a man and woman buy a home together, the woman has the most sway over the decision. If he loves it, and she doesn't, forget it. No sale. However, if she's in love, even if he's lukewarm, the house is as good as sold. That's one of the reasons these "she" rooms are so important. Don't make the mistake of forgetting the masculine, however. You need at least one "he" room, a place that feels manly, where a guy can envision himself relaxing with his feet up, watching the game on a big-screen TV. Create the feeling of a "mens' den": for example, using darker paint colors and accents, staging with some comfortable leather chairs or couch, possibly including a wet bar, featuring a flat screen TV, maybe throwing in a pool table . . . you get the picture. Do what you can to make the man feel at home. You don't want to blow the budget on this room, but do not overlook it.

You do want to use the best you can afford, floor to ceiling, in the kitchen, master bedroom, and master bath: plush carpeting and elegant draperies in the master bedroom; hardwoods or other attractive flooring in the kitchen and bath; baseboards and crown molding in all three rooms, even if nowhere else in the house; beautiful lighting; fine fixtures.

- **Create a feeling of luxury in the master suite.** Think of the master bedroom and bath as the adults' oasis, retreat, private spa. In addition to the fine carpeting (at a minimum, add thicker padding underneath to give a sense of greater luxury) and lovely window treatments, a fireplace can add warmth and set the mood for romance and relaxation.

  In our mansions, the master suite is always quite large; in Acqua Liana, it's the size of the average home in America, about 2,500 square feet, with his and hers everything (dressing rooms, bathrooms, wet bars, and so on). In another, the bedroom was two stories tall, with floor-to-ceiling windows and silk damask window treatments. The 100-percent-wool-imported-from-Holland, $250-a-yard carpet was so plush that more than one billionaire client told us they would be perfectly comfortable piling up some pillows and curling up on the floor to sleep.

- **Spend your money in the kitchen, as well.** This is one of the main selling features of the house, and in my experience, every dollar spent doing the kitchen right returns up to $1.50 when you sell.

Be sure this room is well lit, functional, easy to use, and fresh. Almost every house renovation should include new appliances, cabinets, and countertops to help the kitchen feel contemporary and clean. Nothing dates a house like counters with wear and tear, rough-looking cabinets, or unmatched, old dishwasher, stove, microwave, and refrigerator, so keep the existing ones only if they're like new. A new sink and, if there's room, a kitchen island enhances value, too. Plumbing fixtures in starter home kitchens should be nice, as they'll be touched every day. Include low-flow options to boost real and perceived value. An eat-in area is also a plus, so if you can convert a window space to a breakfast nook, or put a table in the kitchen when you're showing it, so much the better.

When I worked on smaller homes, I usually knocked out a part of the wall that divided the kitchen from the dining or living area to create an informal eating area. A countertop with place settings on the kitchen side, plus a few barstools tucked under the overhang, gave potential buyers a cozy spot they could picture themselves in, enjoying the newspaper and a cup of orange juice in the morning.

So far, the dual kitchens in Acqua Liana are the finest we've ever put in a home. In the main kitchen, the cabinets are made of koa wood, which grows only in Hawaii and can't be taken off the island unless you're Hawaiian, so no one else has it. (We knew someone who knew someone.) It is stunning, with a dark, undulant grain and gorgeous streaks of gold throughout that reflect the light of the kitchen like no other wood I've seen. We've installed gemstone-inlaid granite countertops, a water wall above one of the sinks that appears to flow into the basin, sparkling chandeliers, and iridescent mica wallpaper. There are two of almost every appliance: two refrigerators, two dishwashers, two freezers, two islands (one for cooking and one for eating), and a beautiful Wolf range, cooktop, and griddle. The view of the ocean from the sink is breathtaking, seen through 24-foot-wide sliding glass doors; if you ever decided to wash the dishes by hand, it would be an unprecedented pleasure.

Along with the master bedroom and bath, if you get the kitchen right, your buyers will hardly even notice the rest of the house because they'll be so busy convincing themselves that they can make it work—as long as it's clean and new looking. So, in a starter home, you can focus your budget on those three places and plan to do even the basics beautifully everywhere else. At a minimum, you'll need fresh paint and new carpet throughout. Installing baseboards and crown molding is an inexpensive upgrade that adds a great finish to every room in the house, but it's okay if your budget simply won't allow it anywhere but the master suite and kitchen. Scrape the bumps off of any popcorn ceilings and repaint so that you have a smooth, modern finish. Replace any hanging fixture that looks dated. For showings, use bulbs that maximize the wattage indicated on all fixtures; the additional light makes the house look great.

Going Green, Making a Market

Why not make those bulbs compact fluorescents while you're at it? As a selling point and as a market-making move, you can add resource-efficient features and use environmentally friendly materials all over the home, inside and out.

Remember, we're still in the national anthem stage in the greening of America, so I urge you to get into the ballpark before everyone else has taken their seats. Don't despair about how difficult it is to find new territory from which to make a market these days, because *here it is. Green innovation, environmental responsibility, sustainable* practices: these remain the new frontier for real estate. **You can make that your new mantra: innovation, responsibility, sustainability.** These are values that not only support the planet but can revive a flagging investment portfolio, as even a challenged real estate market could well be turned around with this one practice. Bubble-proofing requires that you get in front of the trends, not behind them, so begin now. This is the new gold rush, or the new industrial revolution; it's like Silicon Valley in '98. It's still so new that even when all the pages of this book are yellowed, we may just be seeing the first pitch.

This is why I think you, or anyone investing in real estate, should capitalize now, start educating yourself now, and begin implementing with your very next property. Done right, this will represent the ultimate in bubble-proofing your real estate life! From xeriscaping to energy-efficient kitchen appliances to water-conserving showerheads and toilets to no-VOC paint to programmable thermostats, more green in and around the home means more green in your pocket, sometimes even before you sell it. Here are the bare-bones essentials:

- **Financial incentives.** Be sure to learn about your state, local, utility, and federal incentives for green improvements. From tax credits to equipment rebates to low-interest loans and more, go to DSIREUSA.org (the website for the Database of State

Incentives for Renewables & Efficiency) to find out how you can save money and profit from the energy-efficiency and renewable-energy improvements you build into the home.

- **Energy audit.** If you're renovating an existing home, your local utility company will conduct a whole-house audit of energy use on the property and give you specific changes you can make that will save the new owner as much as 30 percent on utility bills. Following the audit recommendations means the house will have reduced air leaks, any missing insulation will have been replaced, and any moisture problems will have been addressed. What potential buyer wouldn't want to hear that you'd already implemented the recommendations? Plus, some utilities give rate discounts to homeowners with certified energy-efficient dwellings.

- **Energy-saving appliances.** Buy energy-efficient appliances for the kitchen; look for the blue-and-white Energy Star® label. Many cities offer tax credits when you do this—check with the utility company when you schedule your audit.

- **CFLs.** Use compact fluorescent bulbs in all light fixtures, and you can tell potential buyers that they won't have to replace them for quite a long time—about a decade. (You'll also need to tell them where they can recycle their CFLs; many hardware stores currently accept them. These bulbs must be disposed of properly due to the mercury in them, but soon, none of the bulbs will have this toxic element.)

- **Conserve water.** Go low-flow throughout the house; even luxurious-feeling rainfall-style shower heads come in low-flow now—and it's hard to tell the difference. If you're replacing a toilet, install a dual-flush model, with separate buttons for all-liquid waste (less water usage) and some solid waste (adding a little more water to the flush).

- **Reuse.** Consider using salvaged materials to add unique design elements to the home. I once put a porthole, retrieved from a sunken 1920's trawler off the coast of Key West, into a front door to add interest and novelty. You can do something similar at any price point: check your local used-building-materials yard, architectural-salvage businesses, or Habitat for Humanity "ReStore" location to see if you can find interesting antique or vintage elements—pillars, posts, fencing, flooring, tiles, doors, windows, mantels, etc.—that you could incorporate into the home as part of your artistic vision.

Go all the way and get your house certified as a "green" home. The certification tells buyers that the home meets rigorous standards; it's not just "greenwashed" but a true, high-performance green home. According to the U.S. Green Building Council (USGBC), the homes it certifies offer the following benefits:

- Lower operating costs and increased asset value
- Less waste sent to landfills
- Conservation of energy and water
- Healthier and safer indoor environment for occupants
- Fewer harmful greenhouse gas emissions
- Qualification for tax rebates, zoning allowances, and other incentives in hundreds of cities

Believe me, I'm putting my money where my mouth is. Both Acqua Liana ($29 million) and Crystalina ($30 million) were created as certified green homes. They exceed the mandate as prescribed by the USGBC's Leadership in Energy and Environmental Design for Homes (LEED-H). This program is the nationally accepted benchmark for the design, construction, and operation of high-performance green homes, from small residences on up to our 15,000-square-foot mansions. With the LEED-H program, we promote a whole-home approach to sustainability by recognizing performance in eight key areas of human and environmental health:

- innovation in design
- sustainable site development
- energy efficiency
- water savings
- indoor air quality
- environmentally preferable materials selection
- location
- ease of use/homeowner education

With the creation and construction of Acqua Liana and Crystalina, we're setting new standards for environmentally responsible, luxury building practices around the globe. You can see all the areas where we've earned points toward our certification of Acqua Liana by visiting the Acqua Liana page on Frank-McKinney.com, where you'll find our LEED-H certification worksheet. At Acqua Liana and Crystalina, just some of the green features include:

- **Solar panels and small wind turbines** that generate enough energy to run the entire home on sunny and/or windy days. In sunny, oceanfront Florida, there will definitely be days when the meter "spins backward" and allows the owner to sell electricity back to the utility provider! The owner will be able to quantify energy efficiency in real time via the high-tech automated biofeedback system.

- **Environmentally conscious lighting** that cuts down on fixture consumption and heat generation by 75 percent.
- The use of **water-efficient plumbing** fixtures and an intricate **water-reuse system** that routes excess H_2O to irrigate landscaping.
- **Ultra-high-efficiency air-conditioning, purification, and fresh air intake systems** that make indoor air quality superior to that found in 99.99 percent of homes in America.
- Use of ample **reclaimed and renewable woods,** saving over seven acres of rain forest. The renewable woods we used regenerate at an average rate of every five years—compare that to fifty years for many hardwoods to grow to maturity. (One species of Columbian guadua bamboo regenerates by growing up to ninety feet in a single year!)
- During construction, **85 percent of all debris and trash will be recycled,** and will never reach a landfill.
- A concerted effort has been made to **preserve and maintain the native flora and fauna** that further beautify this oceanfront setting.

This list and the eight areas of the LEED-H program should give you all kinds of ideas for green improvements to be incorporated into your own property. Offer your buyers a way to save money while reducing their carbon footprint, and you've done more than improve the home: you've made it easier to sell that home at a premium, and even improved the world around you. Consider all the ways you can do this . . . .

- How can you incorporate solar or other alternative energy

sources? (A solar-thermal system for heating water is in range for even the most modest starter home, costing only a few thousand dollars.) How can you reduce use of electricity with CFLs or by equipping the home with smart power strips the owners can turn off to limit "phantom load"? (The use of standby power, where appliances and devices are sucking electricity when they're not in use, accounts for up to 15 percent of the average monthly electric bill.) Both will **cut the new owners' bills, essentially putting money back into their pockets**.

- What can you do with the HVAC and filtering systems to produce **better air quality (and overall indoor experience) for your buyers?** You can minimize pollutants, reduce noise, and create indoor environmental quality that will positively affect your buyer's health and comfort by regulating temperature, relative humidity, light, and even sound.

- Can you use renewable or reclaimed woods or other sustainable materials—which you can select not only for their neutral environmental impact but also for their **uniqueness and beauty?** Could you create a rainwater collection system in the backyard that could double as a beautiful water feature, and xeriscape with native, noninvasive plants, both of which would **save buyers money on their water bill?**

With green features, just as with all your other improvement efforts, focus on those items that produce the most bang for the buck on resale. You'll be able to ask more for the house, expand your pool of buyers, and the world will be a better place when someone buys your home. This is not about wearing hemp sandals or eating organic, free-range tofu. This is about an opportunity—maybe your only one—to stay ahead of the trend. To make a market and fortune at the same time. To turn around a troubled industry. To be the first prospector at the new gold mine where the vein is as wide and long as your interstate. It's your Google, Blackberry, iPod, insert-your-favorite-innovation-here. Do it!

Visit the U.S. Green Building Council's website, USGBC.org, or do an Internet search on "LEED-H" to download the current certification application and requirements. There is so much to learn that's available online, so read up. Interview a green consultant who knows all about this new movement and see if they might be a part of your project.

Quality: Realize Your Artistic Vision

On their way to market, a boy sat astride his donkey while his grandfather led them both to town. They passed a small group of people who told the boy, "Shame on you for riding while the old man walks!"

The boy thought perhaps the people were right, so he persuaded his grandfather to trade places. Later, they passed a few people who whispered together, loud enough so they could be heard, "That's terrible! A grown man makes that little boy walk all the way to town!"

They both decided to walk and avoid any more comments. But the next little crowd of people they encountered laughed at them, saying they were stupid to walk when they had a perfectly good donkey to ride. So they both climbed on board.

Next they passed a group of people who said they were awful to burden a poor donkey so. The boy and his grandfather dismounted and undertook to carry the donkey, no small feat of strength for an old man and a little boy. As they crossed a bridge, struggling mightily under the donkey's weight, they lost their grip, the animal fell into the river, and it drowned.

The moral of the story? If you try to please everyone, you might as well kiss your "ass" goodbye.

Or you'll never make the market if you don't listen to your own instincts.

Or you're a total bubble-head if you neutralize your artistry by following everyone else's opinion; in that case, you can kiss the serious money, your reputation, and any shot at differentiation in the marketplace goodbye.

On a lot of TV shows where people are being helped to sell a home, owners are advised to paint everything beige and not push the envelope with anything too out of the ordinary: they strive to make the home feel like anyone could live there. That's absolutely not in line with my bubble-proofing strategy, which requires that you create something unique and magnificent, no matter what size home or type of property you're in. You don't want to blend in; you want to stand out. From the starter home all the way up to the mansions we build, it's innovation and creativity that make a market, drawing people into the home, and then persuading them to pay top dollar.

In entry-level homes, your commitment to quality alone will make you stand out: spending fifteen dollars per yard instead of ten dollars per yard for carpet, putting on two coats of paint instead of just one, replacing the roof instead of merely patching it, laying down sod instead of seed, installing a new mailbox instead of just pushing the old one upright. You want the buyer to think, *I never expected to be able to have that in a home we could afford.*

At the highest end of the market, when I'm envisioning the possibilities for a property, I don't worry if someone won't like what I've done. In fact, creating a genuinely original home practically requires that I include features some people will assure me they hate. But I can assure you I will never sell a multimillion-dollar home to a couple who leaves the property scratching their heads and saying, "That was kinda nice, honey." No way; I *want* them to love it or hate it.

It's okay with me if some people can't stand it as long as some people find it irresistible, stunning, a must-have. I'd much rather hear, "What a magnificent monstrosity!" than "That's nice." Of course, what I most want to hear is, "How soon can we move in?" Neutral reactions don't sell a home—you've got to move people from need to desire, elevating them to a state of subliminal euphoria, where they make a decision to buy almost without realizing that's what they've done.

I've said before that I have no interest in being a starving artist. The artistic vision frequently pushes the budget, squeezing my margins, so, again, any new decision has to be balanced with the question of whether it might materially affect the bottom line. Do I love creative expression, turning my mind loose to design something extraordinary? Yes! Would I put something in one of our homes if I knew no one would appreciate the artistry but me, or if I knew it would flatten my margin? Never. Am I committed to making a masterpiece every time, one with flair and passion, something that could only come from my own imagination? Absolutely. But let me be clear: I never fall in love with any of the decisions, and I don't make them based upon my own lifestyle. (I drive a Yugo, for goodness' sake.) **I encourage you to make your decisions based upon your buyers' tastes, not your own.** Beware of "nesting" in an investment property. Love what you're doing, but don't love it so much that you get attached.

I do some of my best creative thinking when I'm standing in the empty shell of the home, after the exterior walls have been put up, but when it's still devoid of any distinguishing characteristics. I like to be there alone to imagine what it might become, and that's when the ideas start to flow. Early in my career, these brainstorms were largely about how we might use half-walls, counters, aquariums, or freestanding wet bars to separate spaces so that there could be an openness to the floor plan and the house would seem bigger. I would eliminate unnecessary doors to further open the home up.

I still think about many of these same things, but now, I also imagine how we could blow our buyers' minds with something they've never seen before, like the shark mosaic we installed in the glass water floor of an oceanfront home in Ocean Ridge, which looks like it will emerge to devour the bartender. It was behind a tiny wet bar and spanned only about three square feet, but our clients loved it so much that we were inspired to put in the much larger, one-of-a-kind glass floor in the entryway at Acqua Liana, with eighteen inches of water below, flowing over a hand-painted lotus garden motif painted upon glass tiles. Likewise, the cantilevered rooftop Jacuzzi, hanging off the edge of a three-story home, over-looking the ocean, had a similar effect: jaw-dropping. (That's where *Oprah* filmed me in the hot tub with a glass of fake champagne.) Along with its rooftop barbecue, perched sixty feet above sea level, it definitely got buyers' attention and admiration.

Quality is not only about artistry but also about *artisanship*, meaning the excellence of the craftwork in any home, everything from the basics, like whether you've ensured that the cabinet doors

Shark Attack!

Our shark mosaic under water and under the bartender's feet is so realistic and fearsome that it is the centerpiece of this $12 million oceanfront masterpiece that sold in 84 days. The aquarium wet bar surrounding it makes it all come to life.

in the kitchen hang level or tile has been laid with uniform precision, to the more elaborate, like the clarity of the starfire glass in underwater windows at the bottom of a pool over a marble-floored garage. (This was an impressive piece of artistry, too: When you pulled into the garage, you could look up through your pool to see the pool deck—or vice versa, you could peer down through the floor of the pool to see into your garage. Who wants to see their garage? Well, if you've parked your Bentley on a gorgeous marble or reflective black epoxy floor, and the floor windows create an LED display that fires off two million different color combinations to show it off, that's worth looking at.) It's not only about the vision, it's also about the added value of fine workmanship. When I say that my thumbprint is on every square inch of a home, it means that I've imagined it all and then ensured that it was completed beautifully, by combing over every detail.

Mediocre craftsmanship distracts buyers. The fixture that isn't hung quite right, the doorknob that doesn't totally work, the grout in the tile corners that looks sloppy, the single piece of ceiling trim that is crooked by a half-degree, the screws on the light switch cover that don't line up perfectly north-south—they all make potential buyers question their desire, even if they're not consciously aware of it. And at my level, it can kill a sale before someone even has a chance to see the home. At one estate, we hadn't concealed the air-conditioning supply vents, and a high profile woman who came to see the place (and who knew a little something about quality) walked only about six feet beyond the front door, and then turned on her heel without investigating further. She chastised her broker, "If they can't even do that one simple thing, why should I waste my time finding out what *else* they haven't bothered to do right?"

You can assure quality in any kind of home. Just as I began writing this chapter, I had my conviction about this validated again. In Gonaives, Haiti, our nonprofit Caring House Project Foundation has been working to construct a village of thirty-five homes, a nine-classroom schoolhouse, a community center, church, and renewable food and clean water supplies. Only twenty of the homes in this project were completed at the time of this writing, each made of concrete, costing about $5,000 per home. We could have built them smaller and out of wood for less than $2,500 each, but we insisted on the concrete because of the hurricane damage regularly sustained in that area. Wood houses don't fare well in mudslides and flood conditions, while houses with concrete foundation and walls, along with metal roofs and windows, can often withstand extreme weather events. So today, I opened an e-mail from one of our representatives in Haiti, who let me know that in the wake of four hurricanes that had hit the area—Fay, Gustav, Hanna, and Ike—there were three hundred people taking refuge in those twenty completed homes. The homes were acting as an emergency shelter and were saving lives. Because we chose not to cut corners, because we chose to spend a little bit more and take the time to put up the quality of home that could withstand the weather, at a minimum, we made three hundred lives just a little bit easier. Whereas in real estate investing, we gauge success based on ROI (return on investment), we gauge our success as a charity based on ROD (return on donation)—a perfect analogy in this case, where time, budget, and quality came together to ensure we maximized our donations, realizing greater social capital than we would have if we'd let any one of our holy trinity down. It's an incalculable return, one far greater than we even imagined.

Who knows? By honoring the holy trinity of time, budget, and quality yourself—applying perhaps the most important aspect of bubble-proofing your real estate investments—maybe you will experience incalculable returns, too.

Your Chapter 7
Burst of Inspiration

- Clarify your vision and passion into a statement describing your next investment property: what will it represent for you, why will you acquire it, and what are you going to do with it?

8

THE MOST OBSCENE
FOUR-LETTER WORD

"**Y**ou need only two** credit cards: one from American Express that requires you to pay in full every month, and one Visa or MasterCard for those few places that don't take AmEx. You'll want to pay down the balance on this card, too, even though you don't have to. That's it: just two cards, paid off once a month."

When I said this recently at a business roundtable, people laughed out loud. One woman held up her bulging wallet like a trophy, while she nodded and grinned.

"Very funny!" The whole crowd seemed to cheer her on.

Except I wasn't joking.

From consumers on Main Street to lenders on Wall Street to legislators on Capitol Hill, the overuse and misuse of *debt* has been obscene in this country for quite some time. Particularly in the housing industry, which precipitated—and suffered so deeply with—the credit crunch that began in late 2008. There are some harsh lessons to be learned, and debt is no laughing matter. As an individual investor who's bubble-proofing your real estate strategies, you'd be wise to take this very, very seriously. Debt is that sharp pin that can instantly burst even the smartest investor's bubble.

As I mentioned in the previous chapter, one of the most important paradoxes that you must learn to handle is to **be a daredevil and a maverick in making your markets and masterpieces, but be cautious and completely conservative when it comes to debt.** One of the primary reasons I've been able to take enormous and profitable risks for nearly twenty-five years is my responsible, conservative, disciplined approach to debt management. I'm hypersensitive to that four-letter word; I admit I'm deathly afraid of it. So I use long-term credit (and I use a lot of it) in my business for only two purposes: 1) *opportunity*, to augment my own funds in pursuing a worthy investment, and 2) *insurance* while I'm waiting for my pay day. In other words, because I have income only when a property sells, I've established lines of credit, secured by my real estate and other holdings as collateral, that provide me with capital as I need it to run my life, both home and business. This insures that my family eats tomorrow, that my workers get paid, that my world keeps spinning.

Why do it this way? Because, as I am continuing to grow my business, I have very little of my own money sitting in the bank; most of it's been put to work in my investment properties. While that may not sound particularly conservative, I believe that keeping my own money liquid actually would erode my financial future. Why? The historic rates of return on bank deposits or other "secure" investments like CDs or T-bills are abysmal compared with what I have done while investing in myself, putting my money into the markets and masterpieces I create with every new property acquisition. So like most small conglomerates in the United States, I need credit to keep myself moving forward and making markets. And I need to manage my debt carefully and constantly: I need to keep far enough from the sun so that I only tan, not fly so close that I blister.

I have my late father, the banker, to thank for setting me on the right course. He's the one who taught me how to complete a balance sheet when I was twenty-five years old, how to subtract liabilities from assets and keep an eye on my net worth as the ultimate gauge of my financial success. Beginning in 1992, shortly after we started creating homes on the ocean, I've tracked my year-over-year net worth increases or decreases, monitoring my growth, proving to myself time and again that putting my money to work for me in my real estate projects is my best possible financial plan. As of this writing, my average return is a 25.88 percent annual increase in net worth, something very few other investment vehicles could possibly match. In looking at my eighteen-year-old spreadsheet, I see that there was one year when it increased over 102 percent, and a particularly challenging year when it decreased more than 29 percent. (Can you guess when that sharp decline happened?) If I toss out the highs and lows, it is clear that even in some of the more challenging markets, I was still able to increase my net worth well over 15 percent. Over the course of many up and down cycles over the last eighteen years, I've had only three years when my net worth decreased (by an average of 17 percent), whereas I've had fifteen years where my net worth increased (by an average of 34 percent)! If that doesn't prove my real estate investing strategies are bubble-proof, I don't know what will.

My dad also showed me how crucial debt management is to raising that number every year, building net worth steadily over time. At the beginning of my real estate career, as I was transitioning away from the tennis court and buying my first distressed properties, he took me aside for an important father-son talk. Growing up, I'd been rebellious and resented these little chats, but at this stage of my life, I was finally ready to listen. After all, my dad was a prominent bank executive, serving as president and chairman of the board of a small Indianapolis bank, American Fletcher National Bank. He knew so much more about investing, credit, and money management than I did at that time, and I was eager to learn. I wanted to protect my investments and maximize my profits.

In my first few forays into the real estate market, I had tapped several private loan sources, borrowing money from my former tennis students and from my dad, too, to buy properties. Each of the loans carried a different rate of interest, and the loan from Dad had the lowest rate. He knew how each of my smaller deals had been structured, and he had some valuable advice to give me before the numbers got much bigger.

"Ultimately, son, you're going to go to the bank for credit," he said. "But before you get too deeply in debt, you need to turn on all the lights and appliances inside your house and then go outside to look at the electric meter. Just watch that thing spin. Then keep that picture in mind whenever you borrow money, because there's a 'debt meter,' too. Even though you don't see it, it's there, all right, and that wheel's spinning faster every day you're in debt."

With every property I've bought, I've tracked the debt meter that's spinning from the day I purchase until the day I sell. It's one of the reasons I'm such a stickler for keeping to a tight building/renovating schedule, and why I work so hard on marketing my properties so that they'll be on the market for the shortest possible time. Every day you own a piece of real estate, the debt meter is running, and that's money you'll never get back again. Wouldn't it be great if you could just hook up a debt meter to the side of your business to help you evaluate your cash outflow and tell you when to retrench, just like the numbers on a water or electric meter will tell you that you're using too much and need to cut back? Yes, I can make it that easy for you, but you must adhere to my strategy.

How Does Your Debt Usage Compare?

According to the latest figures in the United States, the average credit card holder has eight cards in his or her wallet and carries an outstanding balance of $8,500, accruing interest at annual rates up to 31 percent. (Actually, the balance for most people is probably higher than that estimate. Those numbers are based on Federal Reserve data, which report that the aggregate consumer debt exclusive of mortgages is $2.6 trillion. Divide that number by the total population according to the U.S. Census, including every man, woman, and child, to come up with $8,500 each. But since most children don't carry credit cards (I know there are exceptions), we can conservatively assume that in a household with two parents and two children, the family carries at least $34,000 in consumer debt, giving each adult a revolving credit load of $17,000. It's not perfect math, but you get the idea. And you might get a better idea of the problem by looking at your own credit card bills this month.

Think about households earning an average gross annual income of about $60,000 a year. After taxes, they have approximately $45,000 to meet all their obligations. You can figure that with the average mortgage, credit card payments, car payments, and other miscellaneous debt to service, they're spending around $2,000 a month mostly on interest—more than 50 percent of their take-home pay—spinning that debt meter faster and faster, *but not necessarily reducing their liability*. That leaves around $1,750 a month to pay for "discretionary" items like food, gas, utilities, insurance, medicine, clothes, daycare, car repair, entertainment, and any medical needs that aren't covered by insurance. Is there anything left to save or invest? Depends on how badly their kids want that SpongeBob SquarePants doll, I guess—or if they're fortunate enough to not have any surprises like accidents, rate increases on bills, kids' dental problems, and so on, that will wipe out any possibility of saving anything this month.

You could make this work. Many people do. Still, many people don't. About 43 percent of American families live beyond their means. We've turned into a "charge it today, pay for it never" economy, where personal spending outstrips earnings, where we have a negative savings rate in our country, where monthly payments have become the measuring stick of affordability. This is a B.S. approach to life, the opposite of bubble-proofing. This is bubble-creating-then-popping all over your irresponsible face!

By "B.S.," I mean bad strategy. Very, *very* bad strategy. If you've bought into this B.S., make a promise to yourself right now: No more blaming. You are going to take control of your finances so you actually have money to invest and bubble-proof!

This problem is so rampant that it's the major contributing factor to the late 2008 credit meltdown. Meanwhile, if our country had been managing its own government debt more responsibly, perhaps the speeches from members of Congress would have rung less hollow, as they self-righteously congratulated themselves on standing up for Main Street and for swallowing the bitter pill of assisting Wall Street. Indeed, our national finances are nothing to crow about, with revenues averaging 18.3 percent of gross domestic product (GDP) and spending averaging 20.6 percent of GDP, creating an average 2.3 percent deficit per year. We owe about 45 percent of our debt to foreign investors, including countries that don't always share our national interests: China, Venezuela, Saudi Arabia, Iran, Iraq (yes, although we have pumped $10 billion a month into that country, we still owe them), and Russia, among others. This is further reflection and confirmation of the "charge it today, pay for it never" mentality (whatever happened to "In God We Trust" as our mantra?), which is rapidly becoming a national security issue. Since this book isn't about the imprudent financial practices of the U.S. government, however, I'll leave that for you to explore further on your own.

As Congress wended its way to resolution with a $700 billion lifesaver for Main Street and Wall Street, a lot of people were asking, *Why should taxpayers have to foot the bill? Aren't the banks mostly to blame? Aren't they the ones who were dreaming up the esoteric and eccentric financial products, indiscriminately giving away money, and wrecking the system with their greed? Weren't consumers just pawns in their game?*

First, let's be clear: Wall Street is a conduit of money to Main Street, and the two are closely connected. When money lenders seize up and banks stop loaning money, it affects the ability of businesses to run and pay workers, it constricts individuals' ability to make purchases like cars and homes, and it curtails most expansion that depends on credit. In essence, it removes the key element that is necessary to pursue free enterprise and capitalism: risk taking. So it was somewhat misleading to talk about a "Wall Street bailout" without acknowledging that the whole country was affected, for good or ill, both by the crunch and by the relief package. And the whole country was responsible, for individuals bit off more debt than they could chew just like banks and other companies. Sure, the bailout was hard to swallow: At first, calls to members of Congress were 100-to-1 against the relief package, and then we started to get a little financial religion. Once we realized how the lack of access to credit was affecting us as small business owners and consumers, the ever-nimble lawmakers chose to do the right thing.

Still, I can understand why these questions were asked. Certainly, lenders have an upper hand. They have lawyerese and stacks of intimidating and confusing documents on their side; they can draft paperwork that comes across as very enticing, including the low entry-level interest rate that starts at 1 percent and jumps to 10 after they change their underwear, the negative amortization (owe more each day you pay), and the 125 percent loan-to-value (LTV) where we "come to closing, own a home, and walk away with $20,000 in our pocket." That's unscrupulous and borderline unethical, although it wasn't illegal then.

Accountability also resides, however, with the home buyer, the home owner, the debtor, the consumer. For those who committed to mortgages way beyond their means, who didn't understand that "fixed rate for a year" meant it would be adjusted thereafter, who made all manner of poor decisions and didn't discipline themselves to *learn* about what they were signing, they have my compassion for the tumult they find themselves in now. Facing a home foreclosure or bankruptcy can be sad, embarrassing, and even tragic. But I don't for a moment want to let irresponsible borrowers off the hook. It's not someone else's "fault" if you willingly accept debt you can't afford, if you gamble with someone else's money and lose, if you have to walk away from a home with a mortgage that's ballooned into payments you can't handle anymore, if you don't even attempt to rework the interest rate or principal balance or the tenure of the loan. It's the individual's responsibility to manage his or her finances—not the government's, not the lenders', and certainly not the majority of taxpayers who didn't get caught up in this mess. What happened to due diligence? I have said that I believe in the welfare system, but not the welfare mentality, the mindset that comes from an entitlement approach. No, we must learn financial responsibility. *Learn to earn*, as they say. And it looks like people will be learning it the hard way.

True, some people were too uninformed or too greedy or too desperate to resist the credit temptations put before them every day. And some lenders acted like hookers in the street windows of Amsterdam's red light district. But consumers who chose to go into that brothel made their own decisions. They say that if you lay down with dogs, you get up with fleas. Well, if you climb into bed with a financial whore, you get the fiscal equivalent of venereal disease.

The new *caveat emptor*: borrower beware.

Yes, the culture we live in offers many temptations; easy credit has been just one of a multitude of seductions to which you could succumb, to the detriment of your good health, financial or otherwise. *You have to be on guard.* Yes, the financial literacy in this country is pitiful. Therefore *it's up to you to ensure that you learn what you need to know.* Do your due diligence. While our schools are tied up in knots about teaching kids to take tests, while universities crank out graduates with only a slim chance of seeing a significant return on their student-loan debt, we have a whole segment of the nation that doesn't even know how to create a personal balance sheet or financial statement. It doesn't matter to a standardized test whether students know how to do this net-worth calculation, even though it's perhaps *the most* important mathematical exercise a person can undertake. Knowing your personal net worth—or not knowing it—affects a person's ability to create and act on opportunities for growth, to contribute something unique and meaningful to society, to make decisions that build instead of decimate financial well-being, and to create a legacy of generational wealth.

In the end, *responsibility* has to come back to the consumer. I'm not talking about finger-pointing or finger-wagging or even who should foot the bill for (or, for that matter, profit from) Wall Street's comeuppance, but about who ultimately must take control of and answer for his or her own personal financial situation.

Earlier in this book, you read about the American Dream, how it's alive and well and will never die. Notice I didn't call that dream a "right." The United States got into trouble when the American Dream began to be considered a right of those people who had no business pursuing it to the extent that they did, as in buying the $800,000 house when they should have been living in a $400,000 house. Furthermore, not everyone is entitled or ready to *own* a home. That privilege must be earned and bought through hard work, savings, and restraint. Home ownership can be a dream come true for those who work to achieve it. But as we now know, it also can become a total nightmare when those who can't actually afford a home are enticed into a purchase through some goofy and unsustainable loan product offered by a greedy financial institution. (Such companies became primarily interested in creating large bundles of risky mortgages to sell off to other financial institutions—I actually heard this compared to gift wrapping poop and calling it gold bullion—rather than selling "vanilla" thirty-year mortgages to clients who saved for their down payment and could afford the payments now *and* in the future.)

Unfortunately, the financial services industry had some significant allies in spreading credit around unwisely. In April of 2005, former chairman of the Federal Reserve Alan Greenspan (proudly?) stated,

. . . innovation and structural change in the financial services industry have been critical in providing expanded access to credit for the vast majority of consumers, including those of limited means. Without these forces, it would have been impossible for lower-income consumers to have the degree of access to credit markets that they now have.

He went on to characterize this as "constructive" and "beneficial to consumers." Where was the one word that, if inserted in any line above, may have made a difference: *responsible?* Again, B.S.— baaaaaaaaaad strategy. Do I think people of limited means should be given a chance to build a credit history by proving their ability to handle reasonable amounts of debt? Absolutely. Do I think they need the kind of unfettered access that was available through such outrageous financial instruments as "No Income, No Assets" (NINA) loans, where you signed a lot of papers but didn't have to prove any kind of financial suitability or even any kind of income at all? Absolutely not!

In late 2008/early 2009 the U.S. Treasury committed to go in like a giant vacuum cleaner to suck the bad loans out of the good banks that are still standing (that means, taking over nonperforming loans held by the banks whose better judgment and superior business models have kept them in business during the market turmoil). They also infused the remaining institutions with billions (some received over $25 billion) to secure their solvency and, more important, to insure they would start lending again—responsibly. The goal of this action was not only to save the banks and the credit system of the United States, but also to give creditworthy home buyers another chance. It is my sincerest hope that this effort will result in the resetting of the American Dream to its original parameters. In other words, a twenty-two-year-old just out of college, without a job, can't buy a 1,200-square-foot starter home with no down payment. Thank goodness, we are returning to the days when you had to save for a down payment, and the home loan you received reflected your ability to pay, not just monthly installments for a brief time, but a mortgage over the real lifetime of the loan. That model kept the United States real estate market solidly appreciating over the last seventy-five-plus years. Now, rest assured that free enterprise will prevail, and in a year or so, when the mess seems a distant memory, creative products will start to creep back into the system. Resist them. Recite the post- 9/11 mantra: "We will never forget." A bubble-proofer would be well-served to adopt a new mantra, too: "We will never re-debt."

No doubt you're reading this long after Congress has acted to contain the fallout from the credit crunch. You'll have the benefit of hindsight that I lack right now (as this book is being completed) while we're still in the thick of it. You'll know whether the banks responded by loosening the purse strings and making good loans again, or if they kept credit unnaturally constrained, or if (God forbid) we sunk deep into an extended recession that lasted until you were forced to use these pages as toilet paper.

And if you're paying attention, the real bottom line is this: **the last thing you ever want to be faced with is needing a bailout of your own.** There's plenty I can't know about how the congressional actions will affect real estate and how long it will take to completely play out. Yet there is one thing I can see quite clearly in my crystal ball: I can guarantee that **if you commit to never misusing debt as you may have in the past, or are now warned about the perils of irresponsible debt if this is your first time, you will have taken the first step to bubble-proofing more than just your real estate investments. You will have bubble-proofed your financial life!**

The misuse of debt by an investor is potentially more damaging to a bubble-proofing strategy than anything else. Sure, you could overpay and get lucky in a hot market. Overleverage, though, by borrowing more than you can pay back, and even in a hot market you're going to lose. "Debt up" (there's another four-letter word you could substitute here) in this way, resulting in bankruptcy or foreclosure, and you're screwed for years.

Irresponsible debt is the trans fat of finance. People gobble it up with relish, and tend to pay attention only after they suffer a heart attack. There's a simple answer: read the label, and if you don't know what the contents are, learn them. Understand what you're eating before you put it in your mouth. Make better choices that will foster a healthy, long life. If you don't, you may never recover from the "debt attack" that damages your credit forever.

READING THE LABEL

Not long ago, I watched Larry King interview a consumer advocate who said, among other things, that she was highly educated but unable to understand a mortgage document. She offered this as a reason why many borrowers should be held blameless for foreclosures. I'm sure this woman was very educated—but she also seemed dumb as a box of rocks.

I'm sorry, but I don't care how much time you've spent in school; if you're buying a house, you don't give up trying to learn about the deal you're making. You don't use excuses like "it's too hard," or you're "not a numbers person," or there are "just so many pages and my eyes got tired," or whatever else someone might say to get out of doing the necessary due diligence. No matter how smart you think you are, that's just stupid!

As a committed bubble-proofer and responsible investor, you must scrutinize the deal points in any lending transaction and be sure you know exactly what you're getting ready to take on. Remember, it's your money, and everyone at the table with you wants to separate you from as much of it as possible. The bank wants its piece, the brokerage its piece, the attorneys their piece, and the buyers their piece. All of them want to maximize their returns, which means getting more of your money. You're the only one there as the primary custodian of your interests, so you'd better make darn sure you understand everything that you sign and exactly what signing will mean in terms of your bottom line now and in the future.

Look, I know this is neither easy nor pleasant. I know that the learning curve can be steep and all the technical details of creating a deal can be intimidating. When I first started investing, I didn't understand much of anything I read or what the bankers, attorneys, realtors, etc. were saying. But I was smart enough not to let myself sign anything unless I understood exactly what I was getting into. My early closings took hours, not because they were particularly complicated, but because I wanted to take the time to learn.

Confronted with an intimidating stack of papers (I still find loan documents somewhat daunting), you have a choice: either sign the papers blindly, or ask the necessary questions of your attorney, loan officer, or closing agent. If you don't understand something, get the help you need to sift through all of the legalese. If you don't like the canned answer you're getting, challenge it. Find the relevant financial data and review every financial reference in the loan documents. It's their privilege to have your business, not the other way around.

Even before I had a lawyer to work out legal details regarding my investments, I was relentless when it came to asking questions. For every deal or document, I'd ask, "What does this mean? What's the difference between APR and 'effective annual percentage rate'? Why is one higher than the other?" And on and on I went. *I was scared enough to educate myself.* I'm adept with numbers, but there was plenty to learn, and the deeper I got into this business, the more I took the time to understand the terms that were laid before me. Occasionally, it was confusing and difficult, but it was important to me, so I kept at it. You must do the same for your own real estate deals. It's the only way to ensure the kind of profitability you want, both in the short and long term.

Anyone who ever hopes to be able to say *Burst This!* **needs to be completely informed about every financial aspect of the deal.** At a minimum, the key questions are these:

- Where is my payment information?
- Where is my interest rate information?
- Is there anything that causes the interest rate to adjust? If so, what? Is there a cap? On what index is it based? (My own quirk: I tend to tie mine to prime rate as set by U.S. banks that tie their rate to the federal funds rate, established by the Federal Reserve. I do this because it's simpler to get my head around it than LIBOR, for example, which is the London

Interbank Offered Rate. You can look it up, but England seems kind of far away to me.)

- What's the date my loan is due?
- What's my payment date?
- What's my late date?
- What happens if I don't pay?
- What causes a default, and what happens if I default?
- Is there a built-in renewal clause for the principal balance?

Use your common sense. Even if you're numbers-averse, you can get the information you need by asking the right questions. In the beginning, I used to pore over loan documents, studying the boiler-plate language for hours. By doing that, I've learned that in a thirty-page document, about two pages are important, so nowadays, although I still look closely at every sentence, I spend most of my time ferreting out the essential information of when payments are due, what the grace period is, how long the loan is for, and what happens if I don't pay it back on time. **An easy way to sum it up: Pay on time, and the thirty pages mean nothing. Just make sure you know what you are paying—and that you can afford it.**

If you're already a home owner and you're now planning to purchase your first investment property, prepare yourself for a higher interest rate and more points on an investment property loan than what you negotiated for your own home mortgage. And now that the banks are done handing out loans like lollipops, with no down payment required, plan to pony up *at least* 20 percent and as high as 30 percent as a down payment. Even if your lender requires less, stick with the higher percentages. *Put down as much as you can to minimize debt.* Ideally, you also should cover as much of the improvement costs as you can by yourself (instead of factoring all of them into the loan), which will increase your profit margin when you sell, because you will cut down on total carrying costs.

People often look at me cross-eyed when I suggest this high down-payment strategy. They'll say, "But Frank, isn't the ability to so highly leverage real estate what makes it such a great investment?" Yes and no: yes, leverage is great, but you can overleverage yourself by taking on too much debt (I don't care if it is bank debt or assuming the seller's debt or some combination—it's still debt); and no, because overleveraging isn't the *Burst This!* approach. (Sorry, no-money-downers, I never drank the Kool-Aid and never will.) **Bubble-proofing means you'll keep an eye on that debt meter.** Bubble-proofing also means that you're ready to sacrifice today for a better tomorrow and do what it takes to come up with a sizeable down payment. You'll get a second job if necessary, or reduce your lifestyle temporarily, or sell household goods you no longer use or enjoy. As you read earlier, when I first bought on the oceanfront, Nilsa and I sold everything, including the house we were living in, to finance the purchase of Driftwood Dunes. We lived on next to nothing and put every penny into the renovations. Without our sacrifice, that deal never would have netted us the profit that we then used for the next deal, and the next. To this day we're willing to live modestly and cut back on things to keep personal expenses low and access to capital high. Even now, as my own family is feeling the credit crunch, this "reduced calorie" lifestyle is easier to swallow simply because we've been there before, and really know of no other way.

You have to be willing to do the hard things today so your tomorrow will be brighter. You may have to tap into your savings or pull equity out of other investments and put your money to work for you—banking on the acquisition formula, along with your research and detailed understanding of the local market—to ensure a better return than you'd find elsewhere. That's the bubble-proof approach to investing.

Choosing Your Lender

Once you've responsibly accumulated your down payment and found your property, you'll be looking to a lender for the balance of the investment. I just walked you through reviewing the loan documents, but let's back up a step and detail how to review the lenders themselves. You're going to look for the cheapest source of money and the best terms, negotiating your deal so that there won't be any surprises when you finally sit down with the papers in one hand and a pen to sign them in the other.

Banks: Real Estate Loans and Lines of Credit

An established relationship with a bank has many plusses, not least of which is that you may find you have greater ability to negotiate terms with bankers who know you; after all, there are only a few good ones still standing. If you've done business with them before and have a track record of responsibly borrowing and repaying loans, you can expect to see better terms with each deal. Don't overlook your various checking and savings accounts at your current bank for providing relationship and financial history; even these can help you establish credit with your bank. I suggest that you do business with one of the big four that have strong balance sheets, Bank of America (my bank), Citibank, Wells Fargo, or J. P. Morgan. If you already have a relationship with another, perhaps a regional or even community bank, that is perfectly fine. Be prepared to negotiate every aspect of your next deal, whether it's your first or your fiftieth. Market conditions change, bank personnel move on, and the loans available to you today may or may not be the same as the ones you were offered yesterday; therefore, every deal will require negotiation. Put your greatest focus on the following factors, as they'll have the greatest impact on your profitability.

- **Interest rate.** It's undoubtedly the most important variable because you don't know exactly how long you'll have to carry the property before it's sold. Here you're negotiating how fast your debt meter will spin. Obviously, you want that wheel to turn as slowly as possible.
- **Points or loan origination fees.** Watch out for your bank trying to compensate for a low interest rate with higher points or loan origination fees. Try to keep these fees low: start by asking for zero, and from there go up only gradually, by one-eighth of a point at a time.
- **Loan-to-value (LTV) ratio.** With the resetting of the American Dream, most banks will be loaning no more than 70 percent of a property's value for investment real estate. Always seek to establish a line of credit rather than an outright loan where you have to draw down the full amount at closing. If you can get the bank to the 70 percent level, you'll be doing great, but prepare for an LTV closer to 60 percent. Establish the higher LTV, but try to put down a larger deposit. For example, say you're looking to acquire an investment property for $100,000. You are able to get a loan for $70,000, which means you have to put down a $30,000 deposit. If you are able to put

down $50,000 instead, you can instantly have access to a line of credit worth $20,000, which you can use to make improvements on your investment and build your creditworthiness at the same time. This approach will come in very handy later in your real estate career. (I know this sounds like a large sum, but you will save to get there.)

- **Loan amount.** Always secure more than you think you'll need to help cover contingencies; remember, you need to include the "what if" factor in your budget.

- **Tenure.** How long is the loan for? You need a tenure that extends well beyond the anticipated timeline of your project, so you have time to complete the improvements *and* sell. You've already read in the chapter on the holy trinity of improvements to allow about 1.5 months for new construction per 1,000 square feet and no more than that for renovations. I also tend to include up to a year on the loan from the date of project completion for our artistry to sell; although it's rarely taken that long, I want to ensure that the sale happens long before the loan is due.

- **Other terms.** Negotiate for maximum flexibility about how and where you'll use the funds. If possible, designate the loan for "business purposes" or "real estate" rather than something more specific. Even if the deal you're working on today falls through, or if you find another property with better prospects, you'll still be able to apply the loan to whatever property you ultimately purchase.

If you don't yet own your own home, that should be your first purchase, even if you treat it as an investment property, renovating and reselling within a couple of years. If you do own your own home already, the equity you've built in that property (assuming you still have some), along with your employment income, will be factored into your viability as a loan candidate.

You could also use the equity in your house to secure a line of credit with your current bank, or any number of other lenders, as I have done. Typically, lines of credit are issued for three years, sometimes with an extension. With this kind of credit (called a Home Equity Line of Credit, or HELOC), you pay interest only when you access the funds, and you can use the money for designated purposes, like buying an investment property. Managed properly, lines of credit can provide you with the "dry powder" I've mentioned earlier in the book: ready funds you can use to seize opportunities when they arise. Yet the temptation to abuse this arrangement can be great, so you'll need to be disciplined in spending the money responsibly: only on either *opportunity* or *insurance* (personal and business operating capital) as I've defined them in this chapter. No buying cars or taking vacations until you have sold some properties and made some money.

You'll also maximize your net gain by repaying the line of credit the minute you realize your profit, thereby stopping the debt meter cold. Because I do this, I like to say that I am the bank's best and worst customer at the same time. Whenever a property sells, I go straight to them with a whopper payment. While they're happy to get my money, by paying down the credit line I've effectively cut their return because they're no longer invested in me. The bankers are no fools: they want their money invested in my properties as much as I want my money invested in my properties, because they know we'll profit together.

Mortgage Brokers, Mortgage Products

Given the changing mortgage landscape it might be wise to spend some time educating yourself through a mortgage broker who is up on all the new loan products. (Don't worry, the irresponsible ones are gone for the near term—both products and brokers.)

Indeed, a mortgage broker can be the next best source for investment capital if you can't find a workable arrangement with your bank. Early in my career, I did numerous deals with my mortgage broker, and her assistance was invaluable. Because mortgage brokers get paid only when a deal goes through, they can be highly motivated and offer a wealth of information about available mortgage loans and their terms. I've got a great one for your smaller deals: Call my demolition derby buddy, Eddie Cairo, at (561) 274-0020.

Hard-Money Lenders: The "Expensive" Money

If you feel confident that you can get in and out of a deal within a year, and that you can purchase the property at 65 percent or less of market value, then you might consider working with a hard-money lender. Their loans typically have a 60 to 65 percent LTV based on the property's future value, with a tenure of a year, and, when legal, usually carry a prepayment penalty. As in all loan transactions, terms are negotiable, so you'll want to ask for the best deal possible.

Generally, you should pursue this kind of financing only if others are unavailable to you. Because hard-money lenders typically charge 15 percent plus three to ten points depending on your credit, you need to be exceedingly cautious when availing yourself of this "expensive" money.

Under the right circumstances, however, your mortgage broker may rightly refer you to a hard-money lender, usually an individual or small finance company. Whereas banks evaluate your creditworthiness based 80 percent on your debt service ability and 20 percent on property value, hard-money lenders do the reverse. If you don't have a track record or access to home equity, hard-money lenders can be more willing to take a risk with you, given the value of the property. They also move a lot faster than banks, often closing a deal within days, while banks can take weeks. If you were to come across an unexpected and excellent opportunity and needed to finance it fast so that you wouldn't miss out, then a hard-money lender could be the right choice for you.

In addition to referral from a mortgage broker, you can find hard-money lenders the same way you'd find a plumber: They're in the phone book and advertise in all the conventional ways; on TV, in the paper, online, at bus stops, and so on. Your real estate investment club will, again, be your best bet for quality hard-money-lender referrals.

Sellers: Nice Deal If You Can Get It

Occasionally, a property owner will be motivated enough to sell by holding the note for you. If this happens, take it, assuming the rate and tenure are relatively close to what a bank might offer. This way, you can put all your available cash into the improvements and other costs.

Most sellers, however, are more interested in having cash in hand. One "hybrid" situation is to lease-option the property: Usually, you make a down payment, move in, make monthly payments, and at the end of the lease term, a portion of your monthly payments and the down payment are applied to the purchase price of the property. During the tenure of the lease, you make your improvements, and as soon as you come to the end of the lease, you put it on the market, sell it, use the proceeds to pay off the owner's note, and then take the profits.

Individual Investors: Are You Partner Material?

As I mentioned earlier, I worked with private investors at the beginning of my real estate career: former tennis students and family loaned me money to invest in my first real estate purchases. I had to do it as recently as seven years ago. This provided great flexibility, as I didn't have to worry about the approval processes of banks or other lenders, and my inexperience didn't prevent me from exercising my instincts and making great deals from the start.

With private investors, you may have to give up some control along with a chunk of your profits, but if you can see that the deal will also be worth the time, money, effort, and artistry you'll pour into the project, this can be an excellent financing option. Be sure that you know your investors well—essentially, you're going into business with them for the duration of the project—and even if you're getting money from your mother, father, or best friend, *always put your agreements in writing*, spelling out procedures for settling disputes and the responsibilities of each party. I recommend that you work with people who are content to be silent partners, happy to stay away from the site. The last thing you need as you work to create a masterpiece is unwelcome, intrusive advice on paint color.

You must be willing to sacrifice some upside for a partner or partners that have the staying power to weather the storm, possibly carrying the property for longer than anticipated. I must be clear, however: Take inventory of your own personality. Some people make better partners than others. (I'm definitely not a great partner person.) And remember, a partnership is like a set of rails on a train track. They start out with parallel interests, and are assumed to stay that way throughout the life of the partnership. It rarely happens that way, though, as one often diverts from the other due to an imbalance of contribution.

Keeping Watch:
Calculate Your Net Worth and
Create Your Own Debt Meter

If you take only one thing away from this chapter, or from this entire book for that matter (excepting the final chapter)—if, despite my counsel, you decide to keep using all eight of those credit cards, and you want to play the no-money-down game with crazy LTVs, and you plan to blow off bank financing and go straight to the hard-money lenders—you can forget bubble-proofing, but you can still do yourself an enormous favor and start monitoring your net worth.

If, on the other hand, you're planning to follow the *Burst This!* approach, to buy right and contain your debt for maximum growth, then knowing your net worth is an essential piece of the puzzle.

It's a simple equation—*Assets minus Liabilities equals Net Worth*—yet so few people take the time to run these numbers, which offer you the single most accurate barometer of your financial health and ultimate success. Below, I've included a simple worksheet. Fill it out or find a net-worth calculator online. It doesn't matter which form you use; just be sure to do this at least once a year, with a quick glance at your financial health every month. You need this information, anyway, when you approach lenders, but the real value of the balance sheet is your own conscious realization of financial loss or gain. It's important to know where you stand.

The Burst This! *Personal Net Worth Balance Sheet*

ASSETS

Cash (bank accounts, CDs, money-market funds)	$_____
Primary home value	$_____
Other real estate value	$_____
Stocks and bonds	$_____
Retirement accounts (401(k), IRAs, SEPs)	$_____
Annuities	$_____
Art, collectibles, jewelry, furnishings	$_____
Other (auto, etc.)	$_____
Cash value of insurance	$_____
Total Assets	$_____

LIABILITIES/DEBTS

Mortgage(s)	$_____
Home-equity/line of credit	$_____
Student loan(s)	$_____
Auto loan(s)	$_____
Credit cards	$_____
Tax liability	$_____
Other (liens, medical bill work-outs, etc.)	$_____
Total Liabilities	$_____

NET WORTH

$_____ (Assets) – $_____ (Liabilities) = $_____ Net Worth

Let me warn you: beware of overvaluing such items as cars, collectibles, jewelry, clothes, and furnishings, or other items whose values aren't assessed for you by a third party. Those things may be priceless to you, but let's face facts: on the open market, no one will pay that much for Grandma's prized cuckoo clock or your favorite pair of Manolo Blahniks. Inflating these numbers only gives you a skewed view of your financial reality, so you're much better off being realistic and erring on the side of undervaluing them. If you use high numbers for those items, it red-flags a bank to what a novice you are. Not only do they recognize your own delusion, but they suspect that you're trying to pull the wool over their eyes, too. One hallmark of a competent businessperson is knowing your real value in the eyes of the banker.

As I mentioned, the balance sheet was one of the tools my father taught me to use when I was just getting started. His other timeless idea was the debt meter. Since then, I've turned that metaphor into an actual practice, calculating my blended interest rate and keeping an eye on what my debt costs me every single day. You can do the same.

My debt meter's in the form of a spreadsheet that references down to the thousandth of a percentage point what my blended rate of interest is on all outstanding debt I have on any given day. At a glance, I can tell you to the day, to the dollar, to the one-thousandth of a percentage point, how much money I'm spending in interest. Every time I borrow, every time I pay something back, every time I make a transfer between my two lines of credit, I update this spreadsheet. I also know, if I don't sell something, how long the available funds I have in my line of credit will last.

You probably don't need to create such a detailed spreadsheet. To create your own debt meter, you will need to know:

- **Your annual net income.** What is your "disposable" income—the amount you receive after taxes? If necessary, go back to last year's return to find the actual number, including all forms of income.
- **The total of your minimum monthly payments** to service your debt: house, credit cards, student loans, car loans, liens, hospital bills that are accruing interest—anything that's accruing interest. Remember, this sum is equal to your interest only paid on these items, not principal.

Let's create a debt meter for the average household I mentioned at the beginning of this chapter. We'll call them the Berry family, Yvonne, Edward, and Peekie. They bring home $45,000 a year after taxes, or $3,750 a month. They have a mortgage ($1,500/month), credit cards ($150/month), car payments ($300/month), and a student loan ($50/month), totaling payments of $2,000 per month. Granted, there is some payment on principal, but for the most part, the Berrys are paying recurring interest—the hidden trap of minimum payments. So we can say that their debt meter is spinning pretty fast: Their interest claims about 50 percent of their available money every month.

The most telling figure generated by the debt meter, the one that makes it a meter in the first place is this: *Every day, $66 of their money leaves the house in credit payments.* (They say the devil is in the details; here, add just one more six and you can see it!) That's a tank of gas every day. Or groceries for a couple of days. Or a dinner out for their small family. Heck, forget the SpongeBob SquarePants doll—they could take Peekie to the Nickelodeon hotel and stay in the SpongeBob suite for a few nights, if only they weren't so strapped by their debt.

Do this calculation for your own household and figure your monthly outlay just for interest. Divide that by your monthly after-tax income to arrive at a percentage. You're in good shape if it's under 30 percent. (The Berry family would be okay if they could cut their interest expense to $1,125 a month: $1,125 monthly interest payments divided by $3,750 monthly income = 30 percent.) Much higher than that and you're probably not managing your debt wisely, and it's time to focus on paying it down or shifting your credit to debt sources with a lower interest rate. (Exception: there will be times when you have a higher debt ratio because of a recently acquired opportunity, and that's okay, but work to have that ratio return to not more than 30 percent as soon as practical.)

As I mentioned, I have two lines of credit. One costs me 1.25 percent more than the other because the collateral is different, so any time I can reduce the outstanding balance on the more expensive line, even to the tune of a few hundred bucks, I'll do it. Let's say that I pay down $100,000 from one line to the other, the difference between the interest on the two is just $1,250 annually, or about $3.42 a day. Once I've made the move, every three days I've saved myself over $10 in interest—enough to buy that celebratory pizza. The few seconds it takes me to move the money is completely worth it! That's part of operating a tight ship. It makes the people in my bank a little crazy because I do it so often, but you know what? Over the life of my loan, I will save millions of dollars in interest, bit by bit, day by day.

You, too, will want to look at your most costly and least costly sources of debt and attempt to use one to eliminate or reduce the other. It's the same principle as debt consolidation loans. Save the money on the interest whenever you can! If you can do it, your house is a wonderful place to go for lower rates of interest, far better than tapping unsecured loans like credit card advances. Even if you can't access cheaper sources of credit, you can call your lender and ask for reduced rates. Especially with credit cards, you want to chip away at that 14 to 18 percent interest. Ask for 6 percent and see what you get. People often don't do this because they don't know about it, but probably just as many don't do it because they're lazy. If you're reading this and saying, "I know, I know," then **ask yourself when the last time was that you actually did what you know.**

This is rudimentary, but you've got to start at this level. Practice responsible debt around the house, and I promise you it will positively affect your real estate dealings, from your ability to secure low-interest credit when you need it to your profitability on every project you undertake.

So yes, *debt* is most often a very obscene four-letter word. If you ever need a reminder, look at what its misuse over several years did to the U.S. economy in 2008 and 2009. On the other hand, responsible use of debt separates the flash-in-the-pan, on-paper millionaire from the multimillionaire who extends a legacy of wealth and prosperity into future generations.

Y*our Chapter 8*
Burst of Inspiration

• Stay away from the trap of "charge it today and pay for it never": the most surefire way to create your own bubble and burst it. There are a few financial statements you'll want to keep at your fingertips: your net worth worksheet and your debt meter. What's your net worth? How much are you paying in interest every day? Be sure to consult these as you make decisions, not only about acquiring properties, but also about acquiring new forms of debt. You want that net-worth number to rise year after year.

PART THREE

THE ARTIST AND THE CLOSER

You might think that the marketing and selling cycle starts when our mansions are unveiled, but it begins long, long before then. It's initiated the day I acquire the property. When I was buying and renovating entry-level homes, sometimes it began even *before* the property was mine. I don't recommend you do that—I certainly don't do it any more—but it gives you an idea of just how maniacal I can be about ensuring a bubble-proof investment strategy: from the outset, the goal is to *sell the property*.

In this part of *Burst This!* I'm sharing with you not just the principles behind our ingenious marketing plans, but also the plans themselves.

- In Chapter 9, you learn how to create a standout brand, starting today and extending through your next project, and the next, and the next, until you've reached the real estate utopia of having people so eager to see what you've done next that they line up to see *your* artistry unveiled, just as they do for our masterpieces.

- You'll see both a simple model and the detailed plan for marketing our mansions, which you can apply to *any* property—and any product, for that matter—in Chapter 10, where I deliver the Grade School Compass Approach to marketing, promotion, and sales.

- Chapter 11 reveals to you the necessary planning and key principles of a spectacular showing, where you heighten your buyers' senses to a state of subliminal euphoria, a state where they're inclined to buy quickly and decisively.

- The final chapter in this part of the book, Chapter 12, "Close the Deal, Close the Loop," gives you the essentials for finalizing the deal with your buyer and then reinforcing your brand and the wisdom of your buyers' purchase with some finishing touches almost no one else in real estate bothers to apply.

In every way, this part of the book is about setting yourself apart, doing what others rarely do, thereby shortening your time on market and building a brand that stands strong and tall in any kind of market. In the end, it's all about one thing: getting buyers to your property so they can see it and you can sell it.

9

ARTISTIC LICENSE: CREATING YOUR OWN BRAND

I magine you're one of about 400 people gathered on the beach, sipping "Manalapan mojitos," nibbling gourmet hors d'oeuvres, and anxiously awaiting the grand unveiling of the world's most expensive and opulent green house, Acqua Liana, a $29 million masterpiece. People around you talk loudly, commenting on each other's unusual attire. Some look like characters straight out of a horror film, while others have more of a sweetheart vibe—and a few have figured out how to dress both parts, reflecting the event's theme, "Friday the 13th Meets Valentines' Day." It's hard to tell who's who in this group, given that they're not in their usual "uniforms" of Armani suits and designer dresses, although you know there are power brokers, high-profile media people, and other VIPs in attendance. It's the hottest ticket in town.

The crowd has grown restless, as everyone was instructed to arrive at 7:00 PM *sharp*, and you've all been milling around for half an hour waiting for the show to start. The mansion remains hidden from view, shrouded by a giant curtain, onto which images are projected of the covers for the three books I'm launching at the same event: *Burst This!*, *The Tap*, and *Dead Fred, Flying Lunchboxes, and the Good Luck Circle*. Your anticipation has been building for months, as you've been watching the countdown ticker to this moment on Frank-McKinney.com since summer, and just three weeks ago, you got your invitation in the mail: a heart-shaped black box with red ribbon. Inside, you'd found custom candies and searched through them, looking for one with the word Sold on it, which would have entitled you to a private lunch with me in my oceanfront tree-house office, copies of all three new books, a ride in my 1988 Yugo mini-book-tour mobile, and a private tour of Acqua Liana. Only three of the invitations had yielded these prizes—think Willy Wonka and the coveted Golden Tickets—too bad someone else won all that cool stuff. But still, you are here, standing on some of the world's most prime real estate, ready to see something no one else in the world has created before: a $29 million ultraluxe estate, a gorgeous island-inspired home with unparalleled natural and handcrafted beauty, certified by the USGBC as being constructed to the highest standards of environmentally responsible building.

Finally! A spotlight sears the night sky, runs across the curtain concealing the mansion, and then stops on the roof. There I am, perched high above you. A videographer films me welcoming you so that it can be projected onto the curtain below, kind of like a Jumbotron big screen at a sporting event or concert. As I address my guests, I declare that, despite the world's recent economic troubles, the American Dream will never die. Standing on my creation—the largest green home ever built—I challenge anyone who dares to *try and burst this!*

"Allow me to present the finest ocean-to-Intracoastal home in the world, and remember the American Dream cannot be extinguished: No credit crunch, housing bubble, or market meltdown can kill it . . . For those who think it has been buried, think again!

"Yes! This magnificent masterpiece, Acqua Liana, is the American Dream come to life!"

Then, as fireworks ribbon the heavens with brilliant color and their explosions boom in your ears, the big screen features fast-moving images associated with the Frank McKinney brand: mansions we've created in the past, the good work of our nonprofit Caring House Project Foundation, prior bestsellers, and the new book releases. The three-minute video blast ends just as the last of the pyrotechnics fade, and while you're still reeling from this theatrical assault on the senses, you look down as the ground starts to rumble. Under the tent where you and the rest of the partygoers are standing to watch the show, an eerie fog begins to billow, and the soil erupts as a shiny black coffin slowly pushes through it, dirt and sand giving way as it slowly rises.

It stops just above the surface, and the crowd is buzzing. The top creaks open, and I emerge, wearing a costume that's a collision between Alice Cooper, Marilyn Manson, and Prince Charming (recall the theme for the night). As it's all happening, a live feed, showing me climbing out of the casket, the embodiment of the American Dream revived, appears on the screen.

Standing before the crowd that's raising a collective cheer, I proceed with Nilsa and Laura to escort guests up the driveway of Acqua Liana. As we walk, you're wondering, *How did he get from that rooftop to underground, right under our feet, in a matter of seconds?*

"Now," I say, "let's enter the finest ocean-to-Intracoastal home in the world!"

We drop the curtain to reveal the front of the home, the crowd erupts, and I open the front door. It's then you get your first glimpse of the interior of the house, a jaw-dropping, spectacular foyer unlike any other. *When you cross the threshold, that's when the show really begins.* In the blink of an eye, no one's focused on me anymore, and the home completely steals the spotlight.

* * *

On another day, at another ultra-high-end estate, my friend and direct competitor, Mark Pulte, hosts a more sedate gathering for a handful of people wearing their best "business casual." A harpist plays Debussy's *Arabesque* in the corner. An elegant butler serves wine and caviar from a silver tray. Guests talk softly and walk from room to room, quietly exclaiming over the stunning amenities. Mark, the creator of this most magnificently luxurious home, hardly says a word. He's quiet, understated, discrete—the antithesis of what people see as my flashy public persona. Brokers gently guide guests through an hour-long tour.

Who will sell the home, Mark or me? After all, we're competing in a buyers' pool of only about 50,000 people in the world who can afford the purchase. Yet *both of us* succeed with this market time and again, because both of us have developed a distinct identity in the marketplace, consistently repeated and associated with our top-quality products. **It's that *distinction*—the characteristics that *differentiate* us from the competition, make us *stand out*, and *draw* buyers in—which makes our brands so strong.** In the end, you can bet we'll both sell.

Just what is a brand? I define it not only as the name associated with your product (whether that's your own name or a business name), but also as the collection of attributes associated with that name that make you stand out from the crowd. The ultimate show of successful branding is to create *recognition* of those attributes among your target market, and you do this through the direct experiences you provide with your product, and through the influence of marketing and media (something we'll address in great detail in the upcoming two chapters). A person's experiences— such as walking through the property, seeing and appreciating your artistry, noticing the quality and attention to detail, reading about your latest creation in the paper or what you do to make a difference in their neighborhood—set their expectations as a buyer, influence their opinions, and ultimately help generate demand and desire for whatever you might offer. Whether you choose to build your brand on magic and theatricality, as I do, or understated elegance, as Mark does, or something altogether different, the objective is always the same. *Attract a buyer and sell your property.* Quickly. And at a premium.

Based on the strength of your brand, someday there could be a line of people breathlessly waiting for the finish date on one of your homes, no matter the price point. That's your Shangri-la, your real estate utopia, your *Burst This!* nirvana. The good news is that it doesn't take that much to get there. You simply need to . . .

- **Accentuate more of *yourself*.** This may seem like contrary advice, but it's vital. Not everyone is as theatrically inclined as I am (okay, very few people are as theatrically inclined as I am); you need to find the characteristics and features that make you and your properties unique, and accentuate one or more of them. There's no need to make something up—this chapter will show you how to maximize what you already possess to create a strong personal brand.

- **Create a superior product.** Closely associate your *artistry* and commitment to *quality* with your name or business name. That's one of the things Mark and I do similarly; although he doesn't fully furnish his homes, he does take the same painstaking care with every detail, and they are beautiful. In a seller's market, where properties are scarce, being even a little bit better than your competition will get you a lot more profit because buyers will clamor to bid on your homes. In a buyer's market, where a lot of properties are available and prices are falling, being just a little bit better than the other guy or gal can make the difference between being the house with no offers and the house that gets sold. By creating a superior product, the public (e.g., agents, buyers) will know it's worth their time to see what you have to offer.

- **Share your blessings.** In real estate, you must feature yourself as well as your products. A good reputation in your community will produce both goodwill and good connections that will help you and your properties stand out from the crowd. Make community contributions, volunteerism, or charitable donations part of your business plan. Not only are you able to do good, but you also get to do well. This approach is priceless, with immeasurable returns.

- **Build anticipation.** The branding and selling of a property starts the moment you purchase it and continues throughout building and/or renovations. Anticipation of your next masterpiece is your best friend when it comes to creating a quick sale and a strong brand. You must view every purchase, every sale, every event, every appearance as an opportunity to reinforce your brand and get the public excited about what you might do next.

FIRST, ACCENTUATE MORE OF YOURSELF

My mom used to ask me, "Mickey, why don't you just put out a sign and have an open house like everyone else?" I wish it was that easy, because deep down I am really very shy and would love to avoid the expense associated with our grand unveilings.

Back in the day, I used to don a pink gorilla suit, tie giant helium balloons to the roof, and apply Mylar strips to the fascia of the homes I was marketing. Our directional signs were lime green and sported still more balloons. Garish? Maybe—it was a bit like a used car lot—but there was a method to my madness. My mom's answer was contained in her question: I wouldn't do what everyone else did *because* everyone else did it. Even in the beginning of my real estate career, before I knew anything about branding per se, I understood the importance of getting my buyers' attention. I've never been big on conformity, so it came a little easier when I decided to do something out of the ordinary for my marketing. I also knew instinctively that I'd have to work with what I had: I couldn't be the singing real estate guy (I just don't have the pipes), so I took an aspect of my personality and accentuated that to the hilt. My flair for being contrary in a public forum and not worrying about the naysayers has proven to be one of my greatest business assets and the foundation of the Frank McKinney brand.

Even if I have fun doing what seems to be dramatic stuff, it's all for a purpose. Despite what some may whisper behind my back—

that these grand unveilings are merely a tribute to my ego, or that I am a frustrated actor who likes to play dress up and make a big scene just to aggrandize my own accomplishments—the real point of all this is, again, to bring people to the property *so it can show itself.* The theatrics don't come with the house. Shoot, the guy with the long hair and rock-and-roll front-man getup doesn't come with the house, either. Who would want him? I'm selling the home. But I'd be a fool if I didn't use all that I've got to draw people there, specifically people who are or know qualified buyers. You could say that I'm actually working toward getting a few of them to talk behind my back in another way. Like this . . .

Million-dollar broker on the phone to her best billionaire client: "Listen, I'm at that raucous grand opening of a home in Manalapan . . . yes, in Florida, on the oceanfront. I swear, this guy and his production are straight out of Vegas, and the whole scene is a little over the top for me, but you've got to see this estate! Whew, I'm telling you, it's unlike anything I have ever experienced before, and I know you'll love it. Yes: gorgeous, gourmet main kitchen with two of everything and the most beautiful countertops. And there's Hawaiian koa wood cabinets! Mmm-hmm. One of a kind. *No other estate has anything like them.* Right, the catering kitchen has top-of-the-line appliances, too. I'm going to send you to McKinney's website and mail you a full-color brochure, but let me tell you about this stunning water floor, and OMG, you gotta see the 2,000-square-foot master suite . . ."

That's the *real* objective.

Face it: real estate is a competitive business at every price point, so anything that sets you and your product/property apart from the crowd plays to your advantage. Yet I'm not suggesting that you

"King of the Ready-Made Dream Home"

Here's a more recent version of the pink gorilla suit—this was taken for the cover of USA Today *and designed to sell the $30 million home where it was shot, further reinforcing our brand.*

create an affectation—something that's not innate in you—to help you establish your brand. Instead, take a look at who you are, your individuality, what makes you unique. Don't kid yourself that there isn't anything. Maybe that one spark of uniqueness isn't exactly on fire yet, but that's the trick with branding: you pick one thing and then emphasize it to the point of being strikingly different from those around you. That's what makes a red-hot brand. Is there a distinguishing physical characteristic, like your height or a mustache or the red, white, and blue Uncle Sam's hat you like to wear? A way you interact with people: direct, charming, animated? The way you dress: impeccable with a $2,000 suit and tie with pocket square or couture right off the runway? Something you especially love: motorcycles, flamingos, trombone music? Truly, almost anything works. The tough-as-nails real estate cowgirl. The turtlenecked Euro-pop real estate guy. The one who's balding and grins a lot. The folksy one who winks and says, "gosh-darn it" all the time while calling herself a maverick (I really liked her). And on and on. Just like a politician or a media personality, you should find your standout attribute, and then work it.

Back in the seventies, a fellow named Cal Worthington ran indelibly memorable commercials on West Coast television stations. He always appeared in a wide-brimmed hat, but what was especially unusual always came right after the voice-over announcer saying, "Now here's Cal Worthington and his dog, Spot!" It was never a dog. A gorilla, a whale, a tiger, a goose, a snake, yes. But never a dog. And while Cal made his pitch with his arm around the creature, he always had this wry grin, as if to say, "Hey, at least you're paying attention!" The ad was actually a spoof on a competitor's commercials, but Cal found a way to use his fondness for exotic animals to heighten brand recognition, even though his product had nothing to do with his nonhuman friends.

Think about other familiar personal brands and what they represent. Oprah: uncanny communicator with down-home delivery, someone who gives back. Donald Trump: the hair, the comebacks, *The Apprentice*. Don King: loud, confrontational, self-assured (and he's another one who works the hair). Martha Stewart: organization, taste, style. Rachael Ray: the neighbor next door who could be helping you out in your kitchen. Dr. Phil: drawling straight shooter, "How's that working for you?" It's no coincidence that each of these people also possesses impressive business acumen. Strong branding is a central strategy for any successful business.

An established brand can help you reach buyers during all economic conditions: when your area's inventory is up and everyone vies for the attention of a small pool of buyers, when it's a seller's market and you need to capture the imagination of the one buyer who will pay top dollar for your creation, when area sales are steady but unspectacular and you need to generate some excitement. Branding can be your perpetual unfair advantage over your competition. It provides you a bubble-proofing formula for all times, all markets, always.

CREATE A SUPERIOR PRODUCT

Although I'm advocating that you take a "what works for me" approach regardless of the brand you develop, the infusion of what I call "art" is a critical piece. From the very first property you buy, improve, and then sell, the twin thought processes of artistry and brand originality must be underway. (I assure you, the homes under the helium balloons and behind the Mylar were as infused with my artistry as the ones I unveil now. They weren't as extravagant, but they were as carefully thought out and as aggressively branded. I always made sure that my houses were the nicest on the block, and you'd better believe that was how I marketed them.) The association between your name or your business's name and your unique stamp—between your brand and your artistry—builds the legacy, giving you staying power and the prestige to price your property for maximum profit. Put simply, **buyers always pay more for art and quality**, whether they're looking at a house for $300,000 or one for $30 million.

When I say "artistry," I mean the intrinsic approach you take with every idea, decision, and implemented touch you put on your properties. You are going to consider your work as a craft, just as many artists do. Your canvas is the property to be renovated or built,

Royal Grand Salon

From the beautiful Tuscan marble flooring to the elegant hand-cut crystal chandelier to the unique saltwater aquarium wall and unparalleled view of the Atlantic ocean over the disappearing edge of the 75-foot pool and spa, this opulent grand salon is unlike any other our buyers will encounter.

and your paint is the finishes and amenities you choose. You approach each project with great pride and creativity.

When I wrote earlier in this book that my fingerprints are on every square inch of a property, I was talking about everything from quality checking the installation of an air-conditioning vent to more substantial contributions, like the idea for including a giant water wall, or altering the design of the master bedroom ceiling to create majesty. As the construction of Acqua Liana was coming to a close, I made several changes as things were being finalized, from adjustments on window sizing so that we could get the light to hit the oversized blackened bamboo beams just right, to revisions within a waterfall. That waterfall was made of coral cap rock native to Florida, a beautiful color and texture, but the way the water outlets were placed, the whole thing was starting to look like the brow and eyes of a Cro-Magnon man with a nose like a hawk. We had to remove some of the rock to reshape the falls and their surroundings. Whether someone would have seen what I saw will remain unknown. This is just one instance where it was a chance I didn't want to take. Now, it's completely serene. No more spooky face, just a calm cascade of water over an alluring array of coral cap rock.

As you progress, those things jump out at you, even if you are not trained, if you just stand in the space and silently observe it. Quiet observation of your property may or may not be exactly the way you work, but I can tell you this: You won't create a masterpiece sitting in front of the TV or hanging out with friends. Artistry comes from some quiet recess of the mind, and I believe that you have to get away from external stimulation to let it surface. Allowing yourself this kind of free flow, and then following through with excellent craftsmanship, is what will allow you to sell your property for 10

The Place Where Creativity Flows

My getaway, where I wrote Burst This! *and my four other books, as well as design all of our oceanfront artistry. I find great inspiration in the solitude of my seaside tree-house office.*

percent above its comps, or unload it in a difficult market, and make a name for yourself—a brand for people to remember.

Even if you're still at the pink-gorilla-suit stage, go with it. Do all that you can to promote your brand and stamp your product with your originality and artistry. Stick with the improvement guidelines you've already read in this book, getting the most bang for your buck, making every dollar you spend count with your buyer. Given the competing properties, you need to help people discern yours from the wannabes. Your brand, whether it's represented by a flashing neon sign or an elegant banner whipping in the wind, points to your product: to its beauty, its artistry, its quality, its uniqueness, and its desirability.

SHARE YOUR BLESSINGS

Giving back has always been part of my DNA. Years ago, when I first started transitioning from buying and selling properties for $50,000 to the first property worth more than $2 million, still doing much of the sweat labor myself to save money, I made the time once a week to go out with a van sponsored by a local soup kitchen and hand out meals to the homeless. I didn't do it for the recognition or even to build up my identity in the community; I did it because I'd been raised to share my blessings with other people. It was from my interactions with people who had no homes that I found my charitable "calling": to house those who didn't have roofs over their heads and give them the stability of a place to come home to at night.

The Caring House Project Foundation was the result of this mission. It developed from my sincere desire to "balance the scales," to see my success benefit people other than me, specifically those who weren't enjoying the same advantages. It was inspired by my faith and a biblical passage that says, basically, *from those to whom much is entrusted, much will be expected.* When I gave it some thought, I realized that if you strip my professional calling down to its essence, I'm basically in the housing business. That pointed me to my spiritual calling, a desire to lift up those who suffer in the worst living conditions and assist them in building better lives. What started out as a once-a-week volunteer commitment grew into renting a renovated home to a man who'd been living on the streets, for a dollar a month. Now, with the nonprofit foundation, we build entire villages in some of the most underdeveloped nations around the world, providing a self-sustaining existence for the poorest of the poor.

I wrote a chapter about giving back in my first book, *Make It BIG!*, and it really struck a chord with many readers. In my newer book, *The Tap*, I explored the subject in depth, revealing how God has tapped me (and taps everyone) many times in life, answering prayers and presenting life-changing opportunities. Later, in the last chapter of this book, I'll revisit the subject briefly so you can see how important this aspect of business is to your succeeding in the business of life.

Even if you choose to participate only occasionally in a charitable effort or extend your hand to people in the neighborhood who need your help, being a "good" business is always good *for* business. Not only is it the right thing to do, but it helps the people around you know that while profit may be your motive, it's not your only concern. In short, it creates warm feelings and a deeper connection with like-minded souls in your community. The public has had it up to here with overcompensated and unregulated greed and the attitude of "everyone for him- or herself." Creating an identity for yourself as someone who cares for the greater good, associating compassion and humility with your brand, can not only make you feel good about yourself, but also make others feel good about you. (I have to confess, though, that I've never made others' perceptions of my charitable work a prime motivator. Their positive feelings have been a nice side effect, but they were never my objective. As Charlie "Tremendous" Jones once put it, that would not be true giving; it would be *trading*.)

Think about some of the big brands you know that have built social responsibility into their corporate culture and public image, which fosters customer loyalty and improves their brand acceptance: Target, with its various community giving programs that support nonprofits, disaster relief, schools, and so on; Ben & Jerry's Home-made Ice Cream, which has always made local, national, and international concerns part of its social mission; McDonald's and the Ronald McDonald House charities; as well as Starbucks and its "volunteer to volunteer" program furthering local efforts. There are also individuals who've decided to put philanthropy front and center, altering their personal brand in the process, such as Bono and Bill Gates, who I wrote about in *The Tap*. All of these brands, both corporate and individual, have been enhanced by their ongoing commitment to social values and ideals.

Because I'll revisit this subject in just a few chapters, all I want to do here is plant the seed: What could you do to contribute to those around you? Are there ways for you to give back that would enhance your brand, helping to establish it as a positive force in the local community?

BUILD ANTICIPATION

Effective branding isn't so much about convincing people to buy (although that tends to be the effect), but instead about carving yourself into the buyer's mental space—what marketers call "piece of mind"—wherein your name becomes synonymous with the product you sell. For example, it used to be that when someone thought of outrageously luxurious oceanfront estates in South Florida, they thought of Frank McKinney. Today I'm adding to that brand identity "ultra-high-end green homes that combine sound ecology, low carbon footprint, and guilt-free opulence."

What will make buyers think *of you?*

In an industry that traditionally has approached branding as an afterthought and open houses as an event worthy only of a few directional signs, maybe a cheese tray, and usually a broker either talking or texting on her mobile device—I'm clearly counseling you to do something different. Here's another occasion where you apply the contrarian approach. Forget what everyone else is doing, especially if you're in a crowded market with lots of properties for sale. You must do something different, and this something involves thought and hard work that will set you apart from the crowd and draw people to your open house instead of the others in the area.

As you've read, an open house can provide the sizzle that draws people close enough to the steak so they can go on and take a bite. It's the flash (even if you're not flashy) that transports people close enough to see the substance: your masterpiece, the property you've made irresistible, in which you've invested your hard work, your artistry, and no small amount of money. This is the crescendo and a priceless opportunity to reinforce your brand. Now your masterpiece is finally brought to the attention of your buyers and, in the process, you further entrench your brand and make your marketing for the next property that much more effective.

Yet the open house is hardly your only opportunity to create brand recognition and build anticipation. You want the public wondering, *What will you do next? When will I be able to see it? Can I own it?* Your branding effort must be ongoing. Elements of anticipation should be at work long before the first open house. For Acqua Liana, as with all of our properties now, we created a countdown on our website, ticking off the days, minutes, hours, and seconds to the grand unveiling; we also hosted quarterly brokers' open houses on the last Thursday of every quarter so the better brokers could see our progress toward completion. We sent out invitations by e-mail that were essentially "invitations to receive an invitation" to the grand unveiling, and the invitation itself further built the suspense with a prize contest and plenty of tantalizing descriptions of what attendees would experience. (Even on the night of the grand unveiling, we further built anticipation by *intentionally* delaying the start time, although we asked guests to arrive by seven o'clock sharp.) Still, it goes beyond that. Every home we've marketed before has been a branding effort leading up to the debut of our latest creation. Every media interview, every book signing, every keynote address reinforces the brand, keeps the Frank McKinney name out there, repeatedly associating our brand with our unparalleled product.

This may sound like a lot of activities to keep the brand in the forefront and build anticipation for our next release. And, yes, there are a lot of moving parts to the Frank McKinney & Co. machine—even more than what I've listed above, when you consider everything on our Quality Control checklists, the improvement timeline, and all marketing, sales, and promotion efforts as you'll read in the next chapter. That's why we do all that we can to lock in on the big picture even while we're following through on even the most minute details. In fact, we consider no more than ten "big picture" objectives per year, which helps us keep all efforts moving in the direction of those—and only those—ten initiatives. Even as I type this paragraph, under my right hand on my laptop is our Annual Objective Plan for 2008, right at my fingertips so I see it every day. This kind of constrained, relentless focus is what yields not only a superior product but a highly differentiated brand—one that keeps people excited to see what we'll do next.

Frank McKinney & Company
and Caring House Project Foundation
"The Beauty of Simplicity" Annual Objective Plan, 2008

Objective	Completion Date
1) Grade-school compass approach to marketing, promotion, and sales fully underway	By 6/30
2) Acqua Liana 100 percent complete	By 2/13
3) Host grand unveiling for Acqua Liana	By 2/13
4) Crystalina submitted to DEP	By 3/30
5) Crystalina, commence construction	By 10/1
6) Implement CHPF program of work	By 12/31
7) Hire office assistant for FMC and CHPF	By 1/31
8) Pursue executive apprentice who meets superior standards	Until found or not needed
9) Locate new, longer tenured headquarters	By 6/30
10) Perform quarterly AOP, GSCA, CHPF program of work and semi-annual employee reviews	3/31, 6/30, 9/30, 12/31
Notes:	

I'm convinced that keeping our business focused and stream-lined directly affects our days on market, putting major muscle behind keeping that number low and our margin high.

On average, it takes most sellers about fifty showings before a property sells. So when someone complains to me, "I've shown this house *thirty times*," I encourage them by reminding them they have only twenty more to go. But with a strong brand and clear business plan, you can start to whittle away at that average. Bubble-proof branding leaves averages in the dust. When I first started, I exceeded a 100-showings-for-every-sale ratio. Now, with our brand entrenched and our business laser focused on producing specific results, our ratio of qualified showings to sales is inside of 10 to 1—our efforts are paying off. Yours will, too.

In the next chapter, you'll be reading the nitty-gritty details of our Grade School Compass Approach to marketing, promotion, and sales: every action once the property is ready for market is intended to draw your buyers near, **and then to move them from a state of need or mere interest all the way up to desire by heightening their five senses to a state of subliminal euphoria.** I'll be revealing to you *everything* I do toward this end, from on-site marketing materials to staging the home to getting on national television to showing the property to potential buyers.

When you think about marketing your property, think of your brand as like that Golden Ticket, good for admission in good times and bad, through booms and busts. For now, I'll leave you with the words of Willy Wonka, assuring his Golden Ticket holder:

> Tremendous things are in store for you! Many wonderful surprises await you! . . . [You'll receive] other surprises that are even more

marvelous and more fantastic for you and for all my beloved Golden Ticket holders—mystic and marvelous surprises that will entrance, delight, intrigue, astonish, and perplex you beyond measure. In your wildest dreams, you could not imagine that such things could happen to you!

Your Chapter 9
Burst of Inspiration

• Ask yourself, *How can I stand out?* What elements of your appearance or personality can you accentuate? What parts of your individuality could contribute to your brand? How will you emphasize them in your business? How can you share your blessings with others? What will your golden ticket say?

10

THE GRADE SCHOOL COMPASS APPROACH: Run Rings Around Your Property—and Your Competition

Fact #1: Most people don't take marketing far enough, never closing the loop.

Fact #2: Marketing is so critically important that if you don't get it right, you will do the opposite of bubble-proofing—you will bubble-out: bust, bang, blow it.

Fact #3: Fully and properly implemented, the Grade School Compass Approach (GSCA) can make up for many unintentional shortcomings.

No matter how well you execute your buy, build, or improve, if the right people don't know that you have the best property on the market, and if you don't cause them to make the effort to see it, then what you have is not a piece of artistry or even investment property; instead, it's a beautiful and expensive secret with a debt meter constantly spinning, taking money out of your pocket every day the property's not sold.

On the other hand, marketing genius atones for a multitude of real estate sins, like overpaying (not buying right), blowing your budget, finishing late, and so on. You can't be a total bozo on the front end and hope to market your way out of it, but you *can* make plenty of mistakes and compensate for them when you implement a knockout marketing plan with military-like precision. To do this, you need to follow Frank McKinney's Cardinal Rule of Real Estate: **you must be marketing and selling from the moment you decide to buy.** From that very first hour, your goal is to draw potential buyers' attention to your "diamond" (or your diamond in the rough) with the long-term objective of showing the property and ultimately selling it for a handsome profit.

With every property we acquire, in the first hour we own it, we make sure there's no debris onsite and our For Sale sign is posted. We're ready to close the deal the moment a qualified buyer appears and offers us the right price, even if it's the first day we own the property. Keep that in mind as you read this and the next couple of chapters: The end game for all marketing efforts is to *attract potential buyers and show the property*, so that the selling can begin. The planning should start the moment you make your deposit. And the implementation should be underway the moment you yourself buy the land, or the teardown, or the simple fixer-upper.

Not too long ago, I read an article in *Fast Company* that extolled the virtues of simplicity. It revolutionized the way I look at marketing our properties. Using the lean, minimalist Google home page as an example, it pointed out how much more effective, efficient, and appealing to customers a business can be when it streamlines complex processes. Whereas other search-engine companies have allowed their home pages to be cluttered up with cyber-stuff—

tickers, ads, news, etc.—Google has stuck to the basics. They feature only their logo and a box where you type in your search term. As a result, Google dominates its market space. The point of the article was to suggest that in a world where complexity reigns (we're deluged with information, we have technological devices we have to spend hours learning to use, and so on), you're wise to offer a product that's beautifully simple for users to experience and enjoy—and to do that, you have to instill a culture of simplicity in your company. In short, you have to *zero in on the essentials.*

That's what sparked me to simplify and codify my marketing process into what I call the Grade School Compass Approach to marketing, promotion, and sales. This didn't mean that we took any shortcuts or "dumbed down" our marketing just to make it easy for us to implement. In fact, in a few pages, you'll see exactly how detailed the planning can get. But in the same way that there is an enormous amount of technological sophistication behind Google's home page, you'll put a lot of effort into making sure it's incredibly easy for buyers to see, hear about, visit, and ultimately buy your properties.

On the next page is the model for all of the marketing efforts that go into making sure our 50,000 target customers know about every Frank McKinney masterpiece.

You can see that our marketing is designed as six nested circles. You've heard of "running rings around the competition"? Here's how you do it: Run rings around your property, starting with the marketing tactics you'll deploy closest to home, "home" being the property itself. So the first ring you draw, using your grade-school compass with a metal point on one end and a pencil on the other (or a computer program that can do the same thing), circumscribes your

The Grade School Compass Approach to Marketing, Sales, and Promotion

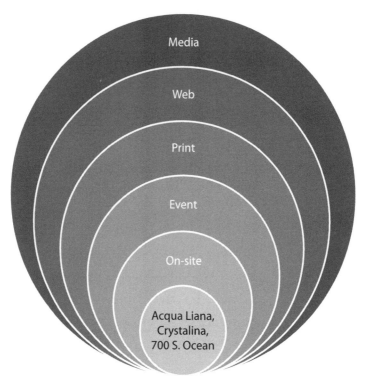

This reflects our efforts at Acqua Liana, Crystalina, and a large plot of ocean-to-intracoastal land at 700 S. Ocean.

property's address. Then, keeping your pencil tip on the bottom of the first ring, you move the metal point up so you're able to draw a larger ring, still touching the first but *widening the angle of attack*. And then you do the same for the next, and the next, until you have six rings altogether. The innermost sphere represents the property itself, and the outer orbits, from smallest to largest, outline five marketing spheres of increasing size and influence: *on-site, event, print, web,* and *media.*

Notice that each ring comes back to touch your property. This is key. While you'll use all five spheres as part of your marketing, you must start with the one closest to the property and move outward, because the property is the center of your universe, and the other marketing efforts are the planets in orbit around it. By approaching it this way, you'll be creating such gravitational force around your property that it begins to work like a black hole, pulling everything around it (your buyers) toward the center.

In other words, you **start closest to home and then expand, ring by ring, into the largest sphere.** You don't begin by thinking about how you'll make headlines in *USA Today*, or do guest spots on *Oprah* or *20/20*, or what the brochure will look like, or what your website needs to include; that's completely random, and this chaos would create complexity you don't want or need. Instead, you begin on-site, right outside the front door of the home or on the vacant lot where you'll build or in the lobby of the condo tower or what have you. Remember your endgame: get people to the property so you can show it. This requires that the property be ready to show at all times, and your marketing must start and radiate outward from there.

When I first created the Grade School Compass Approach, I began by completely rethinking our onsite marketing. For example, the most basic place you can differentiate yourself on-site is through your signage. Look around and see how crummy most real estate signs are. All our properties are on the ocean, and I can tell you that most of my competitors' signs are rusty, with corroded grommets, some hanging by a single hook off of an oxidized post leaning one way or the other, or having fallen down completely. All right, then, we roll up our sleeves and start with the sign.

While this is simple, if you pay this much attention to your sign, imagine how detailed you will be with the rest of your plan! So, how could we make (and keep) all of our signs crisp, clean, and upright? In collaboration with our real estate brokers, Premier Estate Properties (a Christie's Great Estates affiliate), we designed a completely new one made of reflective aluminum, which doesn't rust, uses no grommets, and is inserted into posts made of pressure-treated or recycled plastic lumber. There's no metal frame to tarnish, and the signs themselves are easy to see at night, so that when headlights hit them, drivers can clearly see them. We keep four spare posts and signs on-site so they can be replaced if they ever show any kind of wear, and everyone in our company, including me, carries a level, rag, and a bottle of glass cleaner when it is our turn to visit the property for quality review. Someone checks the signs at least three times a week, with my daughter, Laura, and me making the rounds on the weekends. You'd better believe that I also look at the signs myself every day I drive to the site.

With GSCA, you start by looking at the elements closest to you and expanding from there. Once you have great-looking signs, you need to stand on the property and imagine every angle from which someone could approach, and then place your signage accordingly. Most property sellers are lazy: they put a solitary sign right by the driveway. But what about the two-way traffic? And the fact that people are zipping by at, say, thirty miles per hour? By the time someone turns his or her head to look, it's too late. When you think it through, you realize that you need signs on both sides of the road. And not just *at* the driveway, but before it, too.

Have you ever driven I-95 South through North Carolina? Right over the state line in South Carolina is a funky place called

South of the Border. It's been a fixture on I-95 for as long as the road's been there. Now, there's almost nothing to recommend South of the Border; it's a hokey Mexican restaurant/truck stop with mediocre food, overly expensive souvenirs, and a very ordinary kids' play area and picnic grounds. But South of the Border certainly knows how to market itself. You start seeing billboards at least one hundred miles north of the exit that leads to it. And the billboards are just as silly as South of the Border itself—lots of bad puns, cartoonlike drawings, flashing lights, and animated figures. By the time you actually cross the state line, you almost *have* to stop at South of the Border just to see if it lives up to all its publicity! And you'll see the same kinds of billboards if you're approaching South of the Border from the South Carolina side. Those billboards have been up for so long because they work; they get people to turn off the interstate and head for the restaurant. Your signage has the same goal: to make people take the time to stop and look at your property.

Some people thought I was nuts when I started putting signage on the ocean side of our properties, until I explained that there were plenty of boaters—people in my target market—who cruise by on their yachts with their high-powered telescopes, ogling the oceanfront estates and people on the beach, and I wanted them to know who to contact if they were interested in one of my properties. Not to mention the friends of other oceanfront residents who might be out for a morning stroll and could grab a brochure to pass the time. Again, I was focused on the endgame: *Attract buyers so you can show the property.* To do that, you have to point to the property in every way conceivable, and then ensure that potential buyers know who you are and how to contact you.

You may or may not need to worry about rust and two-way traffic down a coastal road where you live, but my point is this: We spent a fair amount of time and invested a good bit of ingenuity on *a single element*. Know that in our marketing plan we have 165 activities, and this was only one. Each of the 164 others deserves—and gets—that kind of attention, too.

I know this is a lot of attention paid to the lowly real estate sign, but yes, marketing with hyperattention to the details is *that* important.

So much of this falls in the "Really, Frank, I know—I got this" category, but, as I said, most people fall short because they think the most minute details are unimportant. There's that "when was the last time you did something you know" ringing in your head. They don't close the loop; they go 90 percent of the way, and then leave the rest hanging in the wind like a rusty sign. *That 10 percent is the difference between selling after fifty showings, or selling after only ten.* It's the difference between the average days on market, wherever you live, and a blindingly fast sale. I'm telling you, every detail is important, from having impeccable and well-placed signs to whether the screws in your switch plates line up perfectly north-south.

Coming right up, I'll show you *exactly* how we close the loop; I'm giving you the entire Grade School Compass Approach as adapted for Acqua Liana, our $29 million ultraluxury green estate, which you can modify for your own properties, whether they're single-family homes, apartment buildings, commercial space, or any other kind of real estate. Why do I give this to you? No matter the size, price point, or features of your property, the fundamentals of marketing are the same at every level. Once you follow them, you too can drive traffic to your properties and close the deal faster and more profitably than your competition. You will have created such a strong gravitational pull through the implementation of the five rings that your buyers will cluster and clamor for your artistry.

Once you've reviewed the Acqua Liana plan, you'll need to take the time to consider what you'll apply or modify with your own offerings, highlighting every activity from my plan that you want to include in yours. You'll also want to ask yourself the questions I've provided at the end of this chapter to develop additional tactics specific to your offering(s). But you don't have to start from scratch. Don't do that to yourself! Use what I've given you here to ensure that you cover the entire universe of possible marketing avenues, and then give it your own unique spin. And I might have missed some, so please do share with me.

Warning: Don't gloss over any of these areas, assuming that another ring will make up for one that's weak. **Approach each ring as if it's the *only one* upon which you'll be able to rely.**

What follows is the *narrative* version of the GSCA for Acqua Liana. Be aware that a single standard or activity (e.g., "physical site always clean," "grand unveiling," even "rust-proof signs") most always carries with it a whole laundry list of tasks and important contributing parties, which will need to be enumerated so that you and your team can carry them out. We always translate the GSCA narrative into the GSCA *accountability spreadsheet* that we use to track every necessary activity through to completion. That's where all 165 line items get delineated, scrutinized, implemented, and then checked off the list.

For each of the rings of Acqua Liana's GSCA, I've included comments to help you interpret what you're reading and, as they say, *see around the corners* to what may not be immediately obvious simply by reading a list.

THE CENTER OF YOUR UNIVERSE: THE PROPERTY

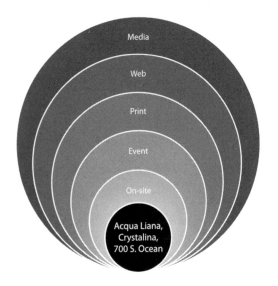

In the narrative version of the GSCA for each property, we include the address and description of what the estate will become.

Acqua Liana, 620 South Ocean Blvd., Manalapan, Florida. Our $29 million, 15,071-square-foot home and guesthouse on 1.6 acres, with 150 feet of direct ocean-to-Intracoastal frontage that reflects Balinese, Tahitian, Fijian, and Polynesian architecture. Certified green by the U.S. Green Building Council and the Florida Green Building Coalition.

You can adapt something from your vision and passion statement to use here, abbreviating it for a concise account of what the property will be and why it will appeal to buyers.

Ring #1: On-site

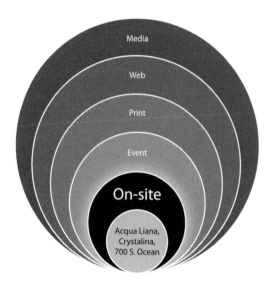

Taking nothing for granted, we're careful to list out the essential standards of upkeep for the grounds, inside the home, and the sales center:

Grounds. New reflective/rust-proof For Sale and Open House signs with rust-proof posts, always clean; four replacements on-site; signs placed at ocean, on street, and on docks. Clean brochure boxes at ocean by stairs, at street entry, on docks (12) full with fresh brochures (200 replacements on-site). Frank McKinney & Co. sign on front and sea walls. Lighted display sign at beach with blow-up photos of model and floor plans; brochure box affixed to display and seawall directly below. Spotlights on house, stairs to beach. Physical site always clean.

Inside Home. Marketing efforts reflected inside when home complete to include brochures throughout, FM books strategically placed; for showings: drinks, chocolates, nicer snack foods, DVDs (narrated home tour and appropriate movies), TV stations, shoe booties, temperature setting, lighting setting, music choice and setting; to include in garage: construction progress photos, home model, framed model photos.

Sales Center. Always clean. Frank McKinney & Co. signs on outside. Brochures (first temporary, then permanent) in stand by front door; four replacement stands on-site. Portfolio of prior projects (two copies). Portfolio of dated construction progress photos. All models (three) neat and clean with mirror on the outside wall of the models. Floor plan (not bent) laminated and set on wall shelves. Model blow-ups framed and hung on walls. Blown up and dated construction progress photos. Material samples in Nilsa's trailer. Framed LEED logo. Full bound set of brochure floor plans (ten sets of each); laminated set of brochure floor plans. Full set of construction drawings. Clean progress camera lens, adjusted for best possible resolution.

Use this part of the narrative to help you avoid making the usual mistakes on-site, which hinder the sale and reflect poorly on your brand. As already noted, these include signage wrongly placed, cock-eyed, or corroded. It's also common to see empty brochure boxes ("Please take one"? What am I supposed to take, air?), or brochures ruined, faded by the sun, soaked by the rain, ripped by the wind. Remember the power of a first impression: avoid an unkempt, uncared-for appearance of the property itself, with overgrown plant matter at the property lines, mail piling up in the mailbox, landscaping untended (e.g., lawn overgrown and bare spots of dirt where mulch should be)—even trash as small as cigarette butts in the neighboring area, on the street or adjacent lots, can make your property less attractive. We go as far as policing our neighboring properties.

Get those things right, however, and you're already well ahead of your competition in attracting potential buyers. Then you're poised to take yourself and your business to the next level by helping people see, even while the property's still undergoing transformation, what it will become. Most properties look a mess up until the last month, with the dust flying and contractors everywhere, so you're wise to post illustrations or photos of the artistry you're creating. A rendering of the finished product, a scale model, photographs of finished details, and photos taken of the model and converted to brochures that make the home look finished. While some of these applications are a little more expensive, giving your buyers the proper first impression is well worth the investment. All these help to tell the "story" of your property and get buyers salivating even before you're ready to show the finished product.

From the word go, you also want to light your property so that even at night, it draws attention. After the sun goes down, you want people driving or walking by to notice it and your For Sale signs. If you're marketing a property during winter in an area where it snows and the leaves fall off the trees, use lighting to make the home festive. Be creative in setting an atmosphere that makes buyers feel as if they've come home for the holidays—and every day

Whether you have a detached sales center or designate a room in the house to serve as one, this also must be inviting, reinforce your brand, and captivate your potential buyers' attention with the story of the property—where it's been, what it's become, what it could be for the person who moves in. You'll stock the sales center with all the information someone might want (brochures, floor plans, blueprints, construction drawings, what have you—more on that when we get to Ring #3, Print) and also give them ways to experience the home even before it's complete—material samples they can touch, progress photos they can see to gain a sense of how far you've come, and so on.

- We always blow up the floor plans to a size of two and a half by three feet so that people can really study the layout of the home, letting their imaginations wander through the rooms. Once we start showing the home, potential buyers also carry a laminated copy of the floor plans, hole-punched in one corner and collected on a key ring, as they walk through. (Occasionally one goes home with someone, but that's okay. They're inexpensive to produce.)
- We also provide a portfolio of our prior projects: it's beautiful and helps to establish credibility for anyone who's unfamiliar with our masterpieces. If you've completed other properties, be sure to create a portfolio of your own, so that buyers can admire your previous work and feel confident in your track record.
- If you're going green, by all means feature that. We have a framed LEED logo in the sales center, and we apply it to all our printed materials, on the Web, and anywhere we promote the estate.

The key principles here are to make the property *accessible* (meaning easy to spot if someone happens by and easy to find if someone is looking for it), *attractive, informative while your buyers are there* (to tell a story while they contemplate purchasing), and *obviously for sale*. Below, I've included a sample Quality Control Checklist, which we use to police the site at least twice a week, and always before a showing, to ensure that it always looks magnificent. (In addition to the QCC, We have a separate Quality Review (QR) Checklist we use prior to showings, and I'll share that with you at the end of the next chapter, in which I reveal all my secrets to creating a one-of-a-kind experience for potential buyers as they see the property for the first time.)

Frank McKinney & Company
Acqua Liana Quality Control (QC) Checklist

Weekly Interior QC (use green cleaning products throughout)

❑ Vacuum all carpet to show perfect lines, carry Chem-Dry spot remover as you vacuum

❑ Vacuum wood floors (don't use rotary head). Remove any streaks, then mop w/ wood floor cleaner

❑ Mop stone floors w/ suggested marble cleaning solution

❑ Light mop glass water floor with diluted solution of vinegar

❑ Wipe down countertops with green glass cleaner (kitchens, baths, bars)

❑ Clean all brass, nickel, stainless, etc., fixtures & hardware

❑ Dust all rooms (furniture, picture frames, window sills, etc.)

❑ Clean all sinks

❑ Clean all mirrors and interior glass

❑ Clean toilets & fold toilet paper neatly to a diamond-tip point

❑ Keep all storage cabinets or storage rooms neatly organized

❑ Have ample supply of shoe booties (floor protection) by front door

Weekly Exterior QC (use green cleaning products)

❏ Rinse & squeegee exterior window glass & frames (including light fixture glass, camera lenses, brochure box glass, etc.)

❏ Pick up all trash by street and on entire property (neighboring properties also)

❏ Sweep or blow off then rinse exterior decks/drives/railings (bedrooms, pool, cocktails bale, summer kitchen, family room, 2nd floor (main and guest), water garden walkways, loggias, driveways)

❏ Wipe down countertops, sinks, and barbecue at summer kitchen & tennis bar (check inside of cabinets for bugs, trash, etc.)

❏ Seal & protect stainless in sinks, barbecue, refrigerators, gate entry keypad, exterior shower fixtures, and all other metal and stainless

❏ Water plants in pots on decks and check sprinkler coverage

❏ Spray Boeshield T-9 on all door hardware, hinges, A/C units, pool equip, aquarium equip, all exterior metal that needs it that is not a part of the mandatory monthly T-9 treatment (see below)

❏ Check exterior light bulbs then clean & trim away leaves & branches to allow ample light

❏ Clean off dock

❏ Clean out waterfalls and ponds and make sure fountains are clear

❏ Freshen up mulch in high visibility areas that need it— always keep some mulch on hand

Periodic Mechanical QC (use green products)

❑ Daily—feed the fish (aquarium & ponds) once a day by hand

❑ Weekly—walk entire property (inside and out) to change burnt-out light bulbs

❑ Weekly—clean filter in pool, waterfalls, and fountain

❑ Monthly—perform water floor full maintenance

❑ Monthly—change all air-conditioning filters

❑ Monthly—T-9/lube: window cranks & parts, door locks, throw bolts, cabinet hardware & hinges, canvas curtain track, pool, spa, winch, waterfall motor equip, front gate operable swing arms, auto garage door chains, exterior A/C units, aquarium equipment, light fixtures, & all exterior metal

❑ Monthly—remove dirt/dust from all central vacuum canisters

❑ Monthly—remove and clean silt, dirt, mulch from fabric covering all drainage grates

❑ Monthly—clean mister heads by bridge and waterfalls

❑ Monthly—start generator

❑ First few months—clean faucet aerators

❑ First few months—test all appliances, toilets, faucets, fireplaces, etc. —"run the house"

I know you're saying to yourself, *Wow! That's a lot of detail. Do I really need all of this?* Maybe not, but I would rather give it all to you and let you decide. Of course, you won't want to cut out what you know will set your property apart. Because of this thorough attention to detail during the maintenance phase, after all construction is complete, our homes tend to continue to look better and better for six months after the grand unveiling. Eventually, they plateau and stay at that very, very high standard until they're sold. We go as far as providing this same list to our buyers after closing so they can keep the house looking magnificent.

RING #2: EVENT

Expanding from the site and now reaching out to potential buyers, you plan events that will get them interested in visiting the property:

While under construction. Quarterly open house for brokers in order to update them on progress; e-mail blast and fax to regional brokers for notice; follow-up; thank-you notes to those who attend. Individual on-site meetings with brokers' offices. Occasional "hard hat" open house for VIPs.

After Completion. Special-event open houses (green education opportunities), special events (showcase cars, art, etc.). Grand unveiling.

I've already described open houses in some detail and will revisit them again in the next chapter, but they're not the only events that help generate local buzz about your property. My schedule is always dotted with keynote addresses, presentations, and other community events. This keeps my name in front of the public and gives me a chance to create interest in the properties we are building.

When I was first starting out, I held free home-buying seminars. I'd put on a pair of my tennis shorts and act as if I was just some guy hired to hand out flyers, going door-to-door in apartment buildings and talking to people as I gave them the event agenda: "Hey, this looks kind of interesting. It says you can stop paying rent and own a home. I think I'll go and see what it's all about!"

At the seminar, which was held in a church meeting room or local school auditorium, I'd talk about the advantages of ownership versus renting and finding a home to fit your budget. I'd explain down payments, closing costs, loan products (FHA, VA, conventional), and what you have to do to qualify to own your own home. I'd tell them what the bank or mortgage company would need from them and introduce my unique "Mortgage Qualifier Program," that basically took them by the hand and led them through the process of obtaining financing: how to apply, how to clear credit blemishes, how to write to creditors to obtain judgment releases, etc. I'd then distribute prequalification worksheets, pictures of houses I had for sale that would fit most attendees' budgets, and information packages on those properties. At the end, I'd collect the prequalification sheets and take questions. You can bet that more than one person asked how soon they could get into one of the houses I'd shown them.

Here's an example of the kind of information I distributed on a home, taken verbatim from one of my old 1986 handouts, which I unearthed recently.

Below is a list of properties that may suit your taste and budget. Please call on any of these if you are interested, as the list is always updated.

Important to keep in mind when looking for or considering any property is the fact that you are talking to the owner. If there is something you want added or changed in the house, all you have to do is ask, and in many cases we will be happy to make that change or addition for you—at no cost to you!

1218 South "F" Street, Lake Worth, Florida

This home is a beautiful, quaint two-bedroom, one-bath home that has been meticulously renovated and maintained. It sits on a nice size lot with a fenced backyard containing grapefruit and orange trees. You may not be able to tell the difference between this home and a new home, except for the price!

Some of the amenities/improvements include:

- Rebuilt kitchen cabinets
- A/C-heat unit
- New carpet and tile throughout
- Screened-in front patio with new roof
- Carport with new roof
- Freshly painted
- New landscaping
- Nearly new appliances
- Rear storage and utility area
- Sprinklers
- And much more

This home happens to be a great starter home that reminds many of the "little cottage" under the ficus tree. A home in this price range is sure to appreciate rapidly. At the price quoted below, this home will sell fast! Call today, (561) 274-9696 (collect).

Selling price..$49,500
Down payment...$1,500
Closing costs......................$1,400—**Guaranteed!**
Monthly payment ....$400 to $499 (approx.)

Although I have to laugh a bit when I see how simple this was so many years ago, I have no doubt that information and seminars like this would work equally well today with potential buyers of starter homes. It's a great way to educate the public about their options; many people who rent have no idea that they could buy, may be worried about the current market and wonder if they will ever qualify for a mortgage, or have heard that the banks aren't lending anymore, and are in the dark about what they could do to fix their credit and start living the American Dream. So you provide a valuable service while getting the opportunity to show your properties to people who are squarely in your target market. This approach works with any property you are trying to sell; it would be wise and cost-efficient to have a mortgage company or bank sponsor the event, with loan officers on-site to prequalify your potential buyers.

In addition to holding events off-site, if you're in a longer project, you'll also want to conduct precompletion events on-site to help build anticipation. We hold quarterly "hard hat" open houses for high-end brokers and even a few VIPs that have bought from us before, or who might be a neighbor to our project and might know someone in the market. We want to keep them abreast of our progress and always build anticipation toward completion. Here's an invitation to one of these that we sent out to promote Acqua Liana:

Frank McKinney and Premier Estate Properties
invite you and your office to a

"Hard Hat Open House Event"

The FINAL in a series of "Hard Hat Open Houses"
to experience the creation of "Acqua Liana," Mr. McKinney's new
$29 million direct Ocean-to-Intracoastal certified "green"
Tahitian/Fijian Estate. Completion 2.13.09.
http://www.frank-mckinney.com/acqua_liana.aspx

Mr. McKinney will be on-site to share completion details.

620 South Ocean Blvd.
Offered at $29,000,000

Manalapan Beach, FL
½ mile south of the Ritz Carlton on A1A
(The road is under construction, so mention the above address.)

Thursday, January 16, 2009
12 PM to 4 PM
Gourmet lunch will be served.
RSVP (561) 274.9696

Hosted by Broker Associate: Pascal Liguori
Premier Estate Properties, Inc.
Affiliate of Christie's

As you can see, we provide good food (always a draw), and I make a point of being there myself to talk with brokers about the home. We write our thank-you notes in advance with a personal message from me and one from our broker, too, so that they can be sent out to attendees promptly the next morning. Below is an example:

Dear Brokers and Agents:

I want to commend you for taking the time yesterday to visit and educate yourself regarding the progress toward completion of our beautiful direct ocean-to-Intracoastal home known as Acqua Liana ("water flower") at 620 South Ocean, Manalapan. (http://www.frank-mckinney.com/acqua_liana.aspx)

It is clear that you came to gather information to allow your clients to make a well-informed decision. That is the mark of a good broker.

The season will be upon us shortly, so be sure to circulate your new knowledge as soon as practical. In doing so, be the beacon of optimism and opportunity that I know you can be. We all know there is plenty to counter this approach that is poisoning our airwaves.

In addition to providing your clients with the brochures you collected, the above link contains stunning photos, two Live Progress Cameras, a Progress Blog that I update regularly, monthly Aerial Progress Photos, recent Media Coverage, a Downloadable Color Brochure, and even a Grand Unveiling countdown ticker.

Should you have a buyer in mind, please contact Pat Liguori directly at (561) 665-8177. As always, we would love to pay you the selling commission!

Sincerely,
Frank McKinney
http://www.frank-mckinney.com/

These precompletion events are so well attended that often I can't give more than a minute or two to each person, so I also meet with a handful of brokers one on one to give them my full attention. (This large attendance is unusual in our industry; the last one we held had more than a hundred guests, which is a testament to our brand recognition.) These are the brokers who have the greatest likelihood of selling the estate to one of their clients, so we invite them for private showings and a sit-down.

The first open house you hold when your property is complete is, of course, the big crescendo. You already know what lengths we go to when unveiling one of our masterpieces—I've jumped my motorcycle, dressed like a pirate, rode ashore on a jet ski, buried myself in a coffin, and done plenty more outrageous things to get all eyes on our estates. What will you do? Even if you're working on a much smaller scale, you can still plan a knockout event: Invite a crowd—prominent people from your area, their friends, some brokers—decorate the house, have a ceremony to declare it's finished and open to see, give a tour, talk about its special green features, and feed folks. You'll want to start planning this event far in advance of your project completion so that you can make it extraordinary and garner some press.

Once the home has been unveiled, we also host special events. At one of our estates, we once allowed Christie's to have an art auction, providing the perfect setting for them—and the right crowd for us to have on-site. Bidders came to consider a handful of pieces of art valued at a minimum of $10 million each; the collection was worth over $200 million. Yes, those were the right people to see our property, which was listed for $37 million. If you were to apply the same principle but at the other end of the price spectrum, you could invite the local PTA or other parent group, community service organizations, book clubs, and the like to meet in a property you're selling. When you get a home green-certified, this opens up still more possibilities, opportunities to invite people who care about environmental issues. You will always be on-site at each event to explain what went into the creation of your artistry.

The whole purpose of events, from repeat open houses to special presentations, is to *raise awareness of your brand and your property* in the local community, especially among those who are in a position to buy and others who know people in your target market.

RING #3: PRINT

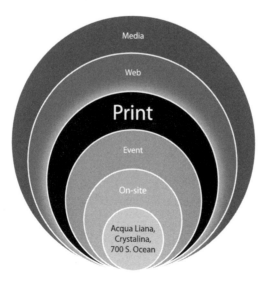

With printed media, you're giving people something they can hold in their hands and possibly take away so that they can refer to it and possibly share it with others, and that includes everything from the ad you place in the local freebie paper to the flyers you post on poles in the neighborhood to the most beautiful, eight-page, full-color brochure you hand out to prospective buyers. It's all about getting people to see the property and imagine that they're in it, touching the smooth countertops, burying their toes in the soft carpet, smelling the flowers, and listening to the birds in the garden ... you get the idea.

Collateral. Brochures (model photos, mood photos, floor plans, captivating text, contact information; text modified/updated/improved prior to reprinting. Other FM property packages (ten). Floor plan—only sets bound in large size for legibility. 8½ x 11 model photos (twenty).

Display advertising/magazines. Luxury Florida Homes, Unique Homes, Palm Beach Real Estate Guide, New York Times Magazine, Homes of the Hamptons, ShowBoats International or marine publication, the *Wall Street Journal, South Florida Sun-Sentinel* or *Palm Beach Post, Palm Beach Daily News* (shiny sheet), brokerage-specific magazine (Estates Portfolio), brokerage-affiliate magazine *(Christie's Great Estates)*, Ritz-Carlton or The Breakers hotel magazines.

For potential buyers and brokers, the brochure gives them a piece of the property to bring home. It's encapsulated in the photos of the details of the place and possibly a photo of a model, your rendering, plans, "mood" photos you include to evoke a feeling of serenity, opulence, and the feeling of their own private resort. It conveys the warmth of "I'm home" with captivating text, and it provides contact information. Over time, this brochure should actually improve—every time you reprint, you must revisit the text, thinking about what you've learned about your buyer and your property since the last time you printed, making new word choices, eliminating what doesn't work, and constantly ratcheting up the property's appeal on paper. In other words, refresh the copy. Even if you're not a great copywriter, you can work with someone who is, and you can explain to him or her exactly what you're trying to do: tap all five senses with your descriptions, put the reader *in* the home, help move people from mere interest to desire.

Even at the entry level, you should have a brochure. A simple, double-sided 8½ x 11 color copy may be sufficient, as long as you follow my suggestions above. Choose pictures over an abundance of words. The higher your price point, the more you should invest in your brochure. Ours are at least eight pages, professionally designed with professionally photographed images, printed in full color on glossy paper, and bound. (You can download Acqua Liana's brochure from our website by going to http://www.frank-mckinney.com/ acqua_liana.aspx.) Consider what your potential buyer is expecting—and then deliver more than that. In an entry-level home, show that it has amenities buyers would never expect to find in a home at this price; in a high-end property, show that it takes luxury and convenience to an unparalleled level.

For those people who respond much more to pictures than to text, you'll also want to have a few photos available in larger format. We blow up the images used in our brochures to 8½ x 11, because the larger photographs show all the amazing detail.

When potential buyers visit the site for showings, hand them a set of floor plans that you've laminated, hole-punched, and bound on a key ring so they can refer to them as they walk through the property. Again, you're giving them something to touch, to hold, so they can start feeling possessive—that's exactly the frame of mind you want to set for your potential buyers.

Another aspect of print marketing helps you enlarge your circle and reach a wider audience: paid advertising. Typically, your broker will foot the bill for most of this, although you may choose to supplement. As you're selecting a broker (and you'll read more about this in the Miscellaneous section of this chapter), one of the questions you should ask is where they typically advertise—and then you need to review those publications. Find like-kind properties and evaluate how that broker's ads stack up against their competition. How do they look? Are they bigger or smaller than the rest? Are they dull (like most of them), or more eye-catching? Does the copy sizzle? Are the ads in good locations within the magazine or newspaper? If you like the way a certain one looks, you go back to the broker and let him or her know that this is what you'll be expecting—is that their intention? You'll also want to ask about the broker's response rates. How often do they get calls from a particular ad? Learn which ads give them the greatest number of leads to follow and convert.

You can see in the Acqua Liana GSCA narrative that we always advertise in high-end publications that cater to the most affluent readers. The most important factors to consider in placing ads yourself or evaluating your broker's choices are these:

- **Demographics.** Choose publications that target readers who match the description of your potential buyers. We place ads in international media because our buyers live all over the world. If your buyers will be local, stay local with your advertising. If you're selling starter homes, think about what renters and young buyers read: the local paper's lifestyle section, the area real estate guide, free publications on family and parenting. Often, such publications will be able to give you their readers' demographics, along with circulation data.

• **Circulation and shelf life.** Be sure to ask your advertising representative for the latest numbers: How many people read the publication? How long do they typically keep it around? We advertise in the Ritz-Carlton's and The Breakers' hotel magazines because some of their customers are in our target market, and because the magazines are published once a year. We pay a single fee for a single ad, and because it's rare for us to take longer than a year to close the deal on a property, we can advertise once and be done with it.

• **Budget.** Obviously, budget is a concern. Full-page ads can run $3,000–$5,000 per insertion for a major national, glossy-back publication, while many local publications offer a run rate at far less than $1,000 per issue. Always negotiate with the assumption that you will be placing your ad more than one time per year, as most publications come out monthly or quarterly. Establish a budget and stick to it.

• **Size.** You'll want to choose the size of your ad over number of publications any day. Given your budget, determine the three best publications, then narrow that to two, but choose to run full-page ads where you can, yet not less than a half-page. I have always opted for much larger ads where possible.

Early in my career, I augmented paid advertising with flyers and direct mail. When I was selling starter homes, I used all three in rental communities and throughout the neighborhood where my property was located. They communicated the details of the home and announced open houses, featuring color photos and, again, captivating text. "Papering the neighborhood" is still an excellent strategy for marketing entry-level properties: you can post flyers in grocery stores, dry cleaners, fitness centers, community centers, and so on, as well as leave them on doorknobs and send them through the mail. Keep these guidelines in mind:

- **Stay close.** Whether you're mailing, nailing to a post, or going door to door, stay within a few miles of your property. Especially at the entry level, people like to stay within the same general area so that they don't have to change school districts, or drive farther to work or church, and so on. Put special focus on any rental complexes in the area.
- **Make it last.** Extend the shelf life of your flyer by including multiple open house dates instead of just one grand opening. You'll be holding open houses every weekend until the property sells, as described in Chapter 11.
- **Stand out.** Feature a color photo of the property, and include at least one other "detail shot," showing the interior. Any open house information should be emphasized with bold type, a box around it, or some other graphic device. Be sure to include the asking price, your phone number, and your web address.

Many realtors will produce and distribute their own direct-mail pieces, targeted toward people who can afford your property; your flyer can be used for that purpose, or you can do this on your own. For my estates, we mail a full package, including brochure, to Fortune 500 CEOs, clients of Christie's auction houses, and clients who have already bought homes in the current property's price range. Mailings are also sent to targeted affluent people in ZIP codes throughout the United States. You can purchase mailing lists based on demographics, income, or location—lists of renters in the area, or people with children, and so on—for your own direct-mail campaign.

Ring #4: Web

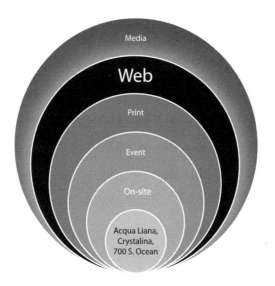

I can understand skimping on printed materials, as some people argue that "nobody pays attention to print anymore," and, to a certain extent, print media have experienced diminished impact in the last ten years or so, but I see it making a comeback as people will want to hold something again. Electronic media, however, just keep getting bigger, more pervasive, more accessible. Anyone interested in buying a property can find plenty of choices online, virtually tour the offering, and not have to contact a broker to do any of it.

Notice how comprehensive this section of the GSCA plan is:

Dedicated page on Frank-McKinney.com. Update captivating text monthly; flash model and mood photos; link to media coverage (brand building and project-specific); grand unveiling countdown clock; live progress camera (two); construction progress photos (most recent and archived); current progress blog; link to Green Giant trailer; link to property-specific video upon completion; LEED logo; link to down-loadable brochures (pre- and postcompletion versions).

Dedicated page on broker's site. Link from broker affiliate to Frank-McKinney.com; feature rotating display on broker's home page.

Other Internet exposure. E-marketing, including blasts to VIPs; affiliate links to luxury websites; search-engine optimization; pay-per-click advertising; buy similar domain names; blog; YouTube, Facebook, MySpace, etc.; Webinars/teleseminars.

You can go to Frank-McKinney.com to see how robust our Web presence has become—it's a crucial part of our marketing strategy, and it will be for you, too. Save yourself a significant amount of time and either copy what we have done there, or have your broker do so. From an administrative perspective, we touch our website *every day* with some new upgrade, text enhancement, photo, link, article, etc. Look at all of our content. This is a living, breathing, ever-evolving domain that can catapult your marketing efforts to gain serious results. I know of at least two instances—a $50 million home and a $10 million home—where sales resulted directly from our online presence. Both owners have told me, separately, that if it wasn't for what they'd been able to see on my site, they never would have made the trip to see the estates in person. One of them viewed the video tour on Tuesday, got the Gulfstream V gassed up and came to see me the next day, and was sleeping in the estate on

Friday. *All because of a video he saw online.*

If we were allowed only one additional marketing ring beyond "on-site," this is the one we'd pick, no question. We average 600 visitors a day (not hits, as those can be misleading), with people who spend more than five minutes looking at the site. Granted, they may be looking at the books, events, the charity, or other pages seemingly unrelated to the estates we have for sale, but it's all brand building. And if someone is interested in the oceanfront estates? The properties are prominently featured, with dedicated pages for each one with pictures, that all-important video tour, descriptive text, progress blogs, and downloadable brochure, as well as a portfolio of prior projects, and an easy fillable form so a qualified potential buyer can receive more information in the mail.

If you have any intention of building a business—if you're buying a property for investment and not your own family's homestead—you must spend the money and hire a top-notch web designer to get your site up and running and looking spectacular. You want to be able to make many changes yourself ("admin" yourself), to update text and at least some photos at any time, and your designer will need to know that in advance. If your designer balks, find one who won't. This kind of site costs a little more up front, but you'll save on time and administration fees in the long run, and your data will always stay current. This is one of *the* most beneficial aspects of marketing online: it can evolve and provide viewers/followers up-to-the-minute information on your offerings and events.

You can find all kinds of information on how to build a following online; I'm not going deeply into that here, but you may find it applicable to your business, so it's worth mentioning. Often, people working toward this start out by offering some kind of freebie (an e-course of my old home-buying seminar seems an obvious adaptation), thereby collecting names of people who are interested in what they have to say and, presumably, could be interested in what they have to sell. It's not useful to merely collect random names and e-mail addresses, however. The question you have to ask yourself is this: *How can I reach out to and* stay connected with *the people who will be interested in buying my properties, or who know others who will?*

My e-mail blasts are highly targeted: I know who has bought a book, who has requested information on our properties, who has actually contacted our office, who has taken a tour. For example, if I'm releasing a new book, everyone who has done any of those things will receive an announcement about that. If I'm conducting a few private showings, however, the recipients will be much fewer, and I'll tailor each note. Similarly, I send out a monthly e-mail update to brokers and a select group of possible buyers, letting them know what's going on with the project in a given thirty-day period.

The use of social networking sites has the same intended effect: build a following of people who are interested in you and what you're delivering to market. Facebook, MySpace, and others offer a free, easy way to conduct a kind of virtual relationship marketing, where you establish online linkages with others whom you may or may not know in person. Microblogging sites and apps, like Twitter, also afford you the chance to easily update multiple sites (e.g., your own website and blog, a Facebook account, etc.) by setting up feeds. This is a simple way to keep your content fresh and your name in front of people who have expressed an interest in you. Again, I encourage you to delve more deeply into how to use these social networking features by investigating them with an online search; I've only scratched the surface here, and the applications are nearly endless.

You'll also want to review potential brokers' sites and evaluate them just as you did with the print advertising. How does it compare with other brokers' sites? Ask about their traffic: How many visits do they get per day? How "sticky" is it—do people click away, or do they stay and look around for a while? Is their site easy to navigate? Does it load quickly? Is it well designed? How will your property be displayed? (See our broker's site at PremierEstateProperties. com. You can view the way they market our properties by clicking on "Atlantic Oceanfront," then "5 Million +." You'll see that they, too, have a dedicated page for each property and, if not already sold, pull elements, like the countdown ticker and the copy, from our own site, in addition to linking to Frank-McKinney.com.) Once you've chosen a broker to represent your property, I suggest you write into your listing agreement the particulars of both web-based advertising and print advertising; although you may not be in a position to command top billing on their site or in other ads, you should insist on having input for the text and photos they'll use. Detail it out so that you know exactly what you're getting and they know exactly what they're expected to provide.

Ring #5: Media

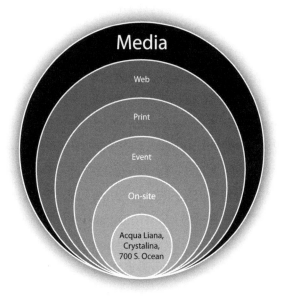

This is the largest ring in the GSCA because it has the potential to reach the largest audience by giving you third-party validation. For most people, local media publicity can be the boost you need to begin to establish your brand. For Acqua Liana, we wrote this simple summary of our media plan:

> Public relations firm to handle major media pitches and inquiries. Produce documentary for network distribution. Feature TV/web/print interviews/coverage. Cross-promotion with book tour.

On the largest scale, this ring represents your chance to jump up and down on Oprah's couch. Your *20/20* feature. Your photo on the cover of *USA Today*. At our current level, we coordinate significant efforts with a public relations firm, although I'll tell you that some of our greatest opportunities weren't secured by anyone in PR. In fact, I've been honored to appear in all three of the high-profile media I just mentioned above (though I didn't jump up and down on her couch, I did have an unusual moment of my own with Oprah Winfrey), and only one of them came through an agency. So don't think that you need big bucks and an outside professional to make big things happen. What you do need is a fascinating story, a great angle, persistence, and a willingness to learn and play the game.

In the past, I used to call the newspapers and a few radio stations using an alias I adopted when I was fifteen years old and long ago retired, Carl Lamet (pronounced like the shiny fabric, and yes, I know it's *lame*). I'd let them know about "an exciting event going on just down the street!" In the very beginning, my marketing director, "Carl," would call the local free paper and tell them, for example, that a pink gorilla (also me) would be on hand working on a special fundraiser at my latest property to benefit breast cancer awareness. Everyone in the neighborhood would be asked to tie a pink ribbon around the new palm tree in the front yard and make a donation. There would be little rides for the kids and pink cotton candy—and that would earn me a little blurb. Then that might get picked up by the paper that goes for fifty cents. And that fifty-cent story would be picked up by, say, the *Miami Herald*, who would like the human interest angle and run a blip there, too. And so on up the media food chain, until I find myself standing in front of a TV camera for a short feature on the local news. Then that local news piece, because of national affiliations, would be picked up by various regional programs across the country, a producer from *20/20* would see it, and the rest is history.

Not that this was entirely my own idea. I was taking a cue from one of my heroes, Evel Knievel, who had done something similar to secure a deal to jump the fountains at Caesar's Palace in Las Vegas. When he decided to make the jump, at first he had trouble getting the attention of the casino's CEO, Jay Sarno, so he established a fake corporation (Evel Knievel Enterprises) with three fake lawyers, who repeatedly called Sarno's office. Evel Knievel himself called Sarno's office, affecting an accent and mispronouncing his "client's" name as "Evvle Nevvle" (both rhyming with *revel*). Other times he called and claimed to be from *Sports Illustrated* or ABC, and expressed interest in filming the jump. Sarno finally agreed to meet, and the jump was set to take place in December of 1967. It would be the site of Evel Knievel's most spectacular crash, which not only left him in a coma for nearly a month but also catapulted him to superstardom.

It all hinges on how you think about your business. What makes it worth hearing about? What can you do to draw media attention? (Hint: two surefire ways are to have an event with a catchy theme and to include a beneficiary of some kind.) Who do you need to tell? Pick up the phone and invite people. Spend some time, go through the phone book, and find your local TV channel and newspaper. Learn who covers your area, who reports on lifestyle, and who could be interested in covering you. When you contact them, be big and bold. Yes, exaggerate the importance a little if you have to. It may be a pink gorilla, but by the time you're done talking it up, it should be an 800-pound gorilla and sound as exciting as one of our grand unveilings.

You must take the time to generate your own publicity, to learn how to pitch a story to a newspaper. You may need to take a class on this or do some reading, but it's not rocket surgery. It's pretty straightforward. You need to learn something about the format of news releases, how to put together a media package, and understand who to call (like the fact that there are desks at a newspaper and you want to call the right person). But even without following or even knowing a lot of "the rules" of public relations, I did pretty well.

The first appearance on *Oprah* came about because we put together a media kit on a $12 million dollar home we were building, and combined that information with the home we renovated and rented as our first Caring House Project Foundation effort. We sent it to about twenty-five of the major news magazine shows. After hearing nothing for a year, *Oprah's* producers called wanting a venue for a shoot, as a backdrop for a segment on the ultrarich. In talking with the producers about it, we completely turned that call into our own story, and Oprah's people loved it. We were able to parlay our fledgling efforts with the CHPF into an interesting hook for the feature on me: the guy who provides housing for the poor as well as for the mega-wealthy, who looks like a rock star and likes to speed along the coast on a jet-black motorcycle and is a churchgoing family man. They thought I was a character, filmed me in that rooftop Jacuzzi I mentioned a few chapters back, drinking (fake) champagne from a beautiful crystal flute, toasting Oprah and her own accomplishments. What a moment!

Great publicity may be the holy grail of marketing: it's free, it strengthens your brand, it gains you greater recognition, and it even helps you sell your product. All are built through third-party validation. And after your fifteen minutes of fame (or three minutes, as was the case for me on *Oprah*), you can either acquire the video or link to it on your website.

MISCELLANEOUS

Although the items here don't neatly fit into any of the rings in the GSCA, you do need to consider all miscellaneous additional tactics. Remember, even this catch-all section can't be treated as an afterthought, since these elements are critically important, too:

Real estate brokerage (listing), independent brokerage with Bob, Bob with brokerage referral. Weekly and quarterly meetings with brokerage for accountability. MLS. Computer-generated walk-through. International travel to present to established and emerging wealth markets. Write additional books. Visit concierges. Turn GSCA into spreadsheet to track due dates/accountability.

I've already touched on a couple of criteria in choosing your broker: how effective is their print advertising, and how will they feature your property/give it the necessary exposure online? But there's more to it than just those two marketing considerations, although the selection of a broker is essentially a marketing decision: who do you feel will best represent you, your brand, and your property to its target market? While I wholeheartedly endorse the use of a broker, at the risk of sounding insensitive, I'm going to put this bluntly: most real estate brokers and agents are C-minus students in life and will do the minimum amount you require to market your property. Realtors are not, as a general rule, the cream of the crop. (If you're a broker reading this, and you feel insulted, then you must be far better than a C-minus. What makes you better is your ability and willingness to implement many of the strategies found in the GSCA. If you are doing this, then I congratulate you, and please accept my apologies. If you aren't willing to do so, then in my book you are average and don't qualify to list one of my or another bubble-proofer's properties.)

So your job is to seek out and find the one broker in a hundred who earns at least an A-minus, who will do a good to great job with marketing and selling your properties.

I suggest you interview at least two candidates and look for the following:

- **Specialization.** A realtor who either specializes in your area or your type of property will bring an added layer of familiarity with your target market. You can find someone like this by driving around and checking For Sale signs, or by investigating brokerage websites to see which realtors are already representing properties with a similar price point or in close proximity to your property.

- **Marketing savvy.** Do the comparisons I've suggested above, reviewing realtors' offerings in the publications where real estate is commonly advertised, including local real estate guides and newspapers. Check their websites to see if you like the way they present other people's offerings.

- **Sales history.** How many buyers do they typically bring to a property? What percentage of their in-house listings do they actually sell? How many times do they show a property before they actually sell it, if they sell it? (Remember that the lower the showing-to-closing ratio, the better, although 50:1 is common.) What is their average time on market for properties in your price range? You want a firm that actively and aggressively sells the properties they represent.

- **Sales avenues and success rates.** Again, find out all the ways a realtor advertises and promotes, and then review the material: print ads, direct mail, website, commercials. How many open houses do they hold per month?

- **References and referrals.** Ask for these, and then check them. How long has this firm been in business? How satisfied have prior property sellers been with this realtor's assistance? If your candidate won't offer you any or you hear reluctant or mediocre reports, you know the broker's in the C-minus category. Look for glowing reports.

- **Better-than-average competence.** What's your feeling about how well this broker will do for you? What's your sense of this person's professionalism and real estate know-how? Will he or she put in the necessary time to learn about your property and be a virtual partner in selling it? Will this person be open to taking your advice and have valuable opinions to offer, as well? How confident do you feel that this person has the ability, honesty, passion, professionalism, and willingness to work with you and sell your property at top price? Finally, and most important, which broker is willing to implement the elements referenced in your GSCA?

In summary, align yourself with someone who breaks away from the herd, who understands what you're doing, who can get behind your asking price and present a unified front to buyers. If necessary, you can explain that the higher price you command isn't based on overconfidence or ego, but instead based on your study of the market, the acquisition formula you use, and your instincts about what buyers want—and it's backed up by a phenomenal property, your masterpiece. See if the broker gets it; trust me, you'll know. This is crucial because you need to be assured that the realtor will talk about your property the same way you do, both when you're in the room and when you're not.

Find a realtor you trust, negotiate a decent commission—and yes, the commission is negotiable, just don't do so to the detriment of your (their) marketing efforts. Pay them well for their work and introduction of the buyer, and then *stay involved*. People often raise their eyebrows when they find out just how involved I am in the sales cycle—I simply don't believe in "hands-off" anything when it comes to my masterpieces, and selling is no exception. I do my best to be at every showing, I map out every footstep of the showing pattern to emphasize a home's most alluring features, and I coach my broker on what to say and how to walk through the home when I'm not there. You'll get these important details on spectacular showings in the next chapter.

Do not, under any circumstances, just hand over your property for someone else to sell. You may not be the world's greatest salesperson, but you know the attention paid, the care taken, the artistry, and the unseen details of the property unlike anyone else. All of these help to capture potential buyers' imaginations, and whether you point these out during showings or your broker does, you need to be intimately involved in deciding what gets communicated. Choose your realtors wisely, develop strong relationships with them, and then monitor their efforts on your behalf.

That's what the GSCA accountability spreadsheet is for: monitoring not only your broker's efforts, but the marketing efforts of every member of your team. Be sure to create one for your property. This is your detailed list of *every single activity* that needs to take place in marketing, from the first day when the first For Sale sign goes in the ground to the quality reviews you'll conduct prior to one-on-one showings. Each activity gets pegged to the initiative (on-site, event, print, Web, media, or miscellaneous), assigned to you or a point person with support personnel noted, and given a due date, along with a column for recording the completion date. I suggest you create both the narrative and accountability spreadsheet, too, so that you can see your overall strategy at a glance (the narrative) and track each activity through its completion, thereby closing the loop on all five initiatives.

Which brings us full circle, right back to the beginning of my advice about the Grade School Compass Approach. You don't go straight from "I bought this great property" to "I'm appearing on *Oprah* next week." No. You start closest to home, on-site, and build from there. You focus on each ring because your whole real estate world revolves there. And then you get out there and *implement.* You close the loop. You do every last thing that you've planned to do, and then some. The net result is the true holy grail of marketing: a potential buyer stands on the threshold of your property. Then, as you'll learn in the next chapter, the show can really begin. . . .

A Few Questions and Tips for Implementing Your Own Grade School Compass Approach

Here are a few key questions to ask yourself for each of the five rings of your GSCA marketing plan.

- On-site. *From the first day you own it, what do you need to do to make this property as appealing to passers-by as possible?* As soon as you buy it, you need to put your property on display and make sure potential buyers can reach you at a moment's notice. How do you ensure that anyone who wants to know more has your contact information? Where do you need to place signage, brochures, special lighting? What do you need to do to make sure the property is accessible and easy to see? Where could you display blueprints, floor plans, material samples, other "props" to help tell the story of the property (either where it's been or where it's going)?

- **Event.** *What event-specific initiative can you undertake to attract buyers and brokers?* Most people think of the open house as the "main event," but how many open houses do you see listed on any given weekend? You must do something (or a lot of something) so you will stand out from the crowd. Think of your open house events as the last step in a series of events designed to generate excitement about your property. What special events can you host leading up to an open house? Do you need to schedule meetings with brokers or prior customers? What do you want to do on the day of your open house? Can you stay open an hour before and after the typical open house times? Can you offer seminars (e.g., "Why Rent When You Can Buy?") or other offsite events to let people know about your offerings? What will be the theme of your grand unveiling?

- **Print.** *How can you best show the property in pictures?* Take a look through MLS websites at competing properties in your area, and try to obtain brochures of homes you like that are competing with yours. Notice how much more time you spend on a brochure that has ten photos than you do on the one with only one photo. Pictures are the easiest way to get buyers excited about your property. You can write a description using adjectives that would make a romance novelist drool, but you'll get more bang for your buck with great photos that show off your property in its best light. (In truth, I like to do both, but if I had to, I'd opt for great photos above great words any time.) What about your property needs to be photographed and featured in your literature and/or displayed during your open house? What other take-home literature do you need to offer to potential buyers (e.g., floor plans, maps of the area, lists of local schools)? What elements of your vision and passion statement (remember, you developed this at the outset, as detailed in the chapter on the holy trinity of improvements) can be expanded into inviting, compelling text to be used in your brochure, flyers, direct mail, and advertising? Where do you need to advertise: how can you reach your target market through newspapers, magazines, real estate guides, or other pay-for-space publications?

- **Web:** *How can you use the Internet to create an "all-access" pass to the property for visitors to your site?* How can you feature this property on the home page of your website? (You do have a website, right? If not, get one!) What will be your dedicated URL (e.g., MyNewProperty.com) that redirects to your main site? What can you do to "invite" users in through the Web's bells and whistles (e.g., web-cam, progress blog, ticker, streaming video, etc.)? Who do you need to link to, and who needs to link to you? Is your site already optimized so that someone searching for what you have can find you? What social and media networks or microblogs will you use (Facebook, MySpace, YouTube, Twitter, etc.)? What e-mail campaigns do you need to plan and implement? How can you use the web to further establish your brand (e.g., webinars, podcasts, e-zines)?

- **Media.** *What kind of coverage will create buzz and reach your target market?* Do you need a public relations professional to help you with publicity, or can you do this yourself? What is your expertise, and how can you make it available to local and, possibly, national media? What kinds of stories will help entrench your brand and make your name ubiquitous among those who are likely to buy your property?

- **Miscellaneous.** (This one's not a circle, but you need to include it to catch any loose ends.) *What's not already covered by each of these circles that would enhance your ability to reach potential buyers and sell the property at top price?* Who and what listing services do you need to utilize? Do you want to take the property off the market at any point? (I often do this a month before a grand unveiling, just to build suspense: for my target market, making the property "unavailable" heightens desire.) What can you do, unrelated to real estate, to raise the visibility of your brand and property?

Plan to spend at least a few weeks on your GSCA marketing plan. If you're new to strategic planning of this kind, it may take a month. You'll need the time on-site, time alone, and possibly time with professionals from some of these disciplines who can advise you and give you additional ideas. If you're a novice in any of these areas, educate yourself: Study, absorb, and then apply. Read books, attend seminars, hire help—do what you must to shore up any of your marketing weaknesses. I can't possibly teach you everything I know about marketing in this book alone—it could be another book altogether (and might be, next year)—so seek out the resources you need to develop a marketing plan that's complete, efficient, and then carried out to the letter.

Let me restate it, because I can't possibly stress this enough: **draw up your GSCA marketing plans so you can start on day one.** You'll need to revisit the plan frequently, at least every few months, and it will become increasingly important as you get closer to your open house date. During the final six months before the grand unveiling of one of our properties, I'm consumed with overseeing the advertising blitz, corralling brokers and educating them about our latest masterpiece, ramping up exposure on our website, confirming details for the grand unveiling, and making myself available for every publicity opportunity. As we go, I'm evaluating current market conditions and adjusting the plan as need be. Acqua Liana's grand opening is a prime example, as we altered some of our events and worked hard to present the property in its best light during some very challenging times. (Keep in mind that Acqua Liana was unveiled right on the heels of the most significant economic crisis we've seen since the Great Depression.) The cross-promotional efforts with my book tour had to be scaled down, too. Instead of touring fifty cities in a four-mile-to-the-gallon luxury tour bus with my family, I decided to make a solo trip cross-country in my cherished Yugo, folding my six-foot-one frame into my compact, forty-miles-per-gallon wonder—a spectacle in its own right. Who knows, this may alter as we draw closer. These new twists caused us to consider all kinds of new marketing angles and avenues, and to do so six months before the unveiling and book-launch party, not at the last minute. We were paying close attention to the times we were in, and even more important, to the psychology of my buyers.

The overriding principle here is the "smart bomb" or beauty-of-simplicity approach: you start by knowing exactly what you want to create (vision and passion statement), the price you want to command for your masterpiece (acquisition formula), and your strategy for reaching potential buyers (Grade School Compass Approach). Every single moment you own a property, you're evaluating and reevaluating its greatest potential for a profitable sale. You've fully mapped out your improvements and marketing in advance, so when someone makes an offer on your masterpiece, you'll be fully prepared to unemotionally assess its validity and profitability. You'll be able to quickly judge the merits of any and all offers against the big-picture goal of your construction or renovation plans and pricing strategy.

Meanwhile, you implement your GSCA to marketing, promotion, and sales with such precision that the astronomical pull of your property becomes irresistible to anyone who enters its orbit. All are drawn to the site with the gravitational force of a marketing plan that's completely out of this world. No one who is a potential buyer escapes—and they wouldn't want to!

BURST OF INSPIRATION

- If you are considering a property purchase right now, you can begin drawing up your GSCA plans even before you acquire it. I don't suggest you start implementing just yet, but creating a plan makes complete sense. And if you don't have a particular property in mind yet, you can still start highlighting all the elements and ideas I've presented here that you'll want to incorporate into your plans in the future. Make it easier on yourself and don't try to reinvent the wheel—you've got my surefire GSCA as your guide.

11

HEIGHTEN BUYERS' FIVE SENSES TO A STATE OF SUBLIMINAL EUPHORIA

The Grade School Compass Approach *will* produce results, generating qualified buyers and putting them exactly where you want them: on the way to your property for your grand unveiling or one of your open houses. (Be sure to host an open house every weekend until the property sells.) When they arrive, what will they see, feel, hear, taste, touch, and smell? Will it be just another house visit that dulls their senses and has them walking out the door and saying they'll "think about it"? Or will they be so intoxicated that they're beyond eager to write up a contract, tell you not to show *their* house to anyone else, and prepare for the closing as soon as humanly possible? Will they leave scratching their heads, or will they be dialing up the moving company before they get to their car?

Using the method of showing that I share with you in this chapter, I've had people sign on the dotted line for a multimillion-dollar home even before they saw the whole property. In fact, this has happened several times. On one occasion, a buyer was so in love with the place that he asked and gained my permission to move in before closing, even before the inspection. There he was putting clothes in his closet and stocking shampoo in a shower big enough to keep any marriage strong, and he wasn't even the owner yet! Still another told me at the closing table, "Hey, by the way, Frank, great job on the house! Would you mind showing me the rest of it? I understand there are three floors and we only got to see the first before today."

The homes I create are big, but they're not *that* big. The man's $12 million had already cleared my bank, and he hadn't even been to the second or third floor yet! Now that's what I call *euphoric*.

But wait, back up to the first guy a second. Why would I allow someone to move in before he owned the house? Well, why not? He was a household name worth hundreds of millions and had a $5 million nonrefundable deposit at risk—and I understood a critical piece: **The impulse window is open for only so long.** I know how to create the environment for a psychological transformation to take place, **where people make the decision to buy even before they're consciously aware of it, where need gets converted to desire, where excitement translates to action.** As soon as that happens, it's best to do whatever's in my power to help my buyer act on that impulse and head off even an inkling of buyer's remorse.

One of the remarkable things I've observed about the people who purchase the homes I create, about people of enormous wealth, is how quickly they make decisions. We can all learn something from this rapid-fire decision-making process. Whereas a new home buyer might take a few weeks or months to mull it over, most decisions to buy one of my estate properties happen on the spot or within forty-eight hours tops. It's due, in part, to the unique psychology and skill set of the ultrawealthy, honed over years of seeing and acting on opportunities they know will benefit them. **But their fast decision to purchase is also the direct result of the experience I create for them during the showing: heightening all five senses to the point of subliminal euphoria,** a state of intense yet subconscious delight, delirium, bliss, ecstasy, and intoxication over my masterpiece. At some point, they are so overcome with the feeling that they delight in acting upon it; they have to have it, a home that many have told me feels like their own private resort.

Of course, that feeling doesn't materialize instantly upon their arrival, nor does it happen by chance. It's built over the tenure of the showing and through careful planning. Remember the Google home page and its "beauty of simplicity"? This is the perfect Google moment, with a *lot* of advance preparation, careful thought, and detailed planning behind what feels to buyers like the most straightforward, uncomplicated experience: the experience of moving to yes. You could even say that you heighten all five senses to awaken the sixth: an extrasensory perception and recognition that *yes, this is right, yes, this is my house, yes, this was meant for me—yes, where do I sign?*

Isn't this what you want from your buyers? An expedited, euphoric yes? An enthusiasm for your property that's so great that it simply will not be denied? In this chapter, I reveal to you all that I do to help my buyers arrive at that point—things that you can do, too, starting from the moment your buyers pull into your driveway.

STOP AND SMELL THE ROSES

Anyone coming to see your property is likely to have done this sort of thing before. Even if it's a first-time home buyer, they'll probably already have visited a few houses before they arrive at yours.

Based on your advance work—the gravitational pull of the GSCA—they will expect to see something "nice." Even and perhaps especially at my price point, potential buyers will be somewhat blasé. Some people feel they've seen it all and might think, *How great could it really be? Hardly anything lives up to its hype these days.* Therefore, the senses lie dormant, and it's up to the seller and the property to awaken them.

All that works in your favor. You'll be delivering the unexpected.

Based on what you've done with the GSCA, when prospective buyers drive up to the property, the first thing they should notice is how clean it is, how everything is in order, how nothing distracts them from feeling invited in to take a closer look. Except, perhaps, a safety cone placed at the end of the driveway. I like to erect this barrier, ostensibly because some detail related to the entrance is being attended to, but really because I want to *slow people down*; I want them to get out of the car and *stroll* so they can appreciate the landscaping and see the main entrance from an especially attractive vantage point.

Without being directed to do it, people walking up to your front door will naturally start to scan the property and take in details: the new or repaved driveway, the sounds of water gurgling in a small fountain to the right, the lovely garden gate with fragrant climbing roses spilling over it to the left. You'll want to start tickling the senses well before the front entrance, so think about ways to add *visual interest, scent, texture,* and *sound* out in the yard, walkway, and driveway. (You can save *taste* for inside the house unless you have your buyers pick fruit from one of your trees.) Even modest touches work if done well: potted plants and flowers, a simple water feature, freshcut grass, resonant chimes hanging in the garden, and so on.

In our case, people might traverse a grass drive, noticing its soft feel underfoot and the silence of their steps across it, similar to what they'd experience on the eighteenth green at Pebble Beach. They'd hear and see the waterfall splashing nearby, flowing underneath the drive into a meandering water garden, and framed by native Florida cap rock. They'd pick up the scent of beautiful tropical flowers and foliage that don't grow wherever they live the rest of the year, set off by the whiff of ocean air from somewhere not too far away. Then there are thousands of other details they might sense and assess without even being aware of it, something Malcolm Gladwell called "thin slicing" in his wonderful book *Blink*. (If you want to learn about quick decision making, both so you can make fast decisions and influence your buyers to do so, this should be your next stop after *Burst This!*) Meanwhile, you can bet that even if they didn't take all that in, I'd point out the most striking features while walking with them, observing their body language and getting to know a great deal about them even before we arrive at the main entry for the home.

Think of the opportunities most people miss by driving potential buyers right up to the front door! Don't make that mistake. If you're conducting a private showing, meet them in the driveway, and if you're hosting an open house, make sure people are parking on the street and walking to the front door. Not only does this give you a chance to show off the landscaping you've done to make the place more beautiful, but it also helps build anticipation for what they'll find once they're inside the house. Remember, slow them down.

If you do that part right, they'll never know what hit them once you open the door: when the hinges swing open, their circuits will start to overload and soon that desirable state of euphoria will begin to come over them.

CREATE A SIGNIFICANT FRONT-DOOR EVENT

Walking over the threshold should be the most compelling moment a potential buyer will experience during the entire showing. I call this creating a "significant front-door event." The moment you open the door, the effect has to be completely stunning: a complete sensory overload where the pulse races but blood pressure drops twenty points, where jaws hit the floor and eyes widen.

At Acqua Liana, for example, within thirty seconds of stepping into the home's foyer, your receptors process the first ever glass water floor and the hand painted lotus-flower motif on the glass tile beneath it; the glass elevator; the twenty-four-foot-tall cascading glass water wall; the 2,500-gallon aquarium wet bar and wine room; the glass see-through fireplace; and the nine-foot-tall, hand-blown glass chandelier dripping water into the reflecting pond that seems to drop off into the ocean, which you can also see as you look through the house across the golf course grass toward the ocean. As long as it took you to read that description, that's how long it takes for the eyes to sweep the entire scene and for the receptors in my buyers' bodies to be brought to full attention. Which is why we keep contracts in a small deck by the front door with everything filled in but the buyer's name and size of down payment.

Clearly, in an estate like Acqua Liana, the visuals dominate the front-door event, but you don't have to rely only on grand architectural and design details, which tend to carry a bigger price tag. Utilize spot merchandising to boost visual appeal—you'll read more about this later in the chapter—along with other sense-sational touches:

- Early in my career, we'd hide an inexpensive CD player behind a silk plant in a corner of the foyer, and play soothing, welcoming music. We'd also hide them in other rooms, strategically placed throughout the house and playing different music in each location. Nowadays, our speakers are concealed behind special drywall that doesn't dampen volume, but in most cases, a discretely placed player of any kind will fill the room with pleasing sound. If it's a nice day, and you hear wind blowing through the trees, or in our case, the sound of rolling waves is filling the air, it's best to turn off the music and invite nature in as your sound system. (Note: Sometimes sound *reduction* can be important, as well. Any unpleasant noises should be eliminated.)

- Right at the door, you should ask your guests to remove their shoes and put on surgical booties, which achieves three objectives: 1) it creates an atmosphere of respect for the home and its future owner, 2) it draws attention to the constant cleanliness and care for the home, and 3) it puts people's feet in closer contact with the floor, sparking the sense of touch. Whether they're standing on glass, gleaming hardwood, $250-a-yard carpet imported from Holland, radiantly heated marble, or any other beautiful material, they're going to feel it underfoot. Later, as they walk through the rest of the house, they will feel the flooring there, too.

- You can also place the laminated floor plans in their hands at this time—another appeal to the senses of touch and sight. As you do this, you can explain generally how the home is laid out and what they can expect to see during the showing. Don't skip this important step of giving them a preview: it helps buyers focus, so they're not distracted by the mental game of trying to piece together a puzzle while they tour the rest of the home.

- Introduce a clean scent (neither sterile nor sickeningly sweet) in the entryway. Natural-smelling citrus, cinnamon, lavender, or floral fragrances work well here—or perhaps you have planted fragrant plants, such as gardenia or jasmine, near the door, where letting the fresh air in will be your best choice, helping the home smell and feel naturally fresh and open.
- Soon after entering the home, involve the sense of taste by offering a beverage. We always have small bottles of Evian and soda available, and if it's a second showing, we're prepared with champagne and wine.

By putting all five senses into play, you can wow your guests right from the start. Many people who experience your significant front-door event will be thinking, *I haven't even seen the whole house yet, and already I love it.* They may or may not know *why* they feel that way—remember, a lot of what you're doing to enhance their experience is subliminal. Now, the order in which you show the rooms of the home is critical to keep building on that state of euphoria.

Establish Then Follow Your Showing Pattern

Every property demands its own, unique showing pattern. You need to think this through, practice it many times, and communicate it to your broker so that he or she can replicate it when necessary. There are two key principles to follow as you're developing a showing pattern:

- **Get to your strongest features first.**
- **Show everything at least twice.**

Because all of our homes are on Florida's Gold Coast, we almost always walk straight from the foyer to the home's oceanfront access. There, a potential buyer can feel and smell the warm, salty air, hear the waves breaking, see the gorgeous azures of the sky and sea, and imagine having all of that within steps of their own front door. Even if you don't have an overpowering natural feature like the Atlantic, you will have at least one standout room, and probably three: the kitchen, the master bedroom, and the master bath, as this is where you will have put most of your attention and valuable improvements. So you'll walk through the front door, straight to the most engaging place on the property, and then create a pattern through the rest that causes you to double back by every room in the house. You may not walk your guests into every room twice, and you may not even go once into the secondary bedrooms, for example, but you'll point them out at least twice as you're on your way to other parts of the home. If you find your buyers feeling pulled toward a particular room after showing it a second time, let them go.

For the key rooms in the house, identify in advance the artistic expressions of which you're most proud. Tell the story of the home like a painter describing a masterwork. If you were in a gallery, listening to an artist describe his or her paintings, you'd love to hear about what inspired the color choices and composition—and would fall asleep if all you heard was, "I used a paintbrush to make that part blue. And then I painted that part green." This means you've got to go beyond saying things like "There are hardwood floors throughout." Yawn. Instead, tell people where the wood came from: "This floor is made with reclaimed lumber from a 300-year-old York, Pennsylvania barn . . ." or "This beautiful strain of bamboo comes from the forests of Colombia and grows ninety feet in a year . . ." or "These are coconut palm floors from trees harvested in the Keys . . ."

I still get very excited about flooring, kneeling down and point-ing to the pock marks on reclaimed river-bottom cypress, or explain-ing the beautiful two-by-two-foot pieces of marble that we've had special cut. I'll pull out a sample of the flooring and show guests the back: "Look how this is bonded so it won't crack!" People want to hear those stories, those country-of-origin stories and what-you-did-to-install-it stories. It's what makes the home unique and mem-orable, so that if they do need to walk away and consider it for a day or two, they can talk about as if it were a piece of art with "that amazing marble floor" or "the gorgeous black bamboo beams." And they can imagine themselves telling their friends those details with pride. A home must tell a story without you or your broker there to prompt it. You create this by taking the time to show your passion as a real estate artist to your buyers, giving them detailed and intrigu-ing descriptions of key elements in the home.

In the end, you can't leave this to your broker, who will be responsible not only for your property but usually twenty more. He or she can't possibly know your house as well as you do and won't be as emotionally invested in communicating the details. Even if you decide to let your broker do most of the talking—if you think he or she is simply a better salesperson—then you still need to be there for backup. You can think of yourself as the color commentator. You can also build it into the realtor's presentation that he or she will turn to you for details, bringing you into the conversation. I always take my brokers through many "mock" showings before the property is finished so their level of knowledge begins to approach mine. We rehearse over and over so that when showtime comes, we're ready to allow the house to shine for buyers.

When I'm showing a home, if the potential buyers seem at all reticent with me—who's this guy with the long hair?—my broker takes the lead, and I'll interject as we go, adding key points. Slowly, I work my way in, and within about ten minutes, my broker will find himself a chair to wait out the remaining hour of the showing. He's already done his job: getting the buyers to the property. At the showing, it's time for me to do mine.

Keep the Flow Constant

Throughout your entire showing, you must continue to heighten the five senses. In every room, what can you do to overwhelm your potential buyer with the experience of *yes*?

One of your most important preparations for showing a property will be "staging." In our estates, this means fully furnishing the home, with Nilsa designing and decorating the interior and supplying all of our buyers' needs, down to the solid gold toothbrushes in the master bathroom, Egyptian cotton linens on the beds, and pillow-soft towels in the closets. You may or may not have the budget to go to these lengths. At a minimum, take a trip to your local Target or Wal-Mart, spend about $500, and spot merchandise throughout the home: towels and soap for the bathrooms, place settings for any eating areas, a TV and a few small appliances for the kitchen (not too many—you don't want to create clutter), silk plants, and any other nice touches that can help your buyer envision how the home might be lived in and used. If you can afford it, a flat-screen TV in the "he" room of the house goes a long way, as do any furnishings you can place in the master suite. Furnishings and accessories heighten the sense of *sight* and the emotional transition your buyer will make from viewing your offering as a house to seeing it as their home.

You'll also want to introduce fragrances throughout, but beware of using overwhelming aromas—no disinfectant spray, no "fresheners" in the air-conditioning vents (believe me, I made that mistake once), no cheap plug-ins. Back in the "old days," we used to put cookie dough in the oven at 150 degrees to make the house smell homey all day (but not actually bake the cookies). Now, companies like Scentevents (Scentevents.com) offer custom aromas, everything from apple pie to floral bouquet to leather. In our homes, especially in the private areas like bedrooms and bathrooms, we also use a tiny paint brush to apply lavender essential oil to every other light bulb, which subtly scents the room only when the lights are on and the heat from the bulbs releases the aroma—an inexpensive enhancement anyone can add but hardly anyone does. (Bonus: A few university studies have shown that the smell of lavender puts people in a better mood. I think it also puts them in a buying mood.)

Throughout the house, we always have food to eat, most notably plates of fine chocolates—another celebrated mood elevator, especially among women. Even when guests are watching their figures, I can usually break the ice by unwrapping one of the chocolates and popping it into my mouth. Even if they don't go for a bite right then, I usually spot them taking, sometimes sneaking, one later. Almost immediately thereafter, the atmosphere gets still more convivial and festive. Spend the money for the good stuff, such as Godiva, Lindt, Ferrero Rocher, Dagoba Organic, La Maison, or artisan chocolates you may find locally. (Maybe your chocolatier would be willing to supply his or her product free or at a discount if you display a discreet sign identifying the candies as local and handcrafted? It tells even those who are not chocolate connoisseurs that you're treating them to the best and provides the chocolatier with some inexpensive publicity.)

Clearly, what you do and say affects your guests' five senses. Do you look crisp and professional? Do you sound relaxed yet excited about what you have to show them? Realize that while you're showing the home, you're part of the buying experience. Keep these guidelines in mind:

- **Represent.** You are your property's best showperson, and you need to look the part. Dress nicely, professionally, neatly. I choose to have my dress reflect that of an artist, but I'm always sure I don't cross the line to looking like a mad scientist. Realize that how you look and act reflects on the quality of the property.

- **Read people.** Some people are just looking; some will appreciate a guided tour; some are truly in the market for a new home. You can't tell by appearances. The first time I met some of the people who bought our estates, I might never have thought they had the means: one rode by on a bicycle and bought a $27 million property from us; many have shown up in cars like the Ford Taurus, wearing jeans and a baseball cap and offering all-cash for a multimillion-dollar home.

  Instead of judging by appearances, try to listen to what people say as they come in. Nine times out of ten, you'll get a good sense of what they really want. At open houses, when you hear "We're just looking," "We happened by," "We were curious," you know that touring your property is probably a way for them to pass the time and may not be represent a serious search—but don't completely discount them. (Such remarks can also be a ploy to tour the house without being "sold to," and you can respect that while keeping an eye on them to see if they need anything, offering an explanation or story if they seem open to hearing it.) On the other hand, "We just moved to town," "We're looking for a bigger place," and "We're tired of renting" indicate real interest—an opportunity to turn their need to desire. Spend your time with these serious buyers, but be careful not to dismiss anyone.

- **Don't rush.** If someone says they have only a few minutes, explain that it takes at least half an hour (or however long) to see the home properly. At an open house, if they're unwilling to make the time to see it with you the way you've planned, give them a tour that might start out quickly, but throttle back to a slower pace once you realize you have piqued their interest.

- **Tell the story of the property without it sounding like a sales pitch.** This may take some practice, but remember: You're an artist describing your masterwork. Point out all the amenities. Call attention to the high quality of improvements you've made. Mention the country of origin, the reasons you selected certain materials, and anything special about the installation. Tell people about the things they can't see or might not notice: green benefits, like improved air quality, energy efficiency, water reuse, renewable material selection, rainforest conservation; the new roof or upgraded plumbing. Open the doors most people wouldn't think to look behind—a broom closet, for example—and explain that you've taken special care with the home, even down to the kinds of details most people overlook. ("We replaced the flooring in here and installed a light fixture and a place to hang your mop to dry.")

- **Talk about the area, neighborhood, and community.** You've done your research and know why this was a great place to invest—tell potential buyers what you've learned about the area's promise. Know where all the neighborhood conveniences are: schools, churches, supermarkets, dry cleaners, and so on. Know where the "insiders" go for great food, a family outing, a veterinarian. Mention any civic or business improvements in the works.

• **Offer people who are serious the chance to see the property at night.** You'll give the keys or the security code to the buyer or broker (whomever is most trustworthy), and let them come back on their own. "Just let me know when you're coming so I can have the lights on," you'll say. And then you'll set the home for a night showing—lights set to the appropriate mood, media room set up, snacks for the kids, wine and cheese for the adults, etc. This can be an extremely powerful experience for potential buyers, driving up to "their" gate and punching in the security code, walking up to "their" front door, putting "their" keys into the lock, walking into "their" home for a relaxing evening. You put the buyer through the exact steps they'd take should they purchase the home. If that sixth sense kicks in—"Yes, this is *my* house"—you're on your way to closing the deal.

• **Send thank-you notes to buyers' brokers.** Most houses are sold through the buyers' broker rather than the listing broker, so be sure to send a personal note to any broker who brings a client to see your property. Build a relationship with buyers' brokers; if this client doesn't buy, perhaps one of the broker's other clients will do so, either with this or some future property.

Your creativity needs to continue and take on a new twist during the selling phase. Think now about how the home can be infused with imagination on top of your artistry. Remember your objective of heightening your buyers' five senses to the state of subliminal euphoria. An extreme but entertaining example: About ten years ago, we decided to play the movie *Independence Day* to show how phenomenal the home theater was at one of our estates. It had ten speakers strategically placed around the room, along with a movie theater-sized screen, plush reclining seats with drink holders, and a device that rumbled sound through the bottom of the seat. It made your bone marrow vibrate! You might remember that there's a scene in *Independence Day* when Will Smith as "Captain Steven Hiller" is standing in front of an aircraft the government has confiscated from the aliens so that he can fly into space and fight them.

"Look," he says, pulling out a gun, "there's a force field around it." When he shoots at the aircraft, the bullet ricochets around the lab and everyone ducks: *bing-bing-bing-bing!*

In our home theater, the ricochet effect was perfect—due to the surround-sound effect, it seemed as if the bullet was flying around and bouncing off the large room's red velvet walls. When the scene had played out, I'd walk over to the speaker that had echoed the last *bing!* and pick up a Coke can I'd stashed there with a hole through it.

"Look how realistic the sound system is," I'd say. "Bullet put a hole right in the can! Here, put your finger in that hole." People loved it!

Go on and rock the house. If you have special features, show them off to the hilt. In this, as in everything you've done up to this point, consider every angle, every detail, every desire your buyer might have but not yet even recognize. In short, give your buyers every reason to say, "Yes, this is my home. Where do I sign?"

Your Chapter 11
BURSTS OF INSPIRATION

• Draw a column for each of the senses on a sheet of paper: *sight, sound, smell, taste,* and *touch.* Now go beyond the suggestions I've given you in this chapter to brainstorm your own ideas for heightening your buyers' five senses. (e.g., "install rain chain over water collection," "place Italian bowl with lemons in foyer," "remove pull chord from overhead fans so they don't hit the blades and make distracting noise," etc.)

• Develop a preshowing checklist, using the following as a guide. You saw a checklist in the previous chapter, which detailed our monthly and weekly maintenance of the property. In addition to that upkeep, there are things that need to be done right before you conduct an open house or one-on-one showing. You may include many or all of the following, tailoring it for your property. As you create your own list, think about being your property's concierge, priming the site so that guests will feel as if their every need has been anticipated.

Quality Review (QR) Preshowing Checklist

❏ Dim or brighten the lights, inside and out, to create a mood and show the property to best effect based on time of day. The objective is to help your guests think and feel, "Yes, I could live here. I *want* to live here." (You'll need to plan this ahead of time and list the best combination settings for both daytime and nighttime.)

❏ If you're conducting a one-on-one showing, set the music according to what you've learned about the potential buyer's age and preferences. If you're conducting an open house, turn on the music you've planned throughout the house.

❏ Likewise, turn on the TVs with preselected programming.

❏ Prepare the scents: dab the light bulbs with lavender, pop cookies in the oven at 150 degrees, start your scent machine—whatever you've planned to infuse the home with subtle, appealing aromas.

❏ Vacuum the floors again if need be. We always vacuum crisp lines in the carpet, and this is especially important if we're having someone visit the home for a second showing when we're not there. We can then see the footprints, which tell us where they went and give us a sense of how long they stayed there. (Almost as good as hiding under the bed.)

❏ Double-check that windows are clean and crystal clear.

❏ Set the temperature for maximum comfort. In cooler climates, you may warm the house more than you usually would to help it feel cozy; in warmer zones, you may cool it more to provide welcome relief from the heat outside.

❑ Turn on all appliances and any special features (e.g., fountain, Jacuzzi, fireplace, etc.). If you have no "special effects," consider drawing a bubble bath or sprinkling a warm bath with rose petals to create an inviting effect with a lovely scent.

❑ Stock the refrigerator with drinks, all labels facing forward.

❑ Nicely present snacks in the kitchen and throughout the home.

❑ If the home is furnished, turn down the bed as a hotel would. Place slippers and a robe nearby.

12

CLOSE THE DEAL, CLOSE THE LOOP

From the first page of this book, we've been working toward one specific objective: closing the sale of your property. Every initiative has been designed to move you closer to that endpoint, when someone recognizes the value of what you have created and compensates you handsomely for it.

Novice real estate investors can be intimidated or overmatched by what's necessary to close the deal, particularly negotiation. Most of them abdicate this responsibility to the realtor. But a bubble-proof investor, even one who's still wet behind the ears, knows that would be foolish; in most cases the broker should be paid very well to make the introduction, and then he or she needs to step aside and the principals should close the deal by direct discussions with each other. This can certainly happen in the presence of both party's brokers as often a broker can help validate points raised during negotiation. Sure, there are times when the chemistry is better between the brokers, so don't be stubborn, but I have learned this is the exception and most often, it's best if I talk with the buyer myself.

This only works, however, when you can do this unemotionally, without being overly identified with your property. There's no "artistic temperament" allowed, no prima donna or prima don who demands a submissive buyer or one who wouldn't dream of offending you with an offer lower than the asking price. There's no loving your artistry so much that you wouldn't sell it. Don't scoff; I have heard about *all* of these scenarios. It's difficult for some people to understand that investing your time, money, and creativity in a property does not mean that you won't gladly part with it for the right price.

I'm frequently asked, "Frank, how could you not stay in that house? Your family could live there . . . " This just tells me that they don't get it: When a masterpiece is done, I want to sell it. I don't want to move in. The love affair ends the day the home is complete. I don't care if the buyer changes the property's name, throws out all the furnishings, or lets the landscaping revert to jungle. That is not what matters. What matters is the negotiation of a solid deal where the buyer walks away feeling like a winner.

Notice I didn't say the buyer needs a "win-win" outcome. I couldn't care less about that; it's meaningless. I want my buyers to feel as if they've won. If they also feel that I've lost, that's fine; I'm unconcerned with their perceptions of my position. (I'm not going to sell a house that isn't a win for me, anyway, and it doesn't matter if they recognize that or not.) If they need to feel as if they've beaten me in order to feel *they've* won, fine. If they need to strut like a peacock, fine. If they want to feel as if they've squeezed every last drop out of me, fine. There's a time and a place for ego, and here is not one of them. Yet most sellers let that little voice get the best of them. Most get caught up with their ego and wind up trying to come off more like Vlad the Impaler than Mother Teresa. (To state the obvious, you should work to be more at the Mother Teresa end of the spectrum.)

As I mentioned earlier in this book, I've always been willing to color outside the lines when it comes to helping my buyers say yes. I'm unconstrained by how things are usually done or, for that matter, by my own ego. I've had buyers practically request the shirt off my back, and I've always been happy to oblige. In the early days, I helped people fix their credit, walked them through the mortgage process, folded past-due medical bills into the cost of the home. More recently, when a buyer told me that he'd pay my price but wanted my two collectible cars that I'd parked in the $15 million estate's show-room-quality garage, I said yes. It was the equivalent of a buyer of a $300,000 home wanting you to throw in a nice $1,500 suit—of course I said yes. Or further down in price, like selling a $100,000 house and your buyer asking you to throw in your nice pair of shoes! The guy was showing off for his new, young wife and her daughter, but what did I care? I turned to my broker and said, "Well, it looks like I'm going to need a ride home." I threw him the keys to the cars and to the front door. At the closing table three days later, the wire transfer cleared and I bought myself a new Yugo. Loop closed!

CAN YOU DEAL?

Let's back up a step. Before you even begin talking with some-one about price and conditions of sale, you want to know that they're prequalified or even preapproved for a mortgage. (*Prequalification* means that a lending institution is of the opinion that the buyer's financial resources allow for purchase of a home in your price point. *Preapproval* means that the lending institution has already okayed a loan up to a certain amount.) Most people interested in buying a home at midlevel or above come with financing in place, and at the highest end, in my target market, they come with cash and no financing contingency at all.

Unless they're working with a realtor, many first-time home buyers have no idea that it would be a good idea to talk to a bank or mortgage lender before looking for a house. They may say to you, "We'd love to buy your house, but we don't know if we can afford it." When you're working with this type of buyer, you'll want to help them out in the same way I did when I was holding those free seminars on home buying:

- **Prequalify buyers yourself.** Ask about income, job stability, credit history (and if it's okay for you to pull a credit report), savings, residence history (where renting), and so on. Given the stricter lending criteria of today, which is likely to continue far into the future, you'll want to be sure you're not wasting time with an unqualified buyer. Set up systems where you collect this data and provide it to your banker or mortgage broker, who can then plug it in to the latest financial product that may suit your buyer. Soon, you will be able to weed out the bad from good, but having that lender relationship is critical in this new age of "back to basics" financing.

- **Explain the importance of investing in a home.** *Outline how it represents not just the biggest expense they've ever had (it's probably the largest purchase they will have ever made), but it's also likely to* *be the greatest contributor to their net worth.* Show buyers the comparative analyses of other properties in the neighborhood, show them historical appreciation figures for your area (ideally a seven-year period, since most people own a home for seven years before they sell and move up to a new residence), demonstrate the difference in equity accumulation between owning and renting, and so on.

- **Walk them through the mortgage process.** As part of my free classes, I used to provide checklists of the financial information needed to qualify for a mortgage. When it came time for buyers to put in an offer on one of my properties, I helped them complete their mortgage application and be sure that when it was submitted, everything was correct and included what was requested. I'd even work with lending personnel on finalizing the deal, oftentimes utilizing my own contacts among bankers, loan officers, and mortgage brokers.

Whether your buyers need a great deal of assistance, as described above, or offer you tens of millions in cash with no financing, as my buyers usually do now, they'll want to feel that they've gotten a good deal, and you need to show them how your property satisfies that condition. This is part of helping buyers feel as if they've won. They need to know that the price they're paying is in line with the value of the property and that they'll be able to sell it for a profit in the future. Some may focus on the price of other homes in the neighborhood, or even the cheapest price in the neighborhood, and worry that they could be overpaying for your property. This means only that you need to educate them on the value of the land and the improvements you've made. You may need to explain how much it would cost and how long it would take for a buyer to acquire a similar tract of land and build with this quality from the ground up, or point out that they don't want to get involved with a messy renovation. You may need to remind them of the unique features in your home, features that you just don't find in other starter homes. You might need to take them back to that state of subliminal euphoria: "Remember how you felt when you first walked into the home? And how much you loved it when you were done with the tour? I can guarantee you, Mrs. Palin, that you won't find another property that makes you feel that way in this neighborhood."

You may even need to point out that the home won't be available indefinitely: "You're welcome to go look at other homes in the area—there's a nice three-bedroom just around the corner. While it may be the oldest line in the real estate sales book, I strongly encourage you to consider our house sooner rather than later, Mr. Palin. This is a great house, and as I'm sure you can imagine, it will likely sell soon. Shouldn't you be the one to put your key in the door?"

When you've represented the property correctly, you aren't likely to receive offers that are too far off the mark—either below market or, in a word, insulting. Yet even if you were to receive an offer like that, which could happen in an extreme buyers' market, you'd be smart to consider how you might convert it. Sure, my first reaction would be to take offense, too, but then the wheels would start turning, and I'd get my emotions quickly back in check. I don't dismiss any offer out of hand.

If, for example, I had priced a home at $30 million, and the buyer offered me $25 million, depending on the strength of the market, I might counter with $29.4 million—98 percent of my original price. Then I could see if the buyer would respond with an offer that's more in line with what I believe to be a realistic price. With this approach, I've been able to stay within 3.8 percent of our asking price for all properties sold in the last decade, and I haven't lowered a price on a finished home since 1998. Often, I've negotiated for what amounted to full price; if the property were priced at $29 million, then the buyer might pay $28 million plus my closing costs. In my book, that's as good as the full amount. Your artistry should be properly priced, not overpriced, so that you should not have to negotiate more than 5 percent off your selling price in any market. Keep that as your goal as you think of the retail price of your property, no matter how much you're asking.

Remember, prices are market-driven, and you need to know the current ratio of asking price to selling price, as well as understand how strong the market currently is in your area. You also want to keep the following in mind as you begin to work out the details of your deal:

- **Don't haggle for the sake of haggling.** *Time is a deal's worst enemy;* I've found the chances of a successful conclusion to a deal will diminish after day two. Talking too much or taking too long usually means the deal falls through just because time has passed. Act quickly.
- **Try to get your buyer to assume as much of the closing costs, including commission, as you can.** Don't be greedy, though. Certain closing costs like title insurance or transfer taxes if applicable in your area should be referenced in the MLS as being the buyer's responsibility. It doesn't guarantee they will pay them, but it is worth referencing. Remember that a key bubble-proofing principle is being willing to hit the single

instead of swinging for the fences. In other words, do what you can to make the deal work. When it's close, you still have some room to deal; I've gone to the brokers, when there was no more margin on my side, and asked them to reduce their commissions slightly. A good broker realizes that a slightly reduced commission is far better than no commission at all. Do *not* lose a deal over a few thousand dollars! I see this all the time. Swallow your pride, and after closing you can swallow that champagne.

- **Don't sell yourself or your property short.** You know what you've done to make this your masterpiece. If a buyer tries to verbally depreciate your property as a negotiation tactic, stand behind the value you've created. Be confident. You may not get everything you want out of a deal, but you're more likely to get more of what you want if you're self-assured and secure about what you have to offer.

- **Sit in the other person's chair.** Prior to any negotiation, I arrive early and sit on the opposite side of the desk. I imagine that I'm my buyer, and everything I've learned from getting to know them up to that point helps me imagine I am that person and consider what their needs or concerns might be—and exactly what they might need to feel as if they've won. After I do this exercise, it becomes even clearer to me what I need to do to finalize a deal.

If you approach all of this with the idea, again, of creating a win for the buyer, you'll find that negotiations are faster and less antagonistic than they otherwise might be. I'll even go so far as to say that you need to *know more about what your buyers want than what you want*. A very important point: As I head to the negotiating table, I never have a bottom-line number in mind. I don't walk in thinking that I won't go any lower than $X. This is a foolish way to negotiate and will kill more deals than it makes for you. Ultimately, the end price will be based on the peripheral terms associated with the deal: the closing date, cash or financing, the affinity (or lack thereof) in the negotiations, buyers' or sellers' market, my predictions about how much postsale "maintenance" this buyer will require (higher maintenance = higher price), the duration of inspections or as-is, and so on.

Generally, I also *know more about what the other person wants than they do*, at least subconsciously. That comes from my years in the business, innumerable showings and all of my purchases, where I've paid close attention to buyers and sellers, noting what the other party desires at the particular phase of life they're in, the kinds of relationships they have, the current state of their business, their family concerns, and so on. Hundreds of layers are communicated without so many words, informing my choices every step of the way. That's why my "chair exercise" can be so helpful: I tap into what I've learned about my buyer and my market, including personality, preferences, background, body language, eye contact, companions, how they treat others around them, handlers, dress, shoes, skin care, nails, color around the eyes, attention span—there's a very lengthy list you will develop over time—even subtle cues that I don't consciously know I know.

Whether a deal goes through or not, I always find out *why*. I always ask the broker: "What could I have done better?" "What did the house need that I didn't provide?" "What were the flaws?" "Could they be corrected?" "What would you have me add if you could?" That last question has yielded some great responses and ideas that have been incorporated into future designs, such as the extra-long, telescoping valet bar in closets so that clothes to be packed for travel can be hung separately, the ability to wash their car *in* the garage, or the display cases that are large enough to house originals of archival collections, such as the Declaration of Independence or the Magna Carta. These are things I never would have thought of myself, but when my buyers told me their ideas, I knew future buyers would be turned on by these accommodations, which say, "I know who you are and what you want."

CLOSE THE LOOP

Real estate deals are notoriously susceptible to what I call "meteor showers," where on any given day, during the pendency of a deal, a meteor could strike the earth. In other words, all kinds of unexpected and even weird circumstances can sour a deal, so you'll want to ensure the briefest passage of time possible between execution of the contract and closing. **Time is a deal's worst enemy!** Avoid haggling for its own sake or drawing out the negotiation for any reason; in addition, you need to remove contingencies quickly, and you need to include a tight timeline for inspections in your contract. Move quickly so that the meteor showers—whether they're individual to your buyer or more global to the market—can't cause your deal to go extinct.

Meanwhile, just as it's important to start marketing and selling the minute you buy, it's also crucial that you continue to market and sell until the wire transfer hits your account.

You never slap a "Sold" sticker on your For Sale sign until the money is in your hands. Don't even think about sticking on one that says "Pending." I've always been amazed by the stupidity of those moves, as it's so common for deals to fall apart. What if another, qualified buyer were to be interested in the property and then wrote it off because of some dumb sticker? Don't deprive yourself of a backup plan. If someone asks you about a property on which some-one else has made an offer, take a contingency contract. If the first deal dies, then you can go straight to the second party. The backup contract also gives you leverage with the first party to ensure that they stay on top of those inspections and move the property to clos-ing: "Hey, look, I just want to let you know that if anything hap-pens here, I've got someone right behind you, so it's in your best interests to get everything done per the contract."

When the deal is done and the new owners are moving in, is your job finished? Not quite.

Every Frank McKinney & Company property carries at least a one-year warranty. Even so, we have been known to fix things upon a reasonable request for three years after the sale. Why? Because that good business practice can cause my buyer to pick up the phone and call his billionaire friend to extol the virtues of Frank McKinney and his artistry.

We also include a comprehensive collection of information on home maintenance specific to the property. Instruction manuals, warranties, contractors' contact information, our own maintenance checklists, even local area resources that go beyond the home are all collected in binders and stored in a shelf we've installed in the mechanical room, especially for this purpose.

With my starter homes, years ago, I'd provide a list of babysit-ters, veterinarians, doctors, dentists, and other services people needed. You want to be a resource to your buyers, yet you don't want to create dependency. Remember, at the entry level, many buyers are used to calling landlords. You are not that, and you need to make that very clear at the closing table.

You've now gone through all the effort I've detailed up to this point, and here you are with the opportunity to close the loop. It's all paid off with a qualified buyer at your threshold. Are you going to sign on the dotted line together, or will it turn out to have been just another showing? If this isn't the ultimate bubble-proof prescription, I don't know what is: *sell your property!* Once sold there is nothing to burst.

Your Chapter 12
BURST OF INSPIRATION

- You're in the business to create value and sell your artistry. You are not a real estate collector or hobbiest. Leave your pride, emotional attachment, and ego at home. Love the process, not the product; save that for your buyers. With confidence, envision your buyer paying top dollar, then calmly work to get them to do so. Then celebrate!

THE
ENLIGHTENED
ABSOLUTIST

*From those to whom much
is entrusted, much is expected.*

When I was writing another book, *The Tap*, I ran across
the term *enlightened absolutist*. It was poetic in its per-
fection—exactly the right words to describe the kind
of businessman I've become. *Benevolent dictator* isn't far off, although
it has some negative connotations. Nor is *compassionate capitalist* so
wrong. Early in my career, I was most certainly dictatorial and a capitalist. I ran a tight ship (still do), accepted no foolishness (still don't),
and was laser-focused on yielding maximum profit by producing a

substantially superior product—so much so that other people's needs were only occasionally on my radar. In time, I did become benevolent and compassionate, too, realizing that having concern for others' lives was not just a nice thing to do, but it was absolutely necessary to giving my work deeper, longer-lasting meaning. Often, it was the best answer to the question, *What's this all for?* It made my continuing high regard for capitalism even more meaningful.

Yet I like *enlightened absolutism*; it just has the stronger ring of truth to it. Historically, the label refers to rulers who were influenced by the Age of Enlightenment and that period's emphasis on the "social contract." People like Eva Peron, Napoleon, and Catherine de Medici were interested in bettering the lives of their subjects, and they believed that what they could do toward that end reinforced their absolute authority over the land. (Some others who may be put into this category—you may remember Mussolini or Castro—were also prone to taking things too far, but that's not what I'm focusing on here.) So I'm taking some liberties with historical meaning by assuming the label for myself, but its spirit fits me ("I know what to do to benefit all concerned," or "Yes, I know what's best for you even if you don't"). Now in my forties, after spending nearly half my life in real estate, I have also attained some enlightenment—some understanding, even wisdom—about not only succeeding in business, but also about succeeding in the business we're all in: the business of life.

That's what this last part of the book addresses. It reveals to you the single most important principle in my incredible rise, the one application that converts any bubble into that impenetrable force field. It started as something basic that my mom taught me while I was growing up, and really began to take shape in the mid-1990s when I experienced what I call an "epiphanous moment"—an experience that rocked my consciousness and changed the way I view the rewards I've received from making markets and creating magnificent homes for the ultrawealthy. And it's continued to evolve from there. Yet the absolutist still reigns with an unwavering commitment to what we call the Frank McKinney Way: a set of standards and a culture in our business of always closing the loop and always seeking ways to innovate to make it better, more cost-effective, as well as more in tune with what our buyers really want—even before they know they want it. You could say this culture has even evolved into a healthy cult, with our business mantra summing up how we approach every day: *often happy, seldom satisfied.*

Having read the first three parts of this book, "The Confident Contrarian," "The Market Maker," and "The Artist and the Closer," you're now ready for the logical conclusion: "The Enlightened Absolutist." All four of these aspects of the *Burst This!* approach and attitude are crucial components for you in creating bubble-proof real estate strategies. This last one is about sustainability, longevity with your chosen field, meaningful wealth, and the dovetailing of your professional highest calling with your spiritual highest calling. Many seek their entire lives to bring these two forces together, and in this final chapter I show you how.

I've written about this concept previously, but never with such precision and depth as when I undertook to write *The Tap*. What you'll be reading next is the result of my concentrated, extended time on this subject, the distillation of a model I created to help you evaluate where you are in the business of life and to show you what will be next for you if you choose it: fulfillment, joy, and the ever-elusive eternal happiness. Isn't that what we're all striving for anyway?

13

FROM RICH
TO ENRICHED

We'd done it. We'd set a new record with the sale of our latest home on the oceanfront, a multimillion-dollar, 12,000-square-foot estate where we were the first to introduce architecture inspired by the great estates Nilsa and I had seen in Loire Valley. Incidentally, this was shortly after the ruckus over the S&L crisis had settled down. A new day was dawning, and my ego was on fire.

Many regional and local papers carried the news. I had been told that I would appear on the front page of the *Miami Herald*, so that morning I sat on the curb at 4:00 AM waiting for the papers to be inserted into the news racks. Pathetic, but true. When the papers arrived, and I spotted my name on the front page, I was genuinely proud of our success. (Yes, of course I emptied the newsstand of all their copies that morning.) We'd worked hard to get there; this was the culmination of many years in the market, spanning from that first fixer-upper in 1986 to our first oceanfront home in 1991. We had sacrificed for a better tomorrow, and now I felt that we had truly made it there. This was the big time.

The story was teased with a headline and paragraph on page 1, and then jumped to page 2, where the paper featured a picture of me posed in front of the house, my grin as wide as it ever had been, my hair as high as it could be, my wife standing beside me as beautiful as she always is. My fists were raised in triumph as I struck a Rocky Balboa pose in my expensive suit. Yes, we had made it!

While I was reading the text accompanying my photo, my eyes were distracted across the fold to another picture. A man stood in line at a soup kitchen, hunched over his dinner. He was unshaven, rumpled, obviously lucky to have received the meal. *And he looked like me.* I couldn't take my eyes off the guy. I couldn't bring myself even to finish reading the story I'd started. You've probably had someone tell you before that you look "just like" someone else. Usually, you can dismiss it: she's too fat, he's too ugly, etc. But on this occasion, I couldn't shake the feeling that this man in the picture didn't just look like me, but that *he could be me.*

"There but for the grace of God go I."

Had I made a few wrong decisions at early crossroads in my life, I certainly could have landed on that page, could have been that man. It stunned me for a moment, the juxtaposition of my photo with his. There I was, with my multimillion-dollar deal, able to afford whatever meal I wanted to eat to celebrate, and there he was, probably living under the interstate bridge and unsure of which dumpster he should pick through the next morning for his breakfast. I felt a rush of heat and a cold chill at the same time. The feeling wasn't altogether unpleasant, but I didn't especially like it, either. There was a choice: ignore what I felt and flip to the back of the paper to see what kind of car I'd like to buy to reward myself for my accomplishment, or take the time to think about what was happening to me.

There's something more to what I'm doing for a living than merely creating megamansions. Could it be that God put me in the position to do this work because He knew I was ready to be a responsible steward, sharing my blessings with those who are less fortunate than I am? Or, now that I have arrived, does this success come with added responsibility and require that I become a responsible steward?

It was a chicken-and-egg type of dilemma. Since I wasn't too philosophical at the time, I came away with a simple answer: *I'm in the housing business, and I should be providing housing to those who don't have it, while at the same time I act on my professional highest calling by providing housing to the world's most wealthy.* It was a realization of the possibility to fulfill a spiritual calling, bound up with my professional expertise. As I thought about it, I really began to embrace the idea and imagine how I could be a sort of modern-day Robin Hood. That mythic persona was deeply etched into my psyche at a young age, as I would gallivant through the backwoods of Indiana pretending I was running through Sherwood Forest. (Yes, I had a bow and arrow, and no, I didn't wear green tights.) I'd be the Prince of Thieves, but with a twist: Sell to the rich, and give to the poor. Yes, that's what I would do!

It was an epiphanous moment.

Isn't that the definition of true success: to realize the potential to dovetail your professional highest calling with your spiritual highest calling? I've certainly seen the other side, people at the absolute top of their game, financially rewarded nearly beyond measure, but estranged from family or in ill health, often feeling soulless, unable to balance their business concerns with their personal ones. They may be succeeding by society's definition, but they're failing miserably by mine. They're failing in the business of life. The people I admire most are those who've figured out how to have it all: astronomical professional achievement, responsible stewardship through the benefitting of others, deep connections with family and friends, vigorously good health, and a sense of both gratitude and personal place in the grander scheme of things.

There's a correlation, it seems to me, between those who survive and thrive, and those who manage to focus on more than just the material acquisition that comes from being excellent at what they do. In real estate, it comes from being able not only to spot enduring value in properties that others dismiss, but also in being able to live the enduring value of sharing your blessings with others—something that's equally easy to overlook, underpractice, or forget.

Those photos in the newspaper made me reflect on a Bible passage I recall hearing first when I was just a child: "From everyone who has been given much, much more will be demanded; and from the one who has been entrusted with much, much more will be asked." (Luke 12:48) In other words, if you've received blessings in life, regardless of their scope and size, implicit in those gifts is a requirement to give back. I was brought up Catholic, but these words probably have a familiar ring to anyone who's ever practiced a great faith tradition, whether Christian, Jewish, Hindu, Muslim, Buddhist, or any of the others that promote service as a way to God and responsible stewardship as a spiritual path. I learned about this while attending Catholic grade school and hearing countless (at the time, also boring) sermons about the requirement to give back through "The Three Ts" of time, talent, and treasure. Although I yawned through these lessons as a mischievous young boy, somehow they stayed with me.

So the question I was asking and answering for myself, and that I ask you to ponder now, is this: *since I've been given these blessings, what do I need to give back?* Indeed, when you've applied the *Burst This!* approach to your real estate investing strategies, and you've reaped the rewards that will come with abiding by its principles and plans, what will it all have been for? For that matter, what is the purpose of everything you've been given already?

When I'd finished staring at the paper, with me on page 2 and the "other me" on page 3, I picked up the phone and called the soup kitchen's sponsor, The Caring Kitchen, ready to relieve myself of some of my success guilt.

"What can I do to help?"

They signed me up to start packing the back of a beat-up old Ford Econoline van full of hot dinner dishes and driving these meals to people in the back alleys and under the bridges of my area. Every week before *Monday Night Football*, I'd go get the van stocked with what was probably the only meal most of my "customers" would have all day, and deliver them to men, women, and children of all ages, including a family with three young girls who lived in an overgrown clump of weeds and scrub trees in a field less than three miles from my own home. That was a turning point in my life, when I started to realize that *sharing* was itself part of the reward you find in great blessings, not just an obligation. I have no doubt that I got much more out of delivering those spaghetti dinners than the people who received them. Yes, it was satisfying for them to be fed—I don't discount their hunger—but I was also feeding a hunger in myself that had been building in me and I hadn't recognized up to that point. I'd known what it meant to be rich and enjoyed many of its perks, but this was something new, something deeply fulfilling: a sense of enrichment.

My beliefs about sharing my blessings evolved from there. When I wrote my first book, *Make It BIG!*, I articulated them in this way:

> I believe God has put all of us on this earth to do great things, but I think He has a special plan for people who are going to take care of those who need it. We are not the end product of our success, merely the conduit for it: we are given the ability to succeed not just for ourselves, but for what we will do for others. Sharing your success is not just writing a check or dropping five dollars in the collection basket (although sharing your wealth is important). It is making a commitment to share whatever resources you have been blessed with. And for many of us, our two most valuable resources are time and personal attention.

Since I first wrote those words, I've come to think about the times when God has reminded me to take care of others as "Tap Moments." These are the points in time when the divine hand lightly makes contact with the mortal self, and we're given a choice: action or denial, sharing or selfishness, evolving or staying within the confines of the familiar. These moments can be as seemingly insignificant as meeting someone who could use some help carrying ice to their car in the 7-Eleven parking lot, or as dramatic as the multitude of opportunities that we find to help the most desperately poor and homeless people from around the world by creating entire villages based upon self-sufficiency.

As I've grown in the years since my experience with the newspaper, I've noticed that advancement seems to come in distinct stages. The more sensitive I've become to The Tap, new incentives for giving, new ways of looking at my contributions, new levels of commitment and compassion have come with each new stage of personal evolution. I like to think of this kind of growth as an eternal, upward spiral, creating a tornado effect with the force of the upper levels determining the degree of impact on the ground.

Before you start thinking that I've gone completely metaphysical, here, let me point out that each of these stages directly impacts to what level you will succeed and will forever change the way you conduct business. That's what I mean by the effect "on the ground." I mean what happens in your day-to-day. How you treat people. Whether you're just a dictator or benevolent, too. If you can be both bottom-line driven and compassionate, too. Whether you can become an *enlightened absolutist*, demanding the best and doing so because you know that when the rewards are doled out for the effort, you will be a responsible steward and ensure that they're shared with those who are less fortunate. It will become part of your business plan, your fabric, your DNA. Your approach to business will have been rewired and reset with correct principles.

The Seven Stages of the Eternal, Upward Spiral

One definition of insanity is doing the same thing over and over again, and expecting different results. Getting stuck at any of the early stages in the upward spiral is like that: if you don't look to progress, the spiral turns into nothing more than a maddening circle, the swirling of the vicious cycle. You stagnate, become frustrated, depressed. Put bluntly, you are failing. Moving up into the higher levels, on the other hand, can be exhilarating, liberating, and oh, so profitable. It's when you start realizing that doing well must include doing good.

As you read the rest of this chapter—number thirteen, always a lucky number for me—see if you can identify your current stage of development, how close you are to living the message from that passage in Luke: *From those to whom much is entrusted, much will be expected.* Furthermore, how are you conducting your business? Be brutally honest with yourself about this. As soon as you've pinpointed your current level, you're in a position to move on to the next.

- **Stage One.** Each of us is born into this world as a need-machine, oblivious to anything other than our own requirements. In time, we develop a limited awareness that others have needs, too, but they're not anywhere near as important as our own nearly bottomless pit of wants and desires. Some people never grow out of this intense self-absorption. They don't learn the most basic lesson of kindergarten: to share. They don't care to learn it, either. In my experience, people at Stage One are rarely in business for themselves or have an interest in entrepreneurial ventures, so I feel fairly confident that you're beyond this black hole of the soul, where there's no social consciousness or concern for other people. If you went looking for Stage One in Webster's, the definition would be just two ugly words: *pure selfishness.*

The Stage One response when some small awareness of others' needs breaks through: *See ya. I wouldn't want to be ya.*

• **Stage Two.** At this stage, other people's needs begin to register more fully, although you're still unwilling to do anything about them. You're adept at denial, and it seems to "work" if you can just turn off whatever awareness you may experience. You change the channel so you don't have to hear about the flood victims. You turn the other way when passing a homeless person. You check the caller I.D. and don't pick up so you don't have to deal with some employee's lame excuse for not showing up at work that day. You delete the e-mail without responding so you don't have to sponsor them *again* in some charity race. (Wasn't once enough to get them off your back?) Someone else's pain or problem or request is no concern of yours, and it's uncomfortable to have it "in your face." You can't or don't want to do anything about it anyway, right? You've got your own stuff to deal with—times are hard and you don't have the money to share, or business is booming and you don't have the time to give, or your deadline is looming and you just don't have the mental bandwidth to think about anyone else. You might think, *Charity is for do-gooders and idealists. I don't want* *to get involved. I have to take care of me first.* Yet if you're even having these thoughts, this means that something is starting to pull at you—you're starting to notice Tap Moments—but it isn't compelling; in fact, it feels like an imposition.

The Stage Two response to Tap Moments, which feel something like an irritating insect: *What is that? Get off me. I don't have the time, the money, or the desire to help.*

• **Stage Three.** In getting to this third stage, you have to cross the threshold of action. In a word, you feel *guilty,* and this motivates you to *do* something. Usually something relatively easy; the less effort, the better. You toss a quarter in a homeless person's cup without looking them in the eye. You bag up some old clothes and drop them off at a women's shelter. You reluctantly agree to contribute a few dollars to your board of realtors Thanksgiving Day food drive. Every Sunday as I perform the duties of usher at our 6:45 AM mass, I get to see Stage Three in action: people crumpling bills into tiny wads and dropping them into the collection, or else folding them so many times and so tightly that the denomination isn't visible, or burying their gift under others in the plate. I've even had a few parishioners *throw* their envelope into my basket with an utter look of disgust on their faces. And no, it's not because my maroon blazer is disturbing—it's clearly a chore to them. It's got to be done, but that doesn't mean they have to like it.

The Stage Three response to Tap Moments, which you're finally beginning to feel with some urgency: *What's the least I can do? Whatever it is, it already feels like too much, so don't ask for more. That's it—I'm done.*

• **Stage Four.** Now you're ready to make some bigger gestures, and you're also eager to be acknowledged for it. You see that contributing to charities or benefitting the needy in some way can yield some very positive attention. You consider good works to be essentially about generating goodwill and public relations, forming an attractive public image, possibly also internalizing a positive self-image. So you share your money with those organizations that will list your real estate business in the "friends of" section of their program. You share your time and talents with those who will help you feel like a hero. You don't waste your time on "small" Tap Moments, so opportunities to do simple kindnesses are completely ignored.

The Stage Four response to Tap Moments: *How will this make me look? Will this benefit my real estate sales efforts? How can it showcase me and my property? Is anyone watching me now? How about now? That's more like it. . . .*

• **Stage Five.** The day after I opened the paper and discovered "myself" on both sides of the fold, I was moved to operating at Stage Five. I was aware of how much I had been blessed to receive and also aware of how much someone else was in need. I was experiencing success guilt, and when I reached out to a charity to show me how to balance the scales (something that took place only in my own mind, of course), it worked. I helped someone else, and that made me feel better about my abundance, about myself. It also felt a little like a hedge against some potential future downturn: "Look, God! I know what to do—don't take away my blessings. When you give me great things, I share them. Keep it coming!"

328 • Part Four: The Enlightened Absolutist

The Stage Five response to Tap Moments: *It feels good to give, and I'll give when the getting's good.*

- **Stage Six.** Now your focus truly begins to shift. The all-consuming "I" starts to give way to a bigger sense of "us" and even "you." You become more willing to share with others even when it's inconvenient, awkward, or expensive. You have the sense that the proper use of the blessings you've received reflects your purpose, both as a professional and as a person placed here on earth to do some good with your life. You now have an inkling of your spiritual highest calling, and you've begun to feel that without this spiritual element, your real estate career will eventually become dry and meaningless. But when you pair the two, it reinvigorates you, both professionally and personally.

  The Stage Six response to Tap Moments, which you now recognize as being an extension of the hand of God: *I feel it, and yes, I think I can act on it.*

- **Stage Seven.** It's about responsible stewardship, highest calling, purpose. Yes, enlightenment. At this stage, Tap Moments are part of your normal life, no longer rare occurrences. Sharing your blessings has become such a part of who you are, so deeply embedded into your conscious and unconscious behavior, that your actions aren't driven by your feelings so much anymore. You realize that, as they say, it's not about you. You have become so sensitized to life's Tap Moments that you treat *every* opportunity, from every "small" gesture to every "grand" calling as important and worthy of your full attention. You can see that the sum total of the actions you take when presented with Tap Moments are what make such a meaningful difference in the lives of others—and in your own life. The "big" Tap Moments are wonderful, yet the "tiny" can be even more enjoyable. You thank God that you have an awareness few have. At this level, there's no longer any dividing distinction between spiritual and professional highest calling. These are not independent, parallel universes anymore, but instead one incredibly expansive, unified world of purposeful good. Your territory grows. Successes come without warning, or explanation, other than the quiet recognition that God understands that you understand. You seek out opportunities to change lives. You can then become a conduit for other people's Tap Moments, the leader of a growing Tap army.

The Stage Seven response to Tap Moments: *Thank you, God, for the awareness.*

Progress through the seven stages can be rapid once you're aware of what they are. This ascent through the spiral and ultimate residence in or near Stage Seven provides insulation from life blowing up in your face, the ultimate bubble-bursting. It's where the force field surrounding your endeavors becomes strongest, once you know that God has chosen *you* as a responsible steward of His blessings. **Yes, you've been tapped.** A healthy sense of stewardship—meaning the responsible use of the resources you've been given—helps safeguard you from some of the traps I've warned against in this book already. It can also keep you from making the grave error of buying into your own hype. I've often been tempted in that way; as I've looked out on the horizon with my hand to my forehead, believing I could see the Bahamas, some days I've felt as if I could walk there, across the water. That's a very dangerous illusion, a threat to sustained success, certainly a problem if remaining grounded is at all important.

The way to stop that, and it's very healthy to stop that, is to realize what the rewards you've worked so hard to earn are for. *From those to whom much is entrusted, much will be expected.*

It's one of the great things my mentor, billionaire Rich DeVos, has taught me: Really, how much food can you eat? How many clothes can you wear? How many cars can you drive? How many houses can you own and use? How many vacations can you take? How many planes can you fly? Or, as in Rich's case, how many sports teams can you own? Again, if you're following the *Burst This!* approach, and you're making it big and earning a great deal of money—once you get to a certain point, whatever that comfort level is for you (and yes, you're going to put some money away for a rainy day, too), you're going to start to experience excess. Which, again, is a dangerous thing; humanity is just not conditioned to handle it. How often have you seen the misuse of excess implode a good life? But there are some who successfully navigate the minefield, and the primary ingredient as I've observed it is that the majority of them use that excess to assist others.

Isn't that the epitome of bubble-proofing?

It's possible that as you grow and move up the spiral, you'll also slip back every now and then. Sometimes you'll go up and down in a single day. To attain consistent, gradual progress, train yourself to think in the ways of the higher stages of Five, Six, and Seven. Once you've attained Stage Five, you're much less likely to go below that baseline in the future.

Perhaps you're thinking that it will be good to pursue this later, after you've made it, or after you've reached the big time, or after some other ambiguous milestone. Perhaps only then will you remember what you've read in this last chapter, the one that's not directly about real estate investing, and be ready to seriously apply it. But I hope not. Recall what were probably your earliest lessons about helping others and the three Ts, and realize that you need not wait until you have the third, "treasure" to share the first two, "time" and "talent."

I hope you're encouraged to start now, instead, and that you can see how the first three parts of this book will certainly help you to attain success in business, but for *lasting* success, you need this final element. I know I need it. It has worked for me and those I look up to, my mentors. During the meteor showers—and I promise you, during your career there will be a few—you'll need to feel as if there's more to your life than all business, as if you're not living in two worlds, one for commerce and one for charity and kindness. Can you do that? To see beyond the bottom line in evaluating your success and that of your business? To be the benevolent dictator? Or the compassionate capitalist? I know you can!

Can you truly bubble-proof your investments by following the acquisition formula . . . being both optimistic and opportunistic . . . ignoring the market's manias and superstitions . . . honoring the holy trinity of time, budget, and quality . . . responsibly managing your debt . . . following the Grade School Compass Approach to marketing, promotion, and sales . . . making markets and masterpieces and then closing the deal?

Can you do all that—and also be enlightened? *Absolutely.*

As you close this book and begin to implement its contents, I wish you the growing confidence in knowing that you can be a *Maverick*, will *Make it BIG!* can feel *The Tap* and can tell all those who doubt you, "Go ahead—try to *Burst This!*"

APPENDIX
Acqua Liana Construction Timeline

**Items may have green components.

Task #	Description	Duration/ Days	Start	Finish	Decision Date	Date Ordered	Received Date
2204.001	Scalp, Fill, Compact**	13	7/21/2007	8/8/2007			
2292	Pile Foundations Layout	2	8/8/2007	8/11/2007			
2304	Pile Foundations -Sub	12	8/8/2007	8/25/2007			
2204.002	Backfill Piles, Grade, Compact**	10	8/22/2007	9/6/2007			
3374	Concrete Sight Wall**	20	9/6/2007	10/2/2007			
15404.004	Plumbing Under- ground Rough**	10	9/9/2007	9/20/2007			
16014.001	Electrical Under- ground Rough	3	9/16/2007	9/18/2007			
15804.001	HVAC Underground Rough**	4	9/16/2007	9/19/2007			
15414.004	Gas Underground Rough**	2	9/16/2007	9/17/2007			
13154.001	Pool Rough Sleeves**	2	9/17/2007	9/18/2007			
3004.001	Concrete Shell**	106	9/20/2007	2/19/2008			
2624.002	Bridge Structure	15	10/16/2007	11/6/2007			

Task #	Description	Duration/ Days	Start	Finish	Decision Date	Date Ordered	Received Date
2204.003	Backfill Grade During Shell	7	10/28/2007	11/6/2007			
7104	Waterproofing-Sub**	3	10/31/2007	11/5/2007			
10304	Fireplaces-Sub**	21	11/5/2007	12/3/2007			
13154	Swimming Pool-Sub**	40	11/7/2007	1/1/2008			
6154	Wood Trusses-Sub**	20	1/29/2008	2/27/2008			
2504	Site Drainage-Sub**	10	1/29/2008	2/12/2008			
2594	Site Util. Gas-Sub	4	1/29/2008	2/4/2008			
2574	Site Util-Electrical -Sub	4	1/29/2008	2/4/2008			
2554	Site Water/Meter-Sub	3	1/29/2008	2/3/2008			
2564	Site Util-Sewer-Sub	20	1/29/2008	2/27/2008			
7814	Gutters Under- ground**	15	1/29/2008	2/19/2008			
7104.001	Waterproofing Pool Deck**	5	2/20/2008	2/27/2008			
2804.001	Landscape A1A**	10	2/20/2008	3/4/2008			
5404	Light Gage Metal Framing-Sub**	25	2/20/2008	3/25/2008			
8604	Wood Windows- Sub**	20	2/20/2008	3/18/2008			
7304.001	Roofing Dry-in	5	2/28/2008	3/4/2008			
15404.002	Plumbing Top Out	17	3/21/2008	4/12/2008			
16014.002	Electrical Rough-In**	25	4/4/2008	5/7/2008			
16444	Home Integration Rough**	25	4/4/2008	5/7/2008			
15804.002	HVAC Rough-in**	20	4/4/2008	4/29/2008			
15414.001	Gas Rough-In**	3	4/4/2008	4/6/2008			
10704.001	Solar System Rough**	5	4/4/2008	4/8/2008			
16414.001	Electrical Generator Rough-In**	3	4/5/2008	4/7/2008			

Task #	Description	Duration/ Days	Start	Finish	Decision Date	Date Ordered	Received Date
16414.002	Electrical Generator Set**	3	4/8/2008	4/12/2008			
7304.002	Roofing Hot Mop**	7	4/13/2008	4/21/2008			
14204.001	Elevator Rough-In	10	4/13/2008	4/26/2008			
11054.001	Central Vacuum System Rough-in**	3	4/13/2008	4/15/2008			
13844.001	Alarm Protection Rough-in	4	4/18/2008	4/21/2008			
7204	Insulation-Sub**	6	5/10/2008	5/17/2008			
6144	Dock-Sub**	30	5/17/2008	6/25/2008			
9254	Drywall-Sub**	30	5/18/2008	6/28/2008			
9104	Stucco-Sub	30	5/18/2008	6/28/2008			
14204.002	Elevator Set Cab**	6	5/19/2008	5/26/2008			
6204	Finish Carpentry -Sub**	65	6/3/2008	9/3/2008			
9904	Painting-Sub**	100	6/8/2008	10/27/2008			
6164	Timber Roof Structures-Sub**	20	6/10/2008	7/7/2008			
4204	Masonry-Sub**	15	6/10/2008	6/30/2008			
6104	Rough Carpentry -Sub**	29	6/15/2008	7/23/2008			
9554.001	Wood Floors Interior**	15	7/8/2008	7/29/2008			
9304	Tile/Marble-Sub**	25	7/13/2008	8/17/2008			
7304.003	Roofing Load Tiles	3	7/21/2008	7/23/2008			
8203	Wood Doors & Frames**	8	7/28/2008	8/6/2008			
8304	Special Doors-Sub**	3	7/28/2008	7/30/2008			
8314	Garage Doors-Sub	3	7/30/2008	8/3/2008			
7304.004	Roofing Set Tile**	25	8/5/2008	9/10/2008			
2204.005	Final Grade**	7	8/18/2008	8/26/2008			

Task #	Description	Duration/ Days	Start	Finish	Decision Date	Date Ordered	Received Date
6404	Millwork/Cabinetry -Sub**	23	8/18/2008	9/21/2008			
4404	Cast Stone-Sub	15	8/20/2008	9/11/2008			
2624	Brick Pavers-Sub**	15	8/27/2008	9/18/2008			
8704	Hardware-Sub	7	8/30/2008	8/9/2008			
8654	Special Windows Water Wall-Sub	10	9/7/2008	9/18/2008			
11504	Wine Room-Sub	10	9/7/2008	9/18/2008			
10704	Solar Systems-Sub**	10	9/11/2008	9/24/2008			
7804	Gutters-Sub**	7	9/11/2008	9/21/2008			
9404	Granite-Sub	20	9/15/2008	10/11/2008			
13994	Stairways – Glass**	20	9/18/2008	10/14/2008			
2814	Landscape- Irrigation-Sub**	25	9/21/2008	10/22/2008			
16534	Site Lighting**	20	9/21/2008	10/15/2008			
13164	Fountain-Sub**	5	9/30/3008	10/5/2008			
9554.002	Wood Floors Exterior**	10	9/21/2008	10/13/2008			
5134	Metal Railing/Hand Rail-Sub	4	10/11/2008	10/14/2008			
5204	Gates-Sub	7	10/11/2008	10/19/2008			
15404.003	Plumbing Trim**	12	10/12/2008	10/27/2008			
13154.002	Pool Finishes	25	10/15/2008	11/19/2008			
2804	Landscaping-Sub**	20	10/18/2008	11/15/2008			
16014.003	Electrical Trim**	40	10/19/2008	12/14/2008			
16444.001	Home Integration Trim**	20	11/17/2008	12/14/2008			
8804	Glazing/Mirrors-Sub	3	11/22/2008	11/24/2008			
11054.002	Central Vacuum Trim**	2	11/26/2008	11/29/2008			
13844.002	Alarm Protection Trim**	3	11/26/2008	11/30/2008			

Task #	Description	Duration/ Days	Start	Finish	Decision Date	Date Ordered	Received Date
15804.003	HVAC Set Equipment Trim**	5	12/1/2008	12/7/2008			
10813	Bath Accessories-Sub**	3	12/6/2008	12/8/2008			
10994	Shower Enclosures-Sub	5	12/6/2008	12/10/2008			
12714	Aquariums-Sub**	20	12/13/2008	2/7/2008			
11404.001	Appliances-Sub**	5	12/13/2008	12/17/2008			
15414.003	Gas Final/Trim**	3	12/15/2008	12/17/2008			
1524	FINAL CLEAN UP**	10	1/3/2008	1/14/2008			
2624.001	Grass/Gravel Drive**	10	1/3/2008	1/14/2008			
12204	Window Treatment-Sub**	10	1/10/2008	1/21/2008			
9684	Carpet-Sub**	2	1/18/2008	1/19/2008			
12604	Furniture-Sub**	10	1/18/2008	1/28/2008			
1524.001	White Glove Clean up**	8	2/1/2008	2/13/2008			

NOTES AND SOURCES

This isn't intended to be a bibliography, as much of what I cite in this book is directly in my area of expertise or readily available information. However, some of the data or more controversial statements have been sourced below. Many of the notes are included to provide additional explanation or to point you in a particular direction for further exploration.

Chapter 3.

1. Blanche Evans, "Realty Viewpoint: Why Buy Now? Media Is Wrong About Housing Slump," *Realty Times* (May 5, 2008).

2. Chris Pummer, "Home-Price Data Has Its Flaws," *MarketWatch* (May 1, 2008).

3. Robert J. Shiller, "Infectious Exuberance," *Atlantic Monthly* (July/August 2008), available online at http://www.theatlantic.com/doc/print/200807/housing.

Chapter 4.

1. To calculate simple interest, use this formula: $P \times r \times t = I$, where P is the *principal* (the amount of the loan), r *is the rate of interest*, t is the *time* (in years), and I is the *interest paid*. In our examples, the computation goes like this: In the first scenario, you were financing $61,470 at an average of 14 percent interest for 2.5 years, so:

$61,470 x 14% x 2.5 = $21,514.50 (total interest paid)
And in the second case, you were financing $36,000 at a fixed rate
of 10.41 percent for 2.5 years, so:

$36,000 x 10.41% x 2.5 = $9,369 (total interest paid)

2. Charles P. Kindleberger's definition of a bubble is from his book (co-authored with Robert Aliber) called *Manias, Panics, and Crashes: A History of Financial Crises*, Fifth Edition (Hoboken, NJ: John Wiley & Sons, 2005), p. 275.

Chapter 8

1. Eight credit cards per person: Kim Khan's "The Basics: How Does Your Debt Compare," *MSN Money*, available online at http://moneycentral.msn.com/content/SavingandDebt/P70581.asp.

2. $8,500 debt per person: "Consumer Debt Statistics," *Money-Zine.com*, available online at http://www.money-zine.com/Financial-Planning/Debt-Consolidation/Credit-Card-Debt-Statistics/.

3. The incredibly high 31 percent rate on a credit card: Lucy Lazarony's "Want a Lower Credit Card Rate? Just Ask," *BankRate.com* (October 6, 2003), available online at http://www.bankrate.com/brm/news/cc/20020415a.asp.

4. Forty-three percent of Americans live beyond their means: Also from Kim Khan's *MSN Money* article.

5. One excellent source of information on the national debt is the movie, *I.O.U.S.A.*, produced by the Peter G. Peterson Foundation. Visit their website, PGPF.org, and download "The State of the Union's Finances: A Citizen's Guide to the Financial Condition of the United States Government" (http://www.pgpf.org/resources/PGPFCitizensGuide.pdf) for an overview of the issues around the U.S. federal debt (that's where the statistics about GDP and debt to foreign countries came from) and some steps for you to take in resolving our national financial condition.

6. Remarks by former Federal Reserve chairman Alan Greenspan are from a speech he gave on April 8, 2005 at the Federal Reserve System's Fourth Annual Community Affairs Research Conference, Washington, D.C. (http://www.federalreserve.gov/BoardDocs/speeches/2005/20050408/default.htm)

ABOUT THE AUTHOR

For nearly a quarter-century, best-selling author, philanthropist, and real estate visionary Frank McKinney has been blessed with the ability to create art in the form of the world's most magnificent multimillion-dollar oceanfront estate homes, each set on the sun-drenched canvas of Palm Beach on Florida's Gold Coast. From his modest first $50,000 fixer-upper in 1986 to his first $2.2 million spec home on the ocean in 1992, to his current multimillion-dollar oceanfront creations, McKinney has created and sold 36 oceanfront properties with an average selling price over $10 million.

The world's wealthiest clamor for McKinney's masterpieces, each inspired by exotic locales and infused with vivid imagination. McKinney was recently recognized as one of the ten most influential people in luxury real estate.

Yet, just a two-hour flight away from these palaces, in the least developed country in the Americas, McKinney builds entire self-sufficient villages through his Caring House Project Foundation (http://www.frank-mckinney.com/caring_project.aspx).

His gift and passion for extraordinary homes extends to his role as the founder and director of CHPF, a nonprofit, 501(c)(3) organization he founded in 1998, which provides a self-sustaining existence for the most desperately poor and homeless families in Haiti, South America, Africa, Indonesia, and the United States. The foundation develops entire communities, complete with homes, medical clinics, orphanages, schools, churches, clean water, and agricultural assets, including both livestock and crops. The foundation started domestically by purchasing run-down single-family homes, refurbishing them, and then renting them for a dollar per month to elderly people who were homeless, completely redefining "affordable housing."

Through seemingly contradictory pursuits, Frank McKinney has come to understand, live, and feel what he refers to as The Tap. In Haiti, for example, where 80 percent of the population lives on less than two dollars a day and 22 percent of children won't see their fifth birthdays, McKinney's foundation works to bring home stability and security to these communities.

"Sure, that's fine for him—he's rich," you might be tempted to say. But he didn't start with building villages; his first tap came when serving meals out of the back of a beat-up old van to homeless families who were living under a bridge.

Before there was the treasure, or even the talent, he was tapped to share his time.

What is most paradoxical about Frank McKinney is that he graduated from his fourth high school in four years with a 1.8 GPA (he was asked to leave the first three schools), never went to college, nor did he receive any formal training in design, architecture, building, business, marketing, literature, or writing. Yet he is the creative force behind the design, creation, and ultimate sale of some of the most magnificent homes in the world, runs a large nonprofit organization, speaks around the world on various real estate, business, and spiritual topic, and has now written five wonderful books.

McKinney is without a doubt one of the most visionary, courageous, and "contrary" business leaders of our time. His latest stateside creations include two of the world's largest and most opulent certified "green" homes (environmentally responsible), priced at $29 and $30 million, and even a $135 million, 70,000-square-foot mansion.

If there were a swashbuckling modern-day Robin Hood, McKinney would be him, selling to the rich and providing for the poor. Armed with a rock star look, a disarming personality, and a willingness to attempt what others don't even dream of, McKinney has defied both conventional wisdom and the predictions of others to achieve success on his terms. Because of his prior bestsellers and the magnificent properties he builds, *USA Today* has called him "the real-estate rock czar," and the *Wall Street Journal* dubbed him "the king of ready-made dream homes."

In 2009, against common practice in the publishing industry, McKinney released three new books simultaneously: *Burst This! Frank McKinney's Bubble-Proof Real Estate Strategies, The Tap,* and *Dead Fred, Flying Lunchboxes, and the Good Luck Circle.*

McKinney lives with his wife, Nilsa, and their daughter, Laura, in Delray Beach, Florida.

INDEX

Accelerate Your Success in the Business of Life

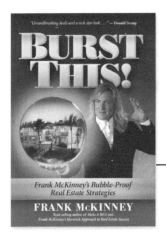

Give copies of *Burst This!* to family, friends and co-workers. . .

Hardcover book (HCI, 2009)
Available at Burst-This.com • $30

Other Exciting Offerings from Frank McKinney

Bestselling author Frank McKinney introduces **The Tap**, a profound spiritual practice leading to success in the business of life. Your prayers for more are answered! *The Tap* shows how to sensitize yourself to feel and then act on life's great "Tap Moments," embracing the rewards and responsibilities of a blessed life. Feel it, follow it and find your highest calling. This book is about accepting the responsibility, and it gives you confidence in your ability to handle your "more," whether it's more wealth, health, happiness, or relationships.

Hardcover book (HCI, 2009) •
Available at The-Tap.com • $25

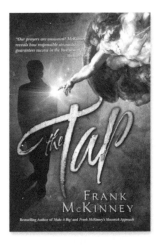

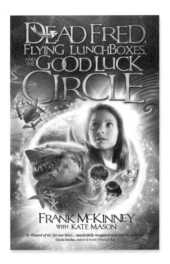

With **Dead Fred, Flying Lunchboxes, and the Good Luck Circle**, Frank McKinney boldly enters young reader fiction in this fantasy novel charged with fairy tale wonder, enthralling magic, page-turning suspense, and the deep creativity he's known for. It will both race and gladden the hearts of readers of all ages. This classic was inspired by real-life Laura McKinney's more than a thousand walks to school with her friends and her father, Frank McKinney.

Hardcover book (HCI, 2009)
Available at Dead-Fred.com • $25

Frank McKinney's Maverick Approach to Real Estate Success takes the reader on a fascinating real estate odyssey that began more than two decades ago with a $50,000 fixer-upper and culminates in a $100-million mansion. Includes strategies and insights from a true real estate "artist," visionary, and market maker.

Paperback book (John Wiley & Sons, 2006)
Available at Frank-McKinney.com • $25

Make It BIG! 49 Secrets for Building a Life of Extreme Success consists of forty-nine short, dynamic chapters that share how to live a balanced life, with real estate stories and "deal points" sprinkled throughout.

Hardcover book (John Wiley & Sons, 2002)
Available at Frank-McKinney.com • $30

Frank McKinney's Succeeding in the Business of Life—The Series™ was recorded in Frank McKinney's tree house by Frank McKinney himself. Twelve hours of audio and video are based on content found in his first two bestsellers, *Make It BIG!* and *Frank McKinney's Maverick Approach*, plus new and expanded information found nowhere else.

Compact Discs • Available at Frank-McKinney.com • $249

The Frank McKinney Experience, Public Speaking, Appearances and **Personal Success Coaching**
One-on-one or group events
Prices and schedule available through Frank-McKinney.com

Please visit Frank-McKinney.com to peruse our entire online store at http://www.frank-mckinney.com/entire_store.asp and take advantage of savings with assorted-product packages. It's important to note that proceeds benefit Frank McKinney's nonprofit Caring House Project Foundation (http://www.frank-mckinney.com/caring_project.aspx).